ENDANGERED SPECIES

RICHARD HEYGATE AND MIKE DAUNT

ENDANGERED SPECIES

The Bart and the Bounder's Countryside Year

JOHN MURRAY

First published in Great Britain in 2007 by John Murray (Publishers)
An Hachette Livre UK company

1

© Bart and Bounder Productions 2007

A CIP catalogue record for this title is available from the British Library

ISBN 978-0-7195-6956-2

Typeset in 13/15.75 pt Bulmer by Servis Filmsetting Ltd, Manchester

Printed and bound by Clays Ltd, St Ives plc

John Murray policy is to use papers that are natural, renewable and recyclable products and made from
wood grown in sustainable forests. The logging and manufacturing processes are expected to conform
to the environmental regulations of the country of origin.

John Murray (Publishers)
338 Euston Road
London NW1 3BH

www.johnmurray.co.uk

For my wife and family
R.H.

For my wonderful children, Seton, Will, Hugh and Tara, with
huge thanks for all the fun we have together
M.D.

CONTENTS

Authors' Note

Like all countrymen, we believe that nothing should stand in the way of a good story. Although everything we write is based on our experiences, occasionally names, dates, characters and locations have been changed or added for the sake of the narrative – just as we would embellish a tall tale in the telling over a pint of beer in a country pub.

INTRODUCTION

THE BOUNDER ON THE BART . . .

It was the Bart, or my cousin Richard as he was then, who shot our grandmother's cockerel with a catapult, and yet I was the one beaten with the back of a hairbrush by Nanny. I was seven; he was ten. It was a fine shot and I bore Richard no grudge because it had always been like that. Richard has forever had the face of an angel. But somewhere, hidden in a neglected attic, I am convinced there is a portrait of him that, like Dorian Gray, shows every sin and peccadillo he has ever committed. That face would probably look rather like mine.

We have always been close. We have shared fishing rods, flats and women, not always in that order. Much of our early life was spent together at our grandmother's house at Welford-on-Avon. Our mothers had divorced from our fathers at almost exactly the same time and they were, as well as being sisters, the closest of friends, too. Richard's mother was my favourite aunt and I know that my mother was his.

Richard was at Oxford when I was an agricultural student nearby, and many times we climbed back into his rooms at Balliol after dinner in some alehouse. I would then sleep on the floor before setting off at dawn on my motorbike, still in black tie, to do the milking.

As boys, Richard and I had done a great deal of coarse fishing in the local weir, but I had gone on to develop a passion for fly-fishing. The break-up of Richard's first marriage coincided with a trip a friend and I were making to fish for salmon on the River Dionard in Cape Wrath, the most north-western river in Scotland. To cheer Richard up I suggested that he come with us.

We arrived on a Sunday night in June at the Cape Wrath Hotel to find the river at a good height after a recent spate and in perfect ply for a salmon. We went into the bar to celebrate. On hearing our accents, a disaffected local who had been celebrating a bit himself started in on us and the rest of the English nation for our centuries'-old oppression of the Scots. There was a long pause, and then a red beard was thrust aggressively into our faces. 'I couldn't agree more,' said Richard. 'We're Irish ourselves.' Red Beard, immediately recognising another downtrodden race, couldn't wait to buy us drinks.

The next morning I gave Richard some perfunctory lessons in fly-casting. He was wholly incompetent, but as I was keen to get going, I told him he was brilliant. We had about an hour's walk to our beat on the river, which contained Heather Point, the best pool of all. Deciding it would be wasted on a beginner, I put Richard on a shallow and hopeless pool from which I had never seen a salmon caught, while my friend Jonny and I fished Heather Point. Two hours later we had had not a touch and were miserably sitting on the bank. At this point Richard appeared. 'Any luck?' he asked. We shook our heads. 'Mind if I try?' he said. 'Go ahead,' I replied, 'but you haven't a chance. We've flogged it to death.' As he made his first, appalling cast, with the line in a tangle on the water, a salmon grabbed the fly.

That fish epitomises our relationship. After sixty years I still love him, despite his supreme competence at nearly everything,

and he still loves me, despite the chaos that has always surrounded me.

AND THE BART ON THE BOUNDER . . .

The manageress of the Chelsea branch of Oxfam was not amused.
'We can only sell clothes that have been sorted and cleaned,' she
said, 'and we don't have the first idea what is in this bag. It was
dumped on us by a very rude lady a couple of hours ago, and I
was not even sure that we should accept it.'

'It's a bit difficult,' I said. 'You see, the clothes belong to a cousin
of mine and he needs them back, as he has nothing else to wear.'

'But if he needs the clothes, why on earth has he sent them
round to Oxfam?' she asked, more puzzled than ever.

I thought for a minute, and then gave her my best smile.
'Would you like to hear a story?' I asked.

The Bounder seemed to have fallen in clover at last, maritally
speaking. His soon-to-be-second wife was beautiful, intelligent
and charming. Yet I had become nervous when I heard that he
had taken up jogging. It was quite out of character. Exercise is
something the Bounder takes only when there is some pleasur-
able adventure at the end of it. I was right, of course: he had been
unable to resist the lure of an attractive actress and ex-mistress.
Eager to start a second performance, matinees only, the Bounder
would head off down Redcliffe Square in his smart new jogging
suit, hail a cab, and return an hour later, sweating nicely.

All went well, until he decided to take the lady to Ascot. Being
keen to show off her finery, she dressed the part, and was snapped
extensively by the *paparazzi*. The Bounder, whose sense of secur-
ity had clearly been lulled by champagne, was visible grinning
sheepishly in several of the shots, later published in *Tatler*. Come
publication day, he was outed by a furious fiancée and his

possessions dumped on the pavement. Somehow he wormed his way back into favour, but had to tell the actress that illicit performances were now off the playbill. She dumped the clothes he had been keeping round at her flat at Oxfam.

The Oxfam lady had the grace to laugh, and I got back the clothes after a small donation to the needy.

My own role in the Bounder's escapades has usually been one of amused participant. The earliest I can remember is when, as very small boys, we were fishing, illicitly, the mill at Welford-on-Avon, near our grandmother's house. We had been worm-fishing for small roach and dace, when suddenly we spotted a pike. It was long and black, and hung dead still by a weed bed. Breathless with excitement, we crept closer and tried it with an old rusted spinner we had found caught in a tree. The pike ignored us completely, until we upped the game and snagged its dorsal fin with a drag across its back. All hell broke loose.

It took us a good 15 minutes to land the fish, and we were just examining our prize when we looked up to find the miller scowling down at us. 'Do that again, and I'll set the dogs on you,' he rasped. Then, with a hint of a smile, he went on: 'But that were rare sport – I never thought you lads would land it! Now put the bugger back and get off home afore I change me mind.' A still cross-looking pike swam slowly back to its hunting grounds, and the pattern for my life long friendship with the Bounder was set.

The idea for this book and the TV programme that preceded it came to us one glorious sunny day by a Hampshire chalk stream. The Bounder had rather rashly bet the editor of the *Field*, Jonathan Young, that it was still possible to poach a prize trout stream, despite all the rules and regulations. We tickled away with some success, had enormous fun, cheated atrociously, and caught our fish. As so often, we ended up telling stories about the real-life poachers, gamekeepers, countrymen, rogues and vagabonds whose paths had crossed ours, and whose love for the English countryside we shared so profoundly. From that conversation arose 'The Bart and the Bounder', our TV special for BBC2, which drew an audience of nearly three million. More importantly, it introduced us to Kate Parkin and John Murray, our much-loved and infinitely patient publishers, who have guided every move of this book's creation and shared endless laughter along the way with us. We hope you enjoy reading it as much as we have enjoyed writing it.

Richard Heygate   Mike Daunt

1

January

RAT CATCHING

'I am just a country boy
Money have I none
But I've got silver in the stars
And gold in the morning sun.'

ANON, contributed by Brian Oliver

THE BART . . .

A bitter easterly wind blew across the hilltop, cutting through clothing and blowing dead leaves in small tornado circles. It whistled through the dilapidated outbuildings of the desolate farmyard, and a lone slate tile fell off the old roof of a barn. A door banged shut, then creaked opened again as the wind eddied. The bleak steading was surrounded by a few trees planted by some optimist years before in the hope of giving shelter from the unfriendly elements. These were unnaturally bent, like old men, by the permanent wind. There were stones missing from the walls, the wooden beams were rotten, and the whole place had an air of cold ghostliness. There was no sunlight to relieve the greyness, just an unfriendly, bitter sky with wintry clouds scudding across. It was a typical mid January day in the high farming country of Yorkshire.

In the middle of this depressing scene two middle-aged men are standing, apparently unconcerned by the cold, occasionally laughing at some shared joke. They are entirely unsuitably and incongruously dressed in full Regency costume. On their feet are highly polished shoes with silver buckles. White stockings lead to black velvet breeches over which hang the long points of dark green embroidered waistcoats. Lace jabots with huge brooches adorn their necks. There is more lace at the cuffs. Black velvet high-collared tailcoats in bottle green complete the ensemble.

This is the uniform of The Ancient and Honourable Society of Ratte Catchers and the two of us – my cousin Michael Daunt (the Bounder) and I, Sir Richard Heygate (the Bart) – have never looked more ridiculous.

That day seven other men and ten terriers also shared the freezing farmyard. They were more suitably dressed, in rough country clothing and flat hats. Their leader was Brian Oliver, a man of medium height with an oval face and a huge, black moustache, and he and his six companions were members of The Royal Albert Rat Catchers.

'We haven't done this farm for several months – let's hope there are a few rats about,' Brian said, turning to us with a grin. He seemed not to have noticed our eccentric dress.

We snapped to attention as the Royal Albert terriers, tough, alert, busy little dogs, were let off the lead. They immediately started snuffling around the yard, sniffing and searching.

'They've got a mark there,' said Brian, with an air of someone who knows what he's doing, as several terriers began to worry at a sheet of corrugated iron which was overgrown with grass and weeds. 'Let's stand on one end and then lift t'other.'

By this time the terriers were frantic, yapping and baying with excitement as we lifted the corrugated iron and started banging it with sticks. Five rats flew out from under it and across the yard, followed by a howling pack of dogs. Everyone was shouting with excitement – 'Go on!' 'Get him!' 'There he goes!' 'Look – that last one's escaped under the door of the barn!' But four of the five were in the bag, killed instantly by a murderous shake of a terrier's head.

'You know, Richard,' said Brian, 'I defy the most anti-hunting, animal-liberating enthusiast not to be excited by a rat hunt. You know why rats are the most universally hated of all creatures? It's because they're the most intelligent, that's why. And it was the fleas on the rat that caused the plague. There's something loathsome about the rat.' He rubbed his hands together. 'I love 'unting 'em,' he said with relish.

By this time the dogs were worrying at an old tractor tyre. As we lifted it, the terriers were climbing on top of one another trying to get into it. 'Put one inside and we'll roll it,' said Brian. Out shot three rats and were instantly dispatched. We caught eleven more in the yard, and then we turned our attention to the buildings. Searching in old corn sacks, under ancient machinery, beneath heaps of junk the terriers had a field day, and killed some sixty rats. Then a nest was marked behind the walls of an outbuilding, but it was impossible for the terriers to get at it and nor could the rat catchers – or not without pulling down the wall, which would not have been popular with the farmer.

'It's time', said Brian, with an air of certain knowledge, 'to use liquid ferret.'

'What the bloody hell's that?' asked the Bounder nervously.

'Just tha wait and see,' replied Brian.

A container was fetched from the car and its contents were sprayed into the rat hole and behind the wall. Then a line of the liquid was splashed onto the ground for about three yards. 'Right,' said Brian. 'Stand well back and keep hold of the dogs.'

As we stood and waited, realisation dawned. Petrol. Brian lit a match and threw it at the line. It lit instantly and a tongue of flame ran to the rat hole. There was a minor explosion and flames shot out – and so, with singed whiskers, did eleven rats. In their dazed and unhappy state, they made an easy prey for the terriers. 'Wonderfully effective, is liquid ferret,' said Brian with an air of complacency. The total bag was some eighty rats – and a good day's hunting.

The Bounder and I had arrived in Yorkshire the night before by train. We had decided to travel first class as the tickets were on special offer ('First Class Tickets for Second Class Citizens,' muttered the Bounder as we set off).

Brian met us at Wombwell station. 'Welcome to the Northern Riviera,' he said. 'I'm taking you to the Dorchester of Yorkshire.' We arrived at one of the seediest guesthouses that I have ever seen. The noise from the sound system could be heard a hundred yards down the street, but inside the pretty, big-busted barmaid made us feel instantly at home. We were just there to unpack – for that night we were going out to dinner at a local country pub to meet the rest of Brian's rat catchers for the first time.

The Royal Albert Rat Catchers number seven in total besides Brian, Yorkshiremen to the heart for centuries, of mining stock, Scargill's men. What the hell were they going to think of us with our 'posh' accents and my title? But when we arrived at the inn, as T. S. Eliot wrote, 'Finding the place it was, you may say, satisfactory.' We were given a typically generous Yorkshire welcome. 'Richard, Mike, I'm Kevin, I'm Pete – what you drinking?'

We might have known each other for years, and the conversation flowed as smoothly as the beer. 'So what's The Ancient and Honourable Society of Ratte Catchers' record day then, Richard?' enquired Kevin affably. I had to admit that I thought it was only one. 'One!' said Brian, aghast. 'You can't call yourselves rat catchers and only kill one fookin' rat!'

The Royal Alberts' amazement at our lack of ratting skill apart, we shared a mutual passion for the countryside. The Bounder found out that Brian collected butterflies, and as he had done the same in his youth they could be heard discussing the extraordinary life of the Large Blue, which is nearly extinct.

'I've never seen one,' said the Bounder wistfully.

'Me neither,' replied Brian, 'but I've got one in my collection.

I bought it as caterpillar from a man who bred them in captivity and he hatched it into butterfly.'

'You lying bugger,' replied the Bounder, outraged. 'That's impossible! They can't breed without the ants that carry them off to their nests where they live on the pupae and in return feed the ants on a sweet secretion from their arses.'

'All right, all right, I know,' said Brian, a bit sheepishly. 'Just trying to catch thee out.'

That night, as I lay in my slightly lumpy bed in the Dorchester of Yorkshire in that strange world between waking and sleeping, I thought back to the origins of The Ancient and Honourable Society of Ratte Catchers, and the larger than life, Pickwickian figure of Cephas Goldsworthy, who had started it all . . .

He was dressed in full Regency attire; green tailcoat with black velvet collar and cuffs, lace at his neck and wrists and an ornate waist-coat. He sported cream buckram breeches and white silk stockings. On his feet were shoes with silver buckles. He stood with two other similarly dressed friends outside the ballroom of Claridge's in London waiting to join one of the most fashionable dances of the debutante season of 1962. After they had passed the doormen, the three headed for the bar and ordered champagne. As they were enjoying their second glasses they were approached by a middle-aged, beautifully gowned lady of obvious bearing and breeding.

'Would you like to dance?' she said to the nearest Ratte Catcher.

The young man followed her to the dance floor. As they began to circle the room she said: 'Do you know whose party this is?'

'Haven't a clue,' he replied airily.

'Well, it's mine. Were you invited?'

'Certainly not!' He was affronted.

'Then I'm afraid you'll have to leave,' said the hostess, who was a duchess and not unamused at the trio's antics.

'Of course,' replied the young buck, with a deep bow. 'And I cannot thank you enough for your kind hospitality. We have enjoyed ourselves enormously.'

He collected his friends and they went outside. 'Don't worry, chaps,' said Cephas, law student, professional gatecrasher of deb dances, and leader of The Ancient and Honourable Society of Ratte Catchers. 'There's another one at the Connaught!'

The Ancient and Honourable was formed by five law students, for no particularly good reason except as an excuse to drink together in the Chelsea pubs and to dine out, in full Regency costume, at the more fashionable London restaurants. It was the Society's pride that they were never allowed to eat in the same restaurant twice. The Bounder and I were invited to join in 1964. There were no real criteria for membership except to drink in the same pub as the Rats (either The Australian in Milner Street or The Nag's Head in Kinerton Street), to have a certain wit about you, and to behave as badly as possible. It was also required of you to support your fellow Rats in times of trouble (usually a bed for the night, or collecting from a police station after a night in the cells for drunk and disorderly).

It was all very well to call ourselves Ratte Catchers, but what rat-catching was really done? The answer, over the years, was 'very little'. On the one or two occasions that we actually left London in pursuit of some sport, more drinking, dining and story-telling was achieved than rat-hunting. We were singularly ill-equipped for the job and knew little or nothing about it. We had no dogs except one or two ill-trained Labradors and they, I suspect, would have run a mile if they had seen a rat.

The Royal Albert Rat Catchers are the very antithesis of the Ancient and Honourable. This group of seven Yorkshiremen (and ten terriers) formed their club in 1996 in Barnsley in a pub of the same name, as a rebellion against the Government's bill banning hunting with dogs. Barnsley and its surroundings have been coal-mining country for centuries, and a Labour strong-hold. But the threat of this bill turned a large majority of the area against New Labour, despite the fact that it later exempted rats. With little money for any luxuries or other pastimes, the hunting of rats with dogs has been a traditional sport in the area for cen-turies. As Kevin Bradley, the Royal Albert's spokesman, told me in broadest Yorkshire: 'We've been hunting rats for years, and our fathers did it before us and our grandfathers before that. The townsfolk know nowt about countryside and we're not having them turning it into a fookin' shithole like the inner cities.'

We first came across the Royal Alberts on the day of the Countryside March in 1997. The Bounder and I were in a pub near Hyde Park waiting to join the tail end, but unable to stir our-selves because we were mesmerised by a vision which had sent us both on a joyous trip down memory lane. Across the crowded bar I had spotted a Very Beautiful Girl. She was not in the prime of youth, but I remembered her when she was, and she had changed little. I pointed her out to the Bounder.

'I know that face, but who is she?' he said.

'Don't you remember?' I said. 'You were Number Two and I was Number Three. And that is what she called us.'

We plucked up courage and went over. The Very Beautiful Girl was every bit as good company as she had been well over twenty years previously and we spent a very happy half-hour, completely forgetting the great national issue we had come to protest. Eventually the Bounder caught sight of the time. As we reluctantly got up to go she gave us each a warm, parting hug. 'Goodbye, Number Two,' she said under her breath to the Bounder.

'Goodbye, Number Three,' she whispered to me. Her husband, we were relieved to see, was out of earshot.

By now we were too late for anything but the conclusion of the march – but how fortunate we were. As we puffed our way across the park to join the other wastrels at the back, we spotted a banner announcing the presence of the 'Royal Albert Rat Catchers'. Brother Rat Catchers? How could we hold back? We went across and introduced ourselves, and all of us abandoned the procession and retired to a pub. It was the beginning of our long and happy association.

The Bounder and I became particularly good friends with Brian – and he has become a particularly good friend of my wife's. He rang her up once: 'Hey, Susie,' he said. 'Dost tha like mink?' Two days later a beautifully mounted and snarling stuffed mink arrived in the post. It was not exactly what my wife had expected. Brian is a quite exceptional human being and full of surprises. I count myself lucky to have met him.

Brian was born in 1954 in the same council house in which he still lives. It is an ugly brute, just big slabs of concrete bolted together and built to last a mere thirty years. 'One of these days I'll fart and t'whole bloody lot will come down,' says Brian. He was educated locally but his real education came from his grandfather, who like all his generation earned his living down the pits. However, he was also a serious poacher and countryman, and made a shilling or two from selling illicit game. He was a great collector of birds' eggs, when that pastime was legal, and had one of the best collections in Britain, which Brian still possesses. He taught Brian all about it, and Brian has added to his grandfather's collection. 'He taught me exactly what was right and wrong,' he says, 'and thus I knew exactly how many eggs to take without endangering the breeding of that bird.'

'In those days,' says Brian, 'almost every miner had a knowledge of birds and every pit had its own caged birds society. It were a question of survival. The miners experimented with different breeding stock to find which one was best at showing the first signs of gas down mine. It were highly competitive between miners, and it gave us all an interest in the countryside.'

The other major pastime of the Yorkshire mining community was rat catching – although it's a sport practised throughout the British countryside. It became popular out of necessity because of pigs. In the 1930s everyone in rural Britain who had a back garden kept a pig in it. The front garden was for vegetables, and the back garden for the pig or pigs, mainly Landrace or Large Whites. Some families had a brood sow that was often cared for and loved more than the children. Each year they farrowed, produced a litter of little pigs, and these young piglets or weaners were sold at market. However, some of the young castrated males or geldings were kept to be fattened up for food. There was always great competition amongst the village as to whose sow could produce the largest litter or which gelding could be fed up to be the heaviest. This pig was part of the family and lived off the swill of each family meal before being ritually slaughtered in October. The slaughtering of the pig was an Event in the villages and people used to turn out to watch as the pig had its throat cut. I can remember even in the 1950s in my home village of Welford-on-Avon the blacksmith slaughtering his pig, whom he had called Ethelred. Why he had chosen this particular name I never knew – except that perhaps he felt that he would always be Unready for slaughter. Tom was a huge man who had tamed many a kicking stallion as he put on the shoes, but Ethelred was the love of his life. Tom cared for him like a son, and he was acknowledged by the village to be the heaviest gelding ever fattened. When the time eventually came for Ethelred to be killed, Tom blubbered for three days beforehand. But although the tears streamed down his face as he drew the knife across Ethelred's throat, it did not stop him from eating every piece of him, from his delicious, vast gammons to his trotters.

Not all pigs are as supine and amiable as Ethelred. Some pigs can be dangerous, particularly when they are weaning, and they have jaws that can bend a spade. There was one man in our village with a huge and bossy wife. One day she disappeared and, despite a long police search, was never seen again. Rumour had it that her hen-pecked husband had finally had enough and had killed her, cut her up, and fed her to his prize sow, who had obediently and contentedly munched her up, bones and all. There was no evidence available, of course, and the man married the pretty petite barmaid at the local pub and lived happily ever after.

The perennial problem with pigs is that they produce a perfect environment for rats, who thrive on their food. 'Thus,' as Brian says, 'we took pride in breeding the best ratting terriers in Britain and The Barnsley Terriers blood line is still extant today. After school each day I used to go ratting with my terrier around the pigsties and the council refuse dumps. It was great fun and cheaper than telly – which we couldn't afford anyway. A lot of what we did at school in those days would be frowned upon now. Our school had a farm and at Christmas every pupil had to kill their own turkey, pluck it and dress it. Can you imagine the fuss that would cause nowadays? Kids think that turkeys come in plastic bags from Tesco's.'

Brian greatly regrets the urbanisation of the modern child. 'My grandchildren don't even know what a magpie looks like,' he complains. 'One Christmas I bought them books on birds and their eggs and told them to read them and learn from them. They never bothered.'

Brian really started taking an interest in wildlife in his early teenage years when he had his own terrier, and every evening after school it was a grab for the banana sandwich on the kitchen table and then off to the woods. As the Bounder and I walked with him past a golf course on our first visit, he turned to us and said: 'That used to be a slag heap. You'd think that wasteland wouldn't hold too many birds but you'd be wrong. That used to be full of oyster catchers, peewits, larks, redshanks, snipe and all sorts. Nowadays most of the wildlife is gone. They much prefer the sparse vegetation.' On the same walk we climbed up a small hill. 'Do you know', Brian said, 'that running up a hill, a hare will beat any dog in t'world; lurchers, greyhounds, anything. But they can't run straight downhill 'cos their back legs are too long. They have to go sideways across the contours.' Brian is one of the greatest amateur naturalists I have ever met.

Brian left the pits after the great miners' strike. Curiously, he remembers this as one of the best years of his life. 'I was supervisor then, so still on the payroll, but had a whole year free to look after my birds and dogs.' He wasn't sorry to leave. 'Mines is closest thing to being blind. All you'd hear in pitch darkness would be sudden noises. "Pink, pink, pink." This was the pressure coming on the props. Laws of physics say that pressure comes in a big arch, 150 yards radius, once you start taking the coal out. This is how mining works. But if the pressure builds up too much, you get a problem, and the first thing you know, rocks are falling everywhere. Funny thing is, when this happens, miners always put up their hands to cover their faces: as if that'd be any use when they are about to be squashed flat.

'What clinched it were the number of men I knew that died at work and the thought that it'd be me next. Brian, I thought, you're selling your life, but for what? By the time you retire, you're well and truly fooked. Doctor told me, if you carry on working, you'll be running around in one of them mobility scooters. He says, you might as well enjoy nature, because that don't cost nowt. Don't worry about the money. You're going to finish on nowt, so you might as well get some practice in now. I thought, you're right. My back is now so bent after accidents, if it gets any worse, I'll be looking up my own arse.'

After he retired, Brian learnt to work a computer and the online auction site ebay. He then started painting pheasant and other easily obtainable eggs to look like rare osprey, golden eagle and other forbidden collectors' species, which he sold on eBay. They were so good that few could tell the difference between Brian's fakes and the real thing. He did not cheat: he always said that they were copies. However, it earned him good money and he had orders from as far afield as Boston and Anchorage. Someone asked him for humming birds' eggs, and these he made from the tiny peppermint sweets that can be bought at any confectioners. When the Bounder and I saw these works of art we couldn't believe they weren't the real thing.

About four weeks after Brian had shown us his collection, he was woken at 8 a.m. by a furious hammering on the door of his house. When he answered it, no fewer than six policemen and three inspectors from the RSPB and the RSPCA confronted him. They searched his house for illicit birds' eggs. He was eventually arrested and held in the local police station all day. After he was released, he rang me, greatly upset. 'They kept asking me where I got the harrier eggs,' he told me. ' "Harrier eggs?" I said to them, "there aren't any bloody harrier eggs. What you seem to forget," I told them, "is that pheasants lay blue eggs." ' It turned out that the inspectors they had sent knew a bit about birds but almost nothing about their eggs. 'When they finally brought an expert in to interview me,' Brian said, 'he told me that he had spent hours looking at my eggs and still wasn't sure whether they were painted or not. I suggested that he bring me a fookin' egg and a knife and watch me scrape the paint off. 'Course, he still wasn't satisfied 'cos he said there were dozens of eggs and any one of them could be genuine. Arsehole.'

The police never charged him, but the RSPB and RSPCA kept the case on file for a year until, finally and reluctantly, prompted by me, they sent Brian back his eggs. The best ones, from his grandfather's collection, were broken. 'It were like desecrating the old man's grave,' he said bitterly.

On our second visit to Yorkshire with Brian he arranged for us to attend a formal meeting of the Royal Albert Ratcatchers. They were incredibly well organised and we were amazed to see Kevin Bradley, their club secretary, with his 'Big Red Book' collecting subscriptions and taking the minutes. When the club started, the members had agreed to pay £5 a week in case their sport was ever licensed. It was a strange insight into life in the mining villages. The miners had taken their sports every bit as seriously as the bosses had running the pits (maybe more so), and organised themselves very well.

The Royal Albert pub is set on a hillside above Wombwell where Brian lives. One of the Royal Alberts, who was a bus driver, drove us there in the club minibus. He had been chosen because it was thought there was a chance he might remain reasonably sober. Inside the pub is small and smoky, with a landlady who takes no prisoners. 'Sit there, behave yourselves and these lads will tell you what to drink' was her opening shot to us. And she was right – a couple of pints of local beer at about half the price of the rest of the country got the Bounder and me settled.

There was a fair amount of catching up to do before the formal business of the club started. One of the Royal Alberts was complaining that his dog had killed a pet rabbit by mistake. 'Most expensive fookin' rabbit I've ever caught,' he said gloomily, to general commiseration. This led to suggestions as to the best way to cook it. Rabbit stew and Yorkshire pudding came up tops. Brian told us his favourite meal: 'Cow heel and stew meat,' he announced with relish. 'My Mum boiled up the cow heels to get the jelly off, cooked up the stewing meat, then added in the jelly until the gravy was so thick it would stick your lips together. It were real nice. We used to have it for Sunday breakfast. The jelly in the pan would be set solid. It just needed warming up enough to melt and it'd be ready to eat.' One of the other lads remembered a shop that served it, where even the knives and forks were fixed on chains to the wall. A long way from MacDonalds!

The growing intrusion of bureaucracy in all its forms was a big source of complaint. One of the biggest local shoots now could only pay their beaters if they gave their National Insurance numbers first. Result, no beaters! 'It's not money. It's bigger than that. Shooting makes millions of pounds for t'countryside, but now it's being ruined by some fookin' idiot who thinks we need more red tape than Russia!'

Kevin called for the more formal club business to be discussed before the beer gained too strong a hold. The Royal Alberts are serious about their role in helping farmers keep down vermin. Apart from rats, the changing face of the countryside has brought some new pests – muntjac deer, for example, have massive appetites and can strip a piece of woodland quick as a flash. Mink are on the rise, and so are foxes. There was one request from a local pub owner to put down a plague of foxes that had caused all sorts of havoc with his kitchen refuse, and even stole directly from the dining room. The club talked about each and decided who would lead the hunt. It was very impressive.

The conversation inevitably turned to coal and the pits, in which many of the men had worked for over forty years. There was talk of reopening some, but a lot of doubt about whether the younger generation would put up with the conditions. Strangely, the Royal Alberts were different. 'I'd start again tomorrow,' said Kevin. 'You don't have mates like miners' mates.' Was it just the drink talking? I don't know, but the meeting of the Royal Alberts had taught me what true friendship meant.

Our memories of the evening get a bit blurred from this point on. I remember Brian, the club's historian, claiming that the 'Pilgrim Fathers' who founded America were named after a pub in Yorkshire, and then it was time for bed. Our bus driver was clearly not up to driving, so one of the long-suffering wives who ran a mini-cab business on the side did the honours. The Bounder and I slept well, the laughter and friendly Yorkshire voices still ringing in our ears.

The next morning Brian was taking us fishing. Apparently none the worse for wear he picked up a distinctly under-the-weather Bounder and me at 7 a.m. As we passed a small patch of scrubby grass at the entrance to a new property development, Brian showed us something we'd have normally passed without a second glance.

'The advantage', Brian told us, 'of keeping birds and butter-flies is that you learn what they eat and become expert in botany. Look here,' he said, bending down to part the grass, 'there's wonderful natural food, despite all the muck and dust. There's groundsel, callomine daisies, goosefoot and Good King Henry. You'd eat Good King Henry before cabbages were domes-ticated. Look at these knot grass seeds, without them, you wouldn't think it were grass at all, but these triangular shapes put them in the same family as dock and bindweed. Understanding seeds will tell you everything about the plants. Here's another one. What you call bilaterally flattened. This is shepherd's purse and over there's Percy Cary, what grows everywhere in 'tatie fields. And there's mugwort, which don't smell very nice, but makes a great midge repellent. See what I mean? This is what they call wasteland, but it isn't wasteland really. At least not to t'birds.'

As Brian's old car rattled through the side streets and then onto an open road, the Bounder and I felt suitably chastened – maybe we weren't quite the countrymen we thought ourselves. Twenty minutes later we turned off onto a small track and there, spread out below us, was one of the most unspoilt valleys I had ever seen in Yorkshire. Thoughts of D. H. Lawrence and *The Virgin and the Gypsy* (always one of my favourite books) sprang into my head. We parked the car and took a big breath of the sweet, fresh air and the smell of new mown grass.

'This were all slag heaps and pit country twenty years ago,' said Brian. 'Now you'd never know they'd been there. It's an extraordinary achievement really. And here's a real test of nature – bum bum flies. They're the flies that hang round cows' arses, and they wouldn't be anywhere that wasn't natural. They seem to like you this morning, Mike,' he said, turning to the Bounder. 'I'm not saying you've got a face like a cow's arse, but you've sure got the flies fooled.'

Brian had more advice. 'If you ever believe in reincarnation, don't come back as a mole. I do a lot of mole-trapping around these fields. A mole leads a solitary life, and a female mole only comes in season once each year, in March for a fortnight. Male has only two weeks to find his mate, get job done and then go back into solitary confinement. So, it's not a very good life being a mole.'

The roar of an engine announced a local farmer on a quad bike. The Bounder nudged me. 'My God! He looks just like a mole! Maybe he's been reincarnated already.'

Brian introduced us and we learnt that mink were now the biggest problem in the valley. They killed first the moorhens and the wild duck, then everything else they could. There was little the farmer could do. As soon as he trapped one lot, another inva-sion would come from the next farm. Brian promised that the Royal Alberts would try to help, and made an appointment for the lads to visit.

The farmer roared off, satisfied, and we followed an overgrown track down to the river, which was small, winding and mostly overgrown with trees. The occasional pool or shallow run gave us a chance to fish. The Bounder was entranced. Despite being a professional salmon fly fisherman, he still likes nothing better than a wild river, small fish and a worm or two. I'm the same. It makes me feel twelve again. Brian agreed. 'You've got to keep hold of your childhood. You become old, else.'

We tackled up, using Brian's home-made maggot dispenser, contrived from an old film container and specially modified for 'trotting' with a float down the narrow stream. We asked him what we might catch. 'There're some beautiful fish in here,' he told us. 'Trout, perch, grayling, barbel, and big eels sometimes, which will break your line.' Brian's favourite fish were grayling, with their graceful dorsal fins. 'The Lady of the Stream', he called them, and said they made great eating.

We soon leant the art. The fish were wild but hungry, and would often snatch the bait right at our feet. It was fantastic fun and, as we now expected with Brian, 'all for nowt'. Between us we caught three small trout, two grayling and some perch. True to his word, Brian kept the grayling for his breakfast, wrapping them in dock leaves to keep them fresh. The rest we released, holding them upright in the current until, with a flick of their tails, they were away.

We kept marvelling about how the countryside around us had recovered from industrialisation. 'Twenty years ago, you wouldn't have recognised it,' Brian said. 'You couldn't drink the water and nothing lived in it. It were full of shit from steel works further up valley. Soapsuds and iron oxide would turn the water brown. It were totally sterile. Now it's clear and the wild life is back. There was a greater spotted woodpecker raising young 'uns in the tree right there last year. Jays, what they call "watchmen of the woods", can be heard shouting most days. I once took some down pit. News travelled faster than a pay rise and soon the foreman was at me. I told him these were genuine "miner" birds, better than canaries. He believed me at first, then found out he'd been fooled. I nearly got sacked that time.'

On the way back to the car, Brian took us through a small patch of woodland. The sunlight was shining in sharp, dust-moted beams through the foliage and the stillness and silence were everywhere. 'Look there!' he said, pointing. 'They're speckled woods butterflies. See the males dancing to attract mates. They do a vertical circle, then a horizontal one. It's like a courtship.' The world was a fairyland as we watched them. Then in a single blink of an eye they were gone, and there was nothing but shadow and flecked, golden light. 'They'll be back,' said Brian. 'It takes more than one dance to get the girls, in my experience.'

As we packed the car Brian heard a bullfinch in the trees, and called it down with the imitation whistling his granddad had taught him. We looked back at the enchanted valley and felt at ease here with the man who was part of that magic land. 'You're in God's Country now,' said Brian.

The Bounder and I returned home, determined to keep in touch with the ratters from the north. With the blossoming friendship that had formed between the two societies, the Bounder and I decided that a revival of the Ancient and Honourable Society of Ratte Catchers was necessary. To this end we invited The Royal

Albert Rat Catchers down south for a rat-hunt and dinner. We also decided to introduce our sons and daughters, to inject some young blood into the crumbling ruin our Society had become.

The Bounder's friend Daniel Busk had land near Stockbridge in Hampshire, on the banks of the Test. Daniel had a major rat problem in all his outbuildings and farmyards. A rat problem for him was a golden opportunity for us, and so it was arranged to hold the first joint rat-hunt between the Ancient and Honourable and the Royal Albert Rat Catchers there. It is necessary to hold rat-hunts in the cold winter months, when there is no foliage to hide the rat holes and the runs are obvious, so on a cold but clear day in January 2006 we all assembled at the farm at 1 p.m. for the meet.

The seven Yorkshire ratters all came down in one minibus with ten terriers. They immediately checked out the farmyard and killed one rat instantly, 'by mistake', before our lot had even appeared. They also efficiently marked many other areas where they found rats, but generously saved them until everyone had arrived.

At last, in dribs and drabs, in a series of vehicles totally unsuited to a farm track, the Ancient and Honourable condescended to roll up and join the party. It soon became very obvious why we had killed so few rats in the past. The Royal Alberts demonstrated their complete professionalism. They had spades for digging in runs. We had swagger canes. They had terriers that dug up rats' nests and killed any rat that appeared with a murderous efficiency. We had one effete and homosexual Labrador who had to be returned to the car half-way through because it was exhausted. They were dressed for the job. We looked like something out of a provincial amateur theatre production. However, it seemed to make little difference to the laughter and enjoyment of good company, and at half time, with hot dogs and mulled wine in our bellies, all of us in the Ancient and Honourable were talking with pride about how many rats 'we' had killed. The total for the day was a magnificent nineteen; or it might have been sixteen rats and three mice, but the Ancient and Honourable claimed they were baby rats. Whether rats or mice, this score was by far the highest ever for the Ancient and Honourable. As I'd admitted to Brian up in Yorkshire, our previous record was one, and even that was a suspicious death as no one had seen it killed.

One of the nicest things about the day was the way the younger generation took to the sport. My son Freddie became such a dab hand at the 'liquid ferret' that the Yorkshiremen made him an honorary member of the Royal Alberts. Tara, the Bounder's adorable eight-year-old, produced the bloodthirstiest remark of the day: 'I loved it when that rat shot out of the hole all on fire,' she said, her little face aglow. 'Can you do it again, please?' Another generation of rat hunters was born.

By tradition that night we had a ratting dinner. This was held in The Three Tuns at Great Bedwyn and, out of keeping with all times past, the police were not called and we are allowed back again. After dinner, the Ancient and Honourable have tradition-ally sung lewd songs. There is one, sung to the hymn tune 'For those in trouble on the sea', which bemoans the downfall of a ducal family. This was normally the point in the past when the police were summoned. There was no such bourgeois reaction on this evening. The management of The Three Tuns seemed to revel in our entertainment and the landlord, an ex-actor and out-standing chef, asked to learn the words.

What neither the Bounder or I knew was that, besides his many other talents, our friend Brian Oliver was also a great singing entertainer, with an unbelievable line in blue Country and Western songs, honed in the stripping pubs round Barnsley. His version of Tammy Wynette's 'Stand by your man' nearly gave me a rupture, I laughed so much.

During a small lull in the singing, as we were sitting there soaking up the atmosphere, Kevin Bradley, the Royal Alberts' loyal secretary leaned over to me.

'You know, Richard,' he said, 'we're seven Yorkshire lads of mining stock and we've joined forces with knights of the realm, landed gentry, and movers and shakers from the City. We're all united in our love of the countryside. Long may it continue.'

I looked around the long, low-ceilinged room and saw the laughing, happy faces of people who share a mutual passion. 'I'll drink to that,' I said.

2

February

WILDFOWLING AND POACHING

They shut the road through the woods
Seventy year ago.
Weather and rain have undone it again,
And now you would never know
There was once a path through the woods
Before they planted the trees.
It is underneath the coppice and heath
And the thin anemones.

RUDYARD KIPLING, 'The Road Through The Woods'

THE BOUNDER . . .

It wasn't a difficult shot, but I muffed it anyway. It was also, I knew, the last chance of the evening as twilight faded to darkness and there was no moon or cloud to silhouette the duck. I had hurried, mis-mounted, and seen the mallard lurch down, a wingtip trailing, a good distance the wrong side of the wire. It would have been better had I never fired, and I can only blame the enthusiasm of youth and the fact that, because of the lack of wind, I had had very few chances that evening.

It was 1966, the height of the Cold War, and I was in Berlin serving with the Royal Green Jackets. I often felt the need to escape the claustrophobia of the officers' mess and, although the smell was unpleasant, there was nothing more refreshing for my soul than to flight the duck on the nearby sewage farm at RAF Gatow. Like so much of Berlin in those days, it was divided by the wire of segregation that ran between West and East and was patrolled by the East German *Volkspolitzei* (the Vopos), who had orders to shoot on sight any unauthorised person near the wire. My duck now lay injured on the wrong side.

I had been taught from an early age that no sportsman worthy of the name should ever abandon a wounded bird, but surely this was beyond the sporting code. If the Vopos spotted me, I would be either shot or captured. If I were captured, I would be

33

interrogated unpleasantly for my meagre knowledge before being spat out and returned to the West and disgrace. I would almost certainly be cashiered. Nonetheless, a combination of childhood training, devilment and sheer stupidity drove me on to the most foolhardy thing that I have ever done in my life.

It was, at least, a very black night. I left my gun and cartridges against a tussock and crawled towards the wire. I commanded the reconnaissance platoon and patrolled the border regularly in armoured cars, so I was pretty certain that this area was neither mined nor trip-wired. I also knew that there were no searchlights. But this did not stop me shaking with terror as I carefully lifted the bottom of the wire high enough to crawl beneath. I stopped and listened. There was no sound at all except the soft sighing of a bitter north wind and the pounding of my own heart. I crept under, and into East Germany. I had marked the direction of the duck and, deciding that speed was of the essence, stood up and ran towards it as fast as I could. The injured duck suddenly erupted in a mêlée of flapping. I grabbed it quickly, broke its neck, and ran back towards the wire, but I couldn't find the hole. I had noted the position of the duck, but not that of my own exit. Forcing myself not to panic, I lay flat, feeling first to the right and then to the left. At last, by a miracle, I found the gap and, drenched in the sweat of fear, wriggled through. Just in time. In the far distance I saw a flare, and a shot was fired. I had been very lucky. The Vopos had been too distracted by some poor devil trying to defect to bother about a fool retrieving a duck.

The romance of wildfowling has hugely appealed to me ever since I was a small boy. I have read all the books 'BB' (Denys Watkins-Pitchford) has written on the sport and revelled in their descriptions of dawns and dusks on the wild coasts of our islands. His writing is so evocative that you can smell the salt of the sea and feel the cold of a January dawn biting into your bones. You can see the fleeting silhouettes of the birds against the black and white scudding clouds, lit by a fitful winter moon, and hear their mournful cries.

With the pull of such tales plucking at my dreams, I knew that as soon as I was old enough I had to go to the marshes and try it for myself. I wanted to spend nights in a hide in a desolate creek waiting for the whistle of widgeon. I longed to linger in a muddy gut, tasting the tang of the tide in that lonely hour between darkness and dawn, with a bitter nor'east wind howling across the barren saltings, alert for the plaintive barking of the wild geese.

Looking back now over the years and the thousands of hours that I have spent in pursuit of every type of game, from patrician grouse to humble woodpigeon, I know that wildfowling is, to me, the most exciting and the most challenging of all country pursuits. It has a strong mystical aura and an empathy with loneliness. Only a man at ease with himself, and at one with wind, mud, frost and tide, can really understand its lure. Once the smell of salt marshes is in his bones, he is lost to their call forever.

To the unknowing and uninitiated, the marshes are dangerous places. That tiny, ebb-tide trickle that is easily crossed on the way out across the mud flats can be ten feet deep and a swirling, unswimmable mill-race with the flood. It can cut a person off from the shore in the wink of an eye. It can move faster than a man can run, and drown him before he knows what has happened. Only a fool goes out devoid of a compass or without telling someone where he is headed and what time he expects to be back, for a sea mist can descend in moments, and suddenly there is no sign of the comforting shore lights. Direction is lost in an all-enveloping grey blanket from which even sound is excluded.

When I was eighteen I was given my first twelve-bore. It was a good, solid English box lock, ejector made by Patstone and, although I had shot a great deal with a twenty-bore, I felt that I had truly come of age when I was presented with it. In November of the winter of 1960 I drove to Norfolk to fulfil my wildfowling dream. I had billeted myself on friends at South Creake, which was ten miles from Wells-next-the-Sea, regarded as the best wild-fowling centre in the country. I had no idea what to do when I reached Wells, but with the eternal optimism of youth I assumed someone would tell me.

When I got to Wells, I walked into the first pub I came to and asked the landlord if he knew of anyone who could take me wild-fowling.

'You'm want to ask for Kenny Cook,' he said, in the beautiful singsong accent of Norfolk. 'He's the best in the county. He drinks in The Eight Ringers and you should find him there any time now.'

I thanked him and found my way to The Eight Ringers. The barman pointed to an alcove where a big man in his mid thirties with dark hair and a weather-beaten face sat alone enjoying his beer. I introduced myself, and bought him a pint. After we were settled I told him what I wanted.

'You'm a bit young, ain't you?' said Kenny Cook. 'You done any shootin' afore?'

I told him that I had done quite a bit. I described all my reading of 'BB' to him. I explained the birthday present of the new twelve-bore. When I had finished there was a long silence as he looked at me and thought hard. I waited in fearful anticipation for his answer.

'Orr right,' he said at last. 'You'm obviously keen enough. I don't need someone out there who's going to want to go home if it's bitter cold or howling wind and rain.'

He paused, looked at his glass, which was empty, and I ordered another pint.

'At the moment it's hopeless,' he said, and my spirits, which had begun to soar, plummeted into my boots. 'You see,' he said kindly, noting my disappointment, 'I'm not taking you out in this weather. It's warm, there's no wind, and we'll shoot nothing. And there's another thing: don't expect no geese. They was over-shot. Everyone used to line the sea wall and they had no peace. Then one year they never came back and they ain't been back since. Give me yer 'phone number and I'll ring you when it's worth it.' And with that I had to be contented.

The call came in early January. 'If you can get here,' said Ken, 'there's a good few widgeon about. It's dirty ol' weather, but the moon and tides are right.'

I drove up the next day.

We met at Ken's house at 5 p.m. in pitch darkness and with a strong north-east wind blowing. Ken had his spaniel Jonkin with him. 'Why "Jonkin" as a name?' I asked. 'Ne'er you mind,' said Ken.

It was almost freezing and there was sleet hitting our faces as we walked towards Ken's van. The moon was due to rise just after 6.30 and the tide was beginning to flood half an hour before that. 'That'll push them ol' duck up,' said Ken. 'Them birds will start to come any time after that.'

We drove to the sea wall, left the van there and walked across the saltings, silent and mysterious in the gloom. 'I hope this sleet eases off,' Ken said gloomily. 'We'll see nothing, else.' It was bitterly cold and the wind cut through our clothes, threatening to blow us over as we battled against it. Occasionally we could hear the sound of wings above us, but in the black sky only flecks of moisture could be seen. We trudged on through muddy creeks, once disturbing a flock of mallard that rose protesting, their wing beats fading slowly as they climbed towards the distant sea. And still the sleet drove into us, until we were wet through. 'We'm nearly there,' said Ken. 'There's a big area of "zos" grass, which has been exposed by the big tides. Them ol' widgeon loves zos grass, or eel grass as some know it.' He stopped and shepherded me into a narrow gut. 'Zos is just in front of us now. You stay here and I'll be fifty yards on your left. Birds'll come in against the wind that way.' He pointed straight ahead. I crouched down on some sea-blite, laid my gun beside me and waited.

I heard the whistle of the cock widgeon at the same time as I realised the sleet had stopped. I looked up and I could see stars. The near full moon showed majestically, silhouetting scudding clouds that were whipped by the freezing wind across the black and white sky. Boom! Boom! Deep roars from Kenny's gun. I peered into the night and suddenly I saw them: five widgeon curling away from Ken's shot, against the clouds. I swung onto the leader, pulled the trigger and was so thrilled to see it fall that I didn't fire the second barrel. It landed near me with a satisfying squelch. A minute later I heard Jonkin retrieve it.

For the next hour the birds kept coming, until I began to worry about running out of cartridges. Jonkin worked non-stop. At last I saw Ken appear through the gloom. 'That's enough,' he said. 'Tide'll be with us soon.' We picked up twenty-eight birds and stored them in sacks before scrambling through the creeks with the tide at our heels. When we reached the sea wall we stopped for a breather. Above us we could still hear wings, but now the clouds were gone and there was only bright moonlight and stars to be seen. 'I don't know if you realise how lucky you are,' said Ken. 'That was the flight of a lifetime, that was. Everything were right, and that's rare.' But I hardly heard him. In my head I was still in that distant creek by the zostera beds, seeing shapes against the clouds and hearing the whistle of wings.

For the remainder of that season I went out on the marshes with Ken as often as possible, but we never came near the success of that first flight. Nor have I since. In the many times that I have flighted wildfowl, either at dawn or at dusk, I have never had conditions as perfect. I didn't see Ken again after the season finished, until he rang me the following November and invited me back to Norfolk. We became good friends over that second season. At the end of an evening's shooting we would go to The Eight Ringers and drink several pints of Bullard's bitter, and talk.

'Ken,' I said one evening, 'you can't make a living out of wildfowling. What else do you do?'

'Bit of painting. Bit of decorating,' he said, and handed me a bent and scruffy card which read: '*Mr Ken Cook, Painter and Decorator. High and Difficult Places a Speciality.*'

The next morning we went on a dawn excursion after some elusive duck, but the wind had dropped with the daybreak, the rain had ceased, and the temperature had soared. We returned early and Ken invited me back to his house for breakfast. He had red eyes and looked tired, and I wondered if he had been drinking the night before, but there was no smell of beer on his breath. While we were waiting for his wife Kathy to cook the eggs and bacon, Ken showed me his guns. There were two twelve-bores with three-inch chambers and a beautiful eight-bore hammer gun, with damascened barrels, for the geese. 'Of course, I loads all me own cartridges,' said Ken, and he showed me the brass cases for the eight-bore and the scales with which he weighed the powder and shot. 'Get it wrong and you can blow the gun up and yerself with it,' he said.

After breakfast Ken said, 'Got one more gun I want to show you.' He disappeared and came back with what looked like an old duelling pistol. He handed it to me. 'What you reckon that is then, Mike?' he asked. I looked carefully at the gun and suddenly realised that it was a four-ten with the barrels sawn off. 'Now,' said Ken, with a mixture of pride and mystery, 'last night you asks me what I does for a livin'. Well, you come along o' me a moment.' And he led me into his and Kathy's bedroom.

I couldn't believe my eyes. The room was knee-deep in pheasants. There must have been nearly three hundred. 'I got all them last night,' said Ken proudly. 'It were perfect for it. A big wind that muffles the shot and pissing rain which discourages the keepers. There's nearly a hundred and fifty pounds' worth there. That's what this little four-ten's for. I shoots them when they're in the roost an' I makes the cartridges meself, putting much less powder in than usual so the bang's quieter. That's why I'm a bit tired today,' he added. 'Didn't get in 'til nearly four.'

'Where on earth did you get them from, Ken?' I asked, still staggered by his haul.

'Same place as I always gets 'em,' Ken replied. 'Lord Leicester's place, Holkham Hall. My father poached his father, an' my grandfather poached his grandfather. It's sort of traditional. We're poachers to the Earls of Leicester.'

'But doesn't he know about you?' I asked. 'Haven't you ever been caught?'

'Course he knows about me!' Ken replied. 'But he's never had me. He knows that I won't let any other bugger on his land, so I think he reckons that I saves him money, and he doesn't try too hard. Imagine what it would be like if every bugger went poaching on his estate! He wouldn't have any pheasants left. His head keeper's called John King, so that's why me dog's called Jonkin. Sort o' keeping it in the family!'

An idea was forming in my head. 'Do you think I could come out with you one night? I'd love to see how it's done.'

'Course you can,' said Ken. 'But you'll have to wait for the next dirty ol' night and then you can help me carry the sacks.'

When I told the Bart about my illicit expedition, he made me promise that I would take him with me. The Bart doesn't shoot, but he is always up for a bit of wickedness.

Ken and I had been on a dawn flight towards the end of January of 1962 and were walking back across the saltings when he turned to me and said casually, 'Weather forecast's for gale force winds tonight and torrential rain. It 'ud be perfect for a bit o' poachin' if you wants to come.' I agreed unhesitatingly and asked Ken if I could bring the Bart. 'Course you can, Mike,' said Ken. 'If he's a mate of yourn, he's a mate of mine.'

I rang Richard, who admitted to being a little nervous as he had just started working for IBM and didn't think that they would be too amused if he were arrested, but he agreed to drive up that day. He made me think, too. I had hitherto lived a relatively blameless life. I was due to join my regiment in March after finishing at Sandhurst in December. If we were caught, I could see myself being the only subaltern to be cashiered without serving a single day as a commissioned officer. I realised that in fact I would be rather proud of this achievement, and my nerves faded. 'You be at my house at 10.30 tonight, Mike, and no drinking aforehand,' Ken instructed. 'We has to be stone-cold sober for this job.'

Wrapped up well and as waterproof as possible, the Bart and I drove to Wells in a high old state of excitement. It was indeed blowing a gale, and the car rocked in the wind. The rain beat against the windscreen and the wipers of my ancient Mini van could only just cope. It took me twice as long as usual, but we arrived at Ken's house at exactly 10.30 p.m. He was almost euphoric, and longing to get going. 'Perfect conditions,' he said, rubbing his hands with glee, 'just perfect! We'll kill a lot of birds tonight.'

We loaded his van with a huge bag of four-ten cartridges, a pile of old hundredweight corn sacks, and the sawn-off four-ten. Then we were away. We drove for about ten miles before we turned off the road and Ken switched off the lights of the van. We bumped down a track and hid the van in a wood facing the way we had come. 'So that we can escape easy, if we have to,' said Ken. 'Now, you bring two sacks each,' he continued, 'and leave the rest here. You can collect them when we've filled these four.'

We started to walk slowly and silently through the covert with the wind howling and the rain lashing down. We had only gone a short way when Ken pulled a slim pencil torch from his pocket and shone its thin, narrow beam into the middle and top branches of the trees above us, bending with the gale. Almost immediately we spotted a line of four pheasants perched at roost, their bodies huddled up and their feathers blown out against the weather so that they looked much bigger than normal. Ken raised the pistol four-ten and fired a careful shot. There was a soft 'phut', like an air rifle, as Ken's specially loaded cartridge went off with hardly any noise at all. The pheasant fell to the ground and I put it into the sack. 'These cartridges are effective only to about fifteen yards,' whispered Ken, 'but we don't need more than that.' Between the wind and the almost silent cartridges the other pheasants on the branch had obviously heard nothing, for they remained fluffed up where they were as Ken picked them off one by one and I put them in the bag. If the pheasants couldn't hear the shot, I reasoned, nor could any keepers.

Every tree seemed packed with birds, and soon the first four bags were full. We dragged them back to the van, brought out four more empty ones, and quickly headed back.

'This is one of the outer coverts of the estate and they don't shoot it much,' said Ken, 'and I haven't done it afore this season either.'

He offered me the gun and asked if I would like a shot. I took it eagerly and we moved on to the next tree. Ken shone the torch and there was the usual line of birds. I aimed at the first one, squeezed the trigger and missed. As Ken had hit every bird at which he had aimed, I was deeply ashamed. 'Go for their feet,' said Ken. I lined up again on the same bird. The tree seemed to be swaying hugely in the wind but I did as I was told and pointed at the pheasant's legs, and to my joy it fell off its perch. I returned the gun to Ken and soon the second four sacks were full. We took them back to the van and returned. I looked at my watch. It was 2 a.m. We continued until 4, by which time we had nearly covered the whole covert and Ken had run out of cartridges. 'Reckon we got nearly five hundred birds there,' said Ken as he started the van, which was low down on its suspension because of the weight. 'That's worth a tidy sum.'

When we arrived at Ken's house we left the pheasants in the van, as he had said that he would take them to his contact immediately the next day. 'Always sell 'em fast,' he said, 'then you ain't so likely to get caught with 'em.'

The Bart and I finally reached our billet at South Creake at 5 a.m. I was shooting at 9 that morning. My long-suffering host was a tenant of the Earl of Leicester and the next day was an end-of-season, cocks only tenants' day. As he did not shoot he had kindly given me his place. The wind had died and an anaemic winter sun broke spasmodically through grey clouds as I arrived at the appointed spot. I left my car and joined the rest of the guns before being taken to the first drive. By luck I had drawn to be in the middle of the line. Behind me was the Earl himself, who always stood at the rear of the centre gun on each drive throughout the day and picked off the missed birds. As we were waiting he introduced himself to me. 'This is always one of the best outside coverts,' he said. 'There should be a lot of birds here, so get ready.' We waited for the first cock to appear. And waited. And waited. At last there was a flurry, and half a dozen pheasants launched themselves into the air, one of which headed straight at me and which I

43

missed. It is the only bird I have ever intentionally let pass in my life, for I had recognised where we were, and I could not bring myself to kill one of the few birds left after Kenny's depredations.

Years passed and I lost touch with Ken – but I did get to know his unwitting employer, the Earl of Leicester, rather better. I taught him to Spey cast along with two Chilean businessmen, to whom I had introduced him as 'Eddie Leicester'. During a coffee break in the fishing hut one of the Chileans asked in very broken English: 'Do you ever teach any sorrs and orls how to fish?' I presumed he meant Sirs and Earls. Not daring to look at Eddie, I replied that I had taught quite a few. 'What are they like?' the Chilean asked eagerly. Before I could reply, Eddie butted in. 'Absolute shits,' he said, with a completely straight face.

At the end of our two days together I asked Eddie if he knew Ken. It transpired that he most certainly did, and was well aware of the part Ken had played in his family's heritage.

Several years later on a weekend visit to Norfolk the Bart and I decided to see if we could look up Kenny Cook. We were told that the person we needed to ask was Diana Foster, who ran a restaurant in Wells. For some reason I had imagined an overweight tweed-clad 'Mother Earth' type with enormous bosoms, but when we met her the next day I couldn't believe my eyes. Diana was one of those women who had been sexy from the age of ten and would continue to be so when they were eighty. There was affection, kindness and mirth in every smile, and a hint of wickedness in every twinkle. Somehow I quenched my baser thoughts and explained my connection with Ken and why we wanted to track him down.

'If he's alive,' said Diana, 'I'll find him by this evening. Oh, by the way,' she added, 'as you're a keen wildfowler, you'll be pleased to know that the geese are back. We'll see them tonight. Each year I always know that summer is over when they return.'

The Bart and I were amazed at the change that had come over Wells-next-the-Sea since we had last been there forty years before. Then it had been a sleepy little fishing community, not much more than a village, visited by few people except wildfowlers. Now it was a thriving holiday town with amusement arcades, fish and chip bars, stalls selling 'kiss-me-quick' hats, and a huge caravan park. Of the people who passed us in the street, only one in four was a local.

That evening we returned to Diana's restaurant. 'I found him,' she said proudly. 'He's in the Scarborough Nursing Home here in Wells. He's seventy-nine now and suffering from Parkinson's disease, but entirely *compos mentis* and very much looking forward to seeing you.'

Naturally we wanted to celebrate, and during the course of several drinks I asked Diana if she minded the change that had overtaken the town in the last forty years.

'It's not what I grew up to,' she said, 'but there was an awful lot of poverty in those days. In the old times we had a bit of money in the summer, mainly from the fishing, and none at all in the winter. Nowadays the visitors come here all the year round and everyone benefits.' She suddenly paused and cocked her head, listening, then she turned to me, her face alight with excitement. 'Can you hear them?' she asked.

I listened, and felt a shiver go down my spine as if a ghost had walked on my grave. In the distance there came a faint cackling as the geese started their evening flight.

The three of us went outside. As I stared upwards, skein after glorious skein of geese was pouring over Wells. In the half-light of the witching hour the plaintive calling of the birds was deafening. They were in their thousands, high in the still air, blocking out the waning sun and filling the sky with the noise of their mournful cries and the beating of their great wings. Even the holidaymakers were moved. Overweight urchins stopped mid-burger, and their parents ceased their chatter and gazed heavenwards in awe.

'Even if we hadn't found Ken,' said the Bart, 'it would have been worth coming here just to see that.'

The next morning we were at the Scarborough Nursing Home at 10 a.m. sharp and were quickly shown into Ken's room. He and I stared at each other and remembered. Great smiles spread over both our faces as we shook hands. We talked of the wildfowling and the poaching. It felt as though we had seen each other only yesterday.

'You know I didn't just do the pheasants,' said Ken, 'I did partridges and hares too. All the game was worth good money in them days. My son-in-law and I poached the partridges with a long net. You need two to watch where the coveys are sleeping at night, and you need two on the net to drag it across the field. Then when you feel the birds hit the mesh you drop it over them. The trouble is that it's easy for the keepers to stop that by putting stakes in the ground or planting bushes where the coveys rest.' He stopped and took a long suck at his tea. Then he seemed to gather his strength and continued, 'Course I had a lurcher for the hares. Best dog in Norfolk. He used to shepherd them hares like a collie and drive them to a gate where I had the nets fixed.'

'What else did you poach, Ken?' I asked. 'What was the most profitable?'

'Deer,' he said without hesitation. 'Them park deer was easy as pie to kill, being nearly tame. I used to shoot them in the head or heart with a .22 rifle with a silencer. But it was getting them off the estate that was the difficult part.' He paused, and started laughing to himself.

There was a story coming. 'Come on, Ken,' I said, 'tell us the secret.'

'All right,' he said. 'It were long ago now anyway, and it don't matter any more.' He paused and then a great smile spread over his lined face. 'I used to dress up as a woman,' he said, 'and then push them out of the park in a pram until I reached my son-in-law's car. I were nearly caught once. I needed a piss and someone saw me doing it standing up instead of squatting down. Luckily it were a mate – but he didn't half pull my leg about it in the pub!'

'So, what was the most you did in one night, and who did you sell them to?' the Bart asked, once he'd stopped laughing.

'Eleven,' said Ken, 'and I always sold them to a Chinaman who used to come up from Norwich.' Our imaginations boggled as we thought of those eleven journeys with the pram, and the venison chop suey served to unsuspecting customers.

There was one question to which both of us longed to know the answer. 'In the end, did you ever get caught?' I asked.

'Just the once in forty years,' said Ken proudly. 'They was waiting for me as I dragged the deer to the pram. Two keepers there were, and a policeman.' He paused. 'I had twisted my ankle real bad and couldn't run, and they had me. I knew the keepers well,' he went on. 'We sometimes drank in the same pub. Not bad chaps. Just on a different side, but they held no grudge. They was just doing their job. That policeman were different. The keepers had to stop him from beating me up. He really hated me. I don't know why, but sometimes when I knew he were lying out in the cold, waiting to try and catch me, I used to think of his pretty little wife curled up all alone in bed.' He smiled wickedly. 'I'll say no more on that,' he declared enigmatically and refused to be pressed further.

'So, what happened to you when you were taken to court?' I asked.

'Fined six hundred pounds,' he said, 'which were a lot of money then.' He smiled again. 'Course, I paid it by going out the next night and shooting six hundred pounds' worth of deer. But there ain't no money in it any more because game sells so cheap, and anyway we was hungry in them days. I had a wife and two daughters to feed and you couldn't do that comfortably on the wages of a painter and decorator. Nowadays the young don't need to poach for food or money; they got plenty of both.'

'Don't you ever miss it?' asked the Bart, perceptively.

A misty look came over Ken's old features and he turned his face to the wall. 'Sometimes I wake up at night here,' he said. 'And when the north wind's howling round the walls and the rain's rattling against the windows, I long to be out in the coverts again.' His voice cracked. 'But I know I never shall be. Not now.'

He looked at us, and suddenly the remembered, mischievous smile spread over his face. 'But I've taught my grandson,' he said, 'just in case.'

That afternoon I rang the Earl of Leicester and asked him if the Bart and I could come over to Holkham Hall and talk to him about Ken. Eddie said that he would go one better and get his old head gamekeeper out of retirement so we could talk to the person who for forty years had done his best to catch Ken.

Edward VII was well known for two passions: shooting, and women. After being invited to shoot at Holkham he wanted to emulate it, and bought Sandringham. It is easy to understand why: the Holkham estate is among the best in Britain. The Leicester lands extend to 14,000 acres, much of it especially laid out for shooting.

We had arranged to meet Eddie Leicester ('Give him my best wishes,' Ken had said cheekily) at the estate office the next day, where he introduced us to John King, the retired head keeper. He was still dressed in the keeper's uniform of knee breeches, waterproofs and tweed cap, having been picking up birds on a neighbouring shoot. As we talked, Eddie and John both wanted to make it very clear that they held no grudge against Ken for all his poaching over the years. In fact, they rather admired him for managing to be caught only once in all that time.

'That doesn't mean to say that we didn't do our best to catch him,' Eddie said. 'We tried and we failed, and I would do the same again with anyone else who poached my land, but Ken was just too good for us, and I respect him for that.'

I could see that he was longing to escape, and wondered why. Suddenly all was made clear.

'I'm going to leave you now,' he said. 'John knows far more than I do about Kenny Cook, and anyway I've found a field that the pigeons are devastating and I'm off to decoy them. It's the most difficult shooting of all and I love it!' And with a cheery wave he was off.

I turned to the Bart and John King. 'When he owns some of the best shooting in Britain, I think the fact that he still wants to kill pigeons is the mark of a true countryman,' I said. 'And talking of countrymen, what did you feel about Ken, John?'

'Same as the Earl,' said the old keeper, without hesitation. 'And remember, I was out in all weathers trying to catch him, and I never did. The one time he was caught I was sick in bed with the 'flu. I was very fed up about that. But his instinct for survival was uncanny. He seemed to know exactly where we were waiting for him every time, and went to another part of the estate. It was as if he had inside knowledge – but we could never prove it. But not all my under-keepers felt the same about him as I did. There was one young one who had just been promoted when Ken poached his beat. He was so angry that he went out and shot Ken's cat. Then he ran it over to make it look as if it was an accident. But Ken was never anybody's fool and he took the cat to the vet and had it X-rayed. Of course that showed that the cat was full of shot. Ken was furious. He stormed in to see the Earl and demanded that the keeper be sacked. The Earl denied all knowledge of the affair, which was true, but Ken was determined on revenge. The next stormy night he wiped out virtually every pheasant in that young keeper's beat. I reckon that was the most expensive cat that ever died.'

'Ken told us that the one person who really hated him was the local policeman,' I said. 'Why might that have been?'

There was a long pause. John shifted a bit. 'Um – he didn't like being out in all weathers with no result?' he offered at last.

'But you were too,' I pointed out, 'and you didn't feel the same way.'

There was another long pause. 'Well,' said John reluctantly, 'that policeman had a very beautiful wife. And that's all I'm saying. Nobody ever had any proof of anything. But there was *talk*.'

As we headed back to Wells we reflected on two mysteries. The first was how Kenny Cook had managed to be caught only once in all the years that he had poached. Ken had undoubtedly become a colossal challenge for the numerous keepers and police-men who had tried to capture him. They had all the resources of a hugely wealthy estate behind them and they only achieved his arrest once and then it was because he had a twisted ankle and couldn't run. It didn't make sense. It seemed impossible without someone on the inside helping him.

Secondly, had Ken regarded the policeman's wife as another richer and more exciting form of game, to be taken illicitly on stormy nights as her husband waited in vain to catch him in some windswept and rain-soaked covert? It would have appealed

greatly to Ken's sense of humour and would explain the policeman's apparently almost pathological hatred of him. But he had
not been caught even once at this form of poaching and we had
not a scrap of evidence to support our theory. I remembered Ken
all those years ago when he was in his prime. He had been a good
looking and personable man. We determined to return to the
Scarborough and ask him.

As we entered his room again he smiled.

'I knows what you two wants,' he said. 'It's the answer to why
I was only caught the one time and whether I was tupping the
policeman's wife. Well, the answer is I'm not telling you; not even
after all this time.' And despite all our persuasion and begging he
wouldn't budge.

When we were outside I said to the Bart: 'Let's ask Diana.
She's bound to know.'

We made our way back to her restaurant and were greeted like
old friends by Diana, but when we told her what we wanted to
know she went quiet and changed the subject. The Bart had the
last word, as usual. 'They are a secretive lot these Norfolk folk,' he
said, 'and they have been fooling the gentry for generations. Just
think of *The Go-Between* with all that naughtiness going on
between the daughter of the house and the lusty young tenant
farmer. Mind you,' he addressed me, 'you randy old bugger, I'll
bet a pound to a pinch of Kenny's black powder that you'll be
back here again soon . . .'

For a moment I didn't understand what he meant, but then I
saw him wink at Diana. I didn't take the bet.

Postscript

A month after this chapter was finished, my old friend Kenny
Cook died. I am so lucky to have known him and poached and
laughed with him. He was a unique countryman.

3

March

HUNTING BOARS

'Dear Pig, are you willing
to sell for one shilling,
your ring?'
Said the Piggy, 'I will.'

EDWARD LEAR, 'The Owl and the Pussy Cat'

There is nothing so domesticated as the pig; fat, pink and friendly, it is one of the most endearing of farm animals, and certainly the most intelligent. A pig can learn to operate an automatic feeder after a single lesson, whereas a cow will probably die of starvation before it gets the trick. Yet in one small corner of south-east England the pig has metamorphosed right back to its primitive ancestor, the boar, and survives where it is against all the odds as a truly wild – and definitely endangered – species. The Bounder and I are recent converts to the boar's point of view, and we joined the movement, as so often happens with great causes, through some people we met in a pub.

We have been rollicking about East Sussex for several decades, for East Sussex was home to the Bounder's beloved mother and my favourite aunt, Elspeth. In his youth, the Bounder was an impossibly daring driver of his black MG TF, scaring the wits out of my future brother-in-law by overtaking him on the wrong side of a blind corner, then buying him a pint at the next watering-hole to help him get over the shock. Over the years and under less critical circumstances we have enjoyed most of the pubs in the county, but after extensive research we eventually settled on Bob's pub near Rye, which became the epicentre of our Sussex world.

It was a bright sunny day and the Bounder and I had decided

to take my disreputable old Land Rover Old Cow (number plate KOW 796Y) out for a bit of a spin. We hurtled into the car park and came to a spluttering stop among Bob's eclectic mix of sixties memorabilia – a primrose-yellow E-type and a white Morgan – and swung into the hop-lined bar with our usual cheery greeting. But no one – not even Jack, the bad-tempered Amazon Green parrot – answered. The atmosphere was all gloom.

'Where's Bob?' the Bounder asked, heaving himself onto his favourite bar stool.

There was general muttering, and then the barmaid reluctantly admitted that he had been taken ill. Further enquiries produced even worse news: Bob had been taken into hospital, where they had discovered a tumour as big as a melon. Inoperable cancer, a matter of weeks. Bob was not seeing anyone. This was a terrible shock. Bob was the life and soul of the whole area. We slunk off, feeling so miserable that the Bounder even forewent his lunchtime pint.

The pair of us lay low for the next few weeks; expeditions to country pubs seemed to have lost their charm. But when eventually I summoned the courage to call to find out about funeral arrangements, to my astonishment Bob answered the phone.

'How *are* you?' I asked, in the breezy, vicarish tones I fancied appropriate when speaking to someone on the brink of eternal life.

'Fine, fine! Never felt better!' Bob was clearly taking the same no-nonsense approach to his last weeks on earth.

'Getting out much?'

'Yes! Taking a long walk every morning.'

This was a brave man indeed. If he could face death with such equanimity, then I could at least confront the reality with him. 'What about the cancer?' I asked.

There was a short pause. 'Oh – *that*! You'll never guess what –

it was all a mistake! The hospital rang me up full of apologies to say they had made a misdiagnosis. Tummy problems – nothing fatal – but I'm not going near that place again. Probably say I'm pregnant next time!'

It was obvious that Bob's Lazarus-like return from the dead deserved a special celebration, so the Bounder and I drove down to Rye and checked ourselves in for B&B at the pub. This was an event that needed some serious planning.

Bob was sitting by the window as usual, taking the first of the countless cigarettes and cups of coffee that make up his staple diet. At first he refused to talk about his near-miss with the Grim Reaper, but eventually I got him round to his brush with death. Strangely, he harboured no resentment of the doctors who had given him such a scare. 'Funny thing,' he said through a haze of blue smoke, 'the whole experience taught me something that surprised me.'

'What's that?' I asked.

'That people like me,' said Bob.

The bar was open by now and so, as is normal at Bob's, the subject of the celebration party became a group discussion. Among the regulars contributing their views was Sam, an old friend of the pub who justified his Saturday-morning pint as a personal contribution to Bob's pension scheme. It turned out he worked for the local council and was responsible, among other things, for issuing gun licences. That morning he had, he said, been asked to approve a .338 Winchester.

The Bounder was astonished. 'But that's an enormous rifle!' he said. 'It will stop an elephant! What on earth would you want it for in East Sussex?'

'Wild boar,' said Sam, rubbing his hands together.

Just then I had a moment of divine inspiration, the sort that strikes rarely but, when it does, should be acted on without hesitation. I had a vision of a boar's head sitting in state on a silver platter, caparisoned with all manner of exotic decoration, being piped in to the dining room by a bunch of medieval eccentrics. In my wild fantasy I even saw a party of jesters and musicians capering about. Surely this would be just the thing for Bob's celebration?

Neither the Bounder nor I knew anything about boar, let alone how to get hold of one, but Sam suggested we try Tim, the head keeper at a large local estate. Tim said he'd be delighted to help and would even take us shooting if we wanted, but suggested that we do a bit of background reading first. What had started off as a flash of inspiration was beginning to feel like rather harder work than I'd intended, but nevertheless when Tim recommended a new book, *The Whole Hog* by Lyall Watson, I bought it dutifully and settled down to some serious study.

I learnt a lot I liked about boars or, to give them their proper Latin name, *Sus Scrofa*, but the thing that clinched it for me was that they seemed to have a sense of humour. In one glorious passage Lyall Watson describes the mating battles of male boars, or 'sounders' as they are called. In Africa, apparently, they settle the contest for a female's favours by backing off about eighty feet from each other, and then charging together with a great clash of heads. The loser in this strange contest slinks off, presumably with a terrible headache, while the winner – who can't have come off much better–grinds his teeth, urinates and then takes a bite out of the other's tail before he disappears.

Lyall Watson is a naturalist, so although I learnt a lot about the habits of the boar, there was not a lot about how I might get one from field to silver salver. For that I needed a proper huntsman. I rang our friend Daniel Busk, who has shot just about anything on four legs.

'Funny you should ask,' roared Daniel down the phone. 'I've just come back from shooting boar in Poland. Fascinating! The boars were driven from the woods by beaters, just like pheasants. We stood outside and shot them on the run with smooth bore shotguns and single bullets – messy business, terrible injuries. I didn't like it much. At night, it's more fun. We sat up in tree hides above open places spread with food and shot in the moonlight – very spooky! The head keeper was marvellous, spoke the most extraordinary English, which he had learnt from a teacher who had last visited England in the Thirties. Talked about "gals", just like my mother, and told me about the "absolutely ripping" boars he had shot. The other huntsmen couldn't fathom him at all – they were all Huns, decked out in those funny green coats.' Daniel snorted in disgust. His idea of appropriate dress for country sport is more along the lines of *Mr Sponge's Sporting Tours*. I suspect he and the Bounder may share a tailor. Daniel lowered his voice a fraction for his next revelation. 'D'you know, after the hunt they made all the huntsmen burn great fiery crosses to appease the trolls of the forest? I ask you! Thought I was in the middle of an episode of *'Allo! 'Allo!*'

Not much the wiser for all this, I returned to my researches, and finally discovered an amateur boar expert in East Sussex. Derek proved to be a mine of information about how the local boar population had got started and was very happy to chat to the Bounder and me.

'It was my wife who spotted them first,' said Derek. 'She was just coming in from a visit to her mother, early autumn, late in the afternoon. "I've just seen a pig down in the garden, a great big black hairy thing," she said. "That's daft," I told her, "the only boar is down on that farm ten miles or so away. You must have been on the sauce". "How dare you!" she says. "You go on out and look."

'So I took the lamp and walked outside on the road. Sure enough – nothing. But then I shone the light into the next-door field and there, standing right in the middle, was a big wild boar. I went back into the house and rang up the farm. "Of course we haven't lost one of our effing boars," the farmer growled. He clearly felt he'd got better things to do than listen to every nutter who couldn't tell a boar from a badger – anyway, he put the phone down.'

Derek was now well into his stride. 'I was buggered if I was going to be treated like that, so I was determined to prove that I was right. Little did I know then that it would take me over six years to do it, but I followed up every rumour I heard and eventually succeeded in filming the first shots of wild boar loose in this country.'

'You mean, since boar were hunted to extinction two hundred years ago,' I corrected him a bit pompously. I was full of my new book-learning.

'That's right,' said Derek kindly. 'There had been a number of sightings by then, all within a few miles of that farm. In the end, the local paper got hold of the story. The boar farmer told them just what he'd told me – without the "effings", I suspect – although he did admit they might have lost one pregnant sow back in 1989. But I'd suspected for some time that the hurricane of 1987 and the storms that followed had knocked down the fences and let a whole herd of boar loose. And my suspicions were confirmed when someone shot a four-year-old boar in 1991 – now, that could hardly be one of the missing piglets, could it?'

'A four-year-old boar should weigh over three hundred pounds,' the Bounder put in. He had clearly been doing his homework, too. 'That would be a fearsome thing to encounter on your way back from the pub!'

'Quite agree,' said Derek. 'But the next "Great Escape" was

even more interesting. Those farmed boars were now being sold in all sorts of upmarket outlets, so they had to be properly slaughtered under EEC regulations. Anyway, one day, the farmer loads up his truck with some chunky specimens and heads for the nearest abattoir. Unfortunately, the animal handlers there were only used to domestic pigs, and as soon as the back of the truck was unfastened, those boars made a dash for it – and a two-hundred pound boar is not something you stop in a hurry.'

'Good for the boar,' said the Bounder, with genuine fellow-feeling. 'What a wonderful scene it must have been. I can just imagine the language. It shows that all that breeding in captivity never touched the primitive survival instincts. Did they catch them all? Hope not – my money would be on the boar every time!'

'Well, they claimed they did,' Derek said, 'but the evidence is against them. They tried again a couple of weeks later. This time, the abattoir people lowered the tailgate very carefully, but once again they were overwhelmed by a great, heaving horde of aggressive, bristly animals, all heading for freedom. It was too much for them: "You can keep your wild boar," they told the farmer. "We're sticking to pigs!" '

'What a lovely story,' I said, thinking sentimentally of Babe. 'So how many of them got away?'

'Well,' said Derek, 'some of the dimmer ones turned up back at the farm looking for food and a few got shot, but a number of them established themselves in the wild and started breeding.'

'How on earth did they stay hidden?' asked the Bounder, clearly wondering if the boar knew any escape-and-evade tips he could put to use.

'They're nocturnal animals,' said Derek, 'and they need dense woodland to lie up in during the day, especially when they're breeding. They seem to have followed the track of the old Kent and East Sussex railway and, luckily for them, found a triangle of land around the villages of Peasemarsh, Northiam and Beckley that gives them exactly the cover they need. Part of it is forestry-owned, but part of it belongs to Paul McCartney.'

The Bounder and I exchanged glances. There seemed little chance that the well-known vegetarian Sir Paul would be interested in providing the main course of our carnivorous feast.

'So what does Sir Paul think about providing a safe haven for Britain's most aggressive new wild species?' I asked. 'They must make a terrible mess of his land.'

'Well, I don't think he wanted them at first,' said Derek. 'But the strong chain link fence he put up around his land probably fenced as many of them in as out, and now he's got poachers as well to contend with.'

We had learned a lot from Derek, but principally established the truth of what until now had been only rumour: that the British boar was indeed in the wild after more than two hundred years and thriving in this little corner of England. We had stumbled by chance on a lovely story of survival of not just an endangered but a previously extinct species. It was time to see for ourselves.

Bob's head keeper friend Tim, who used to be a bouncer at Bob's Rye night club, the Oasis, offered to take us on an expedition into the wild woods. Tim is a friendly but tough-looking countryman who still appears capable of a mean bounce or two. He sat us down with a cup of coffee and started quizzing us about our boar homework. After he was satisfied that we'd moved at least one step up from the basics, we started to talk about how to hunt.

'Boars are canny creatures,' said Tim. 'One or two farmers got pound signs in their eyes as soon as the boar appeared, but the truth is that the herds move around too much from cover to cover, and you can never guarantee that they'll stick to one spot. I know a farmer who got them feeding regularly, using whole maize, acorns and the like, but as soon as he organised a shoot they vanished completely.'

'Is it something to do with their feeding patterns?' I asked.

'Often it is,' said Tim. 'It's been very dry in the woods this year. They feed a lot on grubs, earthworms, acorns and the like, which they root for with their snouts.' He leant forward earnestly. 'A boar's snout is an extraordinary thing,' he said. 'There are stories of captive boars uprooting concrete, but usually they will go where the rooting is easiest.'

The Bounder opened his mouth. I kicked him hard on the shin. I could see where that silly smirk was leading, and we had serious business to attend to. 'And what sort of size do they get to?' I asked. I wanted our boar to be spectacular.

'A typical one-year-old boar will get to a hundred and fifty pounds, but I have seen sounders with their hackles up as high as the bonnet on my Land Rover, and I have shot them over four hundred pounds.'

'But aren't the big ones dangerous?' asked the Bounder nervously.

'It's a big fallacy,' said Tim. 'There have been no reported attacks on humans since boar have come back to the wild. They are very wary, and no casual walker would ever get close to them. The only time you'd be seriously at risk I suppose would be if you tried to catch a young boar out of a family – then you'd have the female after you in a big way. Mind you, those big sounders are pretty scary and could give an old lady a nasty shock, but the truth is that a boar is much more likely to tear off at a rate of knots than attack humans.'

The Bounder looked a little more reassured, and cheered up

immensely when Tim told us that all the shooting is done by night from a hide up in a tree. 'Although you can use the top of the Land Rover,' he conceded. 'But the main thing is not to be around on the ground if one gets wounded. A wounded boar can get very cross indeed.'

'And what sort of money would they be worth?' I asked. Perhaps we could fund Bob's celebration with a bit of entrepreneurial boar-marketing . . .

'Game dealers pay about £1.50 a pound on the carcass for the younger boar up to a hundred and fifty pounds,' said Tim. 'Bigger than that, they get pretty tough and are only good for sausages. Mind you,' he said, with a stern look at both of us, 'I've no idea where the poachers sell them – they probably get about half the market rate.'

Remembering where Kenny Cook's poached deer ended up, I decided to check out the local Chinese restaurants for 'Boarbecue Pork'.

'So with all this shooting, is the population declining?' I asked.

'The numbers peaked about eight years ago, when you could see as many as fifty boar at a time, but they seem to have levelled off. I reckon they are governing their own numbers, like all wild life, according to food availability. In a year with plenty of acorns and chestnuts around, a sounder will breed with up to five females and all will have piglets. In a bad year only the dominant sow, who comes into season first, will have piglets, and maybe one other. It's a matriarchal society, and the dominant sow rules the roost. The families can get quite large if they include progeny from the year before and assorted relatives. The sounder just stays around during the mating season.'

'Good grief!' mused the Bounder. 'Birth control for boars! What extraordinarily intelligent animals. Almost human!'

'It's a pity to shoot them, really,' said Tim, 'but they do cause an immense amount of damage. The farmers get justly pissed off with the damage to crops.'

'What about a shooting season?' asked the Bounder. 'Any regulations?'

'None at all,' said Tim. 'All you need is for the police to put a variation on your firearms certificate so you can shoot boar and have access to land, just like for rabbits. Don't forget – officially wild boar still don't exist.'

'So, what's the future for genuine wild boar?' I asked.

Tim thought for a minute. 'Like you,' he said, 'I'm on the side of the boar. It's extraordinary that they've come back and adapted so well to the modern world. You can't wipe them out, as there are too many and you'd get a conservationist uproar. But they are much harder to manage than deer, where you would typically cull about a third of a herd every year. If you start harassing them, they just vanish, and pop up somewhere else. It's really in the hands of the police. If they hand out too many licences, especially to people who are irresponsible about shooting females with litters, then the population will start to decline. Their best hope for survival will probably be on protected land.'

A couple of weeks later, Tim called us to invite us out on a boar shoot. We drove down to East Sussex full of excitement, swapping awful boar jokes all the way. We'd rather hesitantly brought Old Cow along for the ride, but Tim met us at Bob's pub in a far more professional-looking Land Rover, topped with a sort of platform for carrying back the prize. He checked we had enough warm clothing, told the Bounder his old army face camouflage was probably a bit over the top, and encouraged us to have one last pint. Duly primed and with a couple of flasks of Bob's malt whisky put aside for the colder parts of the night, we crammed ourselves into the front of the Land Rover and set off.

Tim, who has a reputation as the Wyatt Earp of East Sussex, had had a call the day before from a local farmer about extensive boar damage to one of his fields. He wanted them shot or driven off. Nick was a rangy, quietly-spoken man whose family had owned land hereabouts since the Norman Conquest – not untypical of the area. The Conqueror landed here, and it seems a number of his army liked it so much they stayed. It gives the place a sense of continuity that means it is not overwhelmed by the wealthy incomers.

After a glass or two of excellent red wine, Nick showed us where the boar had been rooting. It was easy to understand his concern: a large area of one of his fields near the woods was churned up as if a mad rotivator had been at work. Looking at the damage, it was difficult to imagine how he was ever going to plant his new season's crops. The boars were not popular – but Nick had another problem as well.

'I've lost more than twenty lambs recently,' he told us. 'They just vanished without trace. A few every three days, regular as clockwork. Can't understand what could be doing it.'

'That's the feeding pattern of a big cat,' said the Bounder. 'My spies tell me there have been lynxes reported down here.'

Nick and Tim exchanged a glance. 'You've been talking to that Derek, haven't you?' said Tim. You could see there was no love lost between the two of them. 'He's moved on from boars to lynxes and big cats. Lot of old rubbish, if you ask me.'

I wasn't so sure. I'd heard enough about big cats to send shivers running up my spine. I'd be looking for more than boars in the woods tonight.

'The thing I like about this', said the Bounder as we lurched along the track in the Land Rover, 'is that it is totally alien to all the slaughtering of tame animals by City folk dressed in Edwardian suits that gives the country such a bad name.' He had declined to wipe off his camouflage paint, and presented a truly frightening sight in the moonlight. 'Can't see any of them, mobile phone and all, sitting up a platform freezing his nuts off night after night, can you?'

'No,' said Tim. 'If I had a pound for every hour I've sat watching and not shot anything, I'd be a wealthy man.'

Perhaps my get-rich-quick scheme was not a goer after all. 'How many do you shoot on average?' I asked.

'Usually five or six a month in the winter, and even fewer later in the year,' said Tim. 'Most people only get the occasional one or two, despite all the bollocks that is talked in the pubs.'

Oh, well, I thought as the Land Rover came to a halt and we climbed up on to the shooting platform. It was the experience that counted.

'It's after the mating season,' Tim said to us as we settled in, 'so we should leave the families to raise their progeny. They'll be much more wary anyway. I would hope we can find a young sounder, about a year old and around a hundred and fifty pounds in weight. He should make good eating.' He rubbed his hands in anticipation. 'Now,' he said, 'which one of you wants to take a hand at shooting?'

I haven't used a gun since I shot and wounded a rabbit in Ireland a lifetime ago. It fled inside its burrow and I can still hear the poor little thing's screams. The Bounder, on the other hand, is an excellent shot, and much given to slaughtering things. He couldn't wait. He took Tim's big .308 Winchester (Tim had clearly thought the .338 'elephant gun' was too much for us to handle) and checked it out most professionally, which seemed to impress Tim. I was assigned the lowly task of being 'lamp man'.

'Now, where should I aim for?' the Bounder asked, squinting down the sights. 'Head shot,' said Tim, 'otherwise you run the risk of only wounding the animal. Boar are tough beasts and they can run a long way when wounded. Also, if we are going to roast this one at Bob's, any damage to the main body will ruin the meat.'

I was more interested in the end-product than its method of dispatch. 'Do they taste good?' I asked.

'If you know what you are doing,' said Tim. 'But it's like venison – country people know how to prepare game to make it tender, but most others don't. A quick kill is vital – all the modern thinking on stress hormones proves the old ways right – and then you need to hang it at least a week in good refrigeration and understand how to marinade and slow cook. Do all this right, and you'll have a feast; do it wrong, and you'll have a nasty tough lump of strong-tasting rubbish.'

The hide was just inside the wood, with a good view out into the moonlit fields, where we could just see Nick's sheep still munching their way through their evening meal. I asked Tim about best locations for setting up such a contraption.

'Boars have long race-memories,' he said. 'In the Domesday Book, a village was assessed by its "pannage", the amount of natural acorns and other pig food around it. Boars will keep on coming back to the good spots until they are sure there is nothing there – so, if a dairy farmer has been growing maize, for example, then sells his land to some country gent, that gent'll have boars visiting him for a long while. They also like to lie up on high ground to watch what's going on around them. The hill up back of us is used as a Christmas tree plantation and that provides brilliant cover. We should be right on the paths they'll take when they come down to feed here.'

The Bounder and I settled ourselves in as comfortably as the space allowed, and so started what proved to be a long wait. At first the nearby road gave out a constant hum of activity, then we could hear just the occasional racing engine of the late night pub returnee – then nothing. The birdsong stopped, and for a time the bats flitted effortlessly past us through the thick trees. Once they had gone the real night started, and I felt a sudden sense of increased awareness and anticipation. It may have been Tim's stories, but out here in the woods the veneer of civilisation is paper-thin in the quiet of the night. Every sound stirs long discarded instincts that still remain deep in our unconscious.

I remembered a holiday I had spent working in Canada, building a new highway north of the Great Lakes, country which had only seen Indians and the occasional trapper since man's first arrival. My lowly task had been fetching and carrying water for the men's tea during the night shift, then oiling the ugly brute of a mechanical shovel during their break before attempting a few hours' kip on the machine's gear box – the only warm spot available. The first time I had gone into the forest for the water, I noticed that even the roaring of the shovel and its attendant dump trucks was masked completely by a few feet of trees. Rustlings, scratchings, the occasional screech of a bird hunting, all assumed nerve-twitching importance – especially as I remembered the great black bears that would raid the camp dustbins in broad daylight. I could have won an Olympic record for water-fetching, and was as alert to the sounds of the forest on the last day of my stint there as I was on the first. I have never treated nature with indifference again.

Helped a little, I must confess, by occasional nips from the silver hip flask our Yorkshire ratting friends had given me, I started to fall asleep, but was jerked awake with a start. A great white barn owl swooped so close to our platform that I felt the draught of its wings. The night had taken on a sense of increased expectancy.

Tim was staring intently along the tunnels between the trees. A fox loped towards us, bold as a brass, glanced up at the platform, then padded off down to the farm without a backward look. Suddenly the Bounder leant forward, and I heard the soft click of the safety catch being taken off. An indistinct white shape had appeared between the trees.

Tim stopped him with a whisper. 'Just an albino rabbit,' he said.

The Bounder looked a bit sheepish, but then a much larger shape emerged – then another, then another. Tim kept his hand on the rifle. It was a truly magnificent sight: a whole family of about ten boar. The dominant female, black and hulking, could, I swear, sense us. She stood stock-still facing towards us, her snout sweeping to and fro, taking sharp audible sniffs of the night air. Around her the piglets were less nervous, running in short bursts from tree to tree, their striped camouflage (which wears off as they grow older) making them almost invisible in the bracken.

'Leave them!' whispered Tim, and we watched in silence as they went on their way.

It must have been an hour or more before we saw anything else, and a full moon was high in the sky and casting sharp shadows around the trees. Time for the trolls, I thought – then a group of three boar appeared so fast that we almost missed them. 'Lights!' hissed Tim. I duly obliged, and lit up the great hairy brute in the middle. The crash of the Bounder's rifle deafened me. He shot well, and the boar slumped instantly to the ground and lay still.

'Good shot,' said Tim. 'Let's see what we've got.'

Tim and the Bounder climbed down to inspect their kill. I stayed behind for a moment to assemble my thoughts. Just before the shot had been fired, I was sure that I had seen a much larger patch of darkness move by the old beech tree at the mouth of the clearing. Had I imagined it, I wondered, or was I still remembering Charlie's story (Ch. 11) about the 'Beast of Bodmin' and its yellow devil's eyes glowing in the moonlight? My heart was beating hard, and I could still feel the hairs on the back of my neck and cold gooseflesh all over my body.

I shook my head to clear the fancy and climbed down to help the hunters. The Bounder had shot exactly what we had been after – a one-year-old sounder of about a hundred and fifty pounds. It was a heavy weight to drag back to the Land Rover and load onto the roof rack. As we struggled to lift it I happened to glance towards the farmhouse, to see the most extraordinary sight: the sheep, which had been scattered over several fields, were now wedged into a triangle of hedges, close to the house lights, clearly terrified. The ones on the outside were literally climbing on the backs of those further in to get away from what ever it was that was frightening them. I watched them until the Bounder's jibes about 'not pulling your weight' bit home, and we finally heaved the carcass up. The roar of the Land Rover's engine seemed to reassure the sheep, who began to fan out again. I kept my thoughts to myself on the way back. Call me a superstitious fool, but I was with Derek on this one. I knew I had just seen a big cat, whatever Tim might say.

A week later, the Bounder and I were down at Bob's again for some party planning. The two of us sat with our host, his pretty daughter Morgan, his chef Dean, and Stuart 'the Bus'. Stuart drives an extraordinary eleven-bed air-conditioned coach on hire to pop groups around the country, and Bob lends him the cottage behind the pub. Stuart has also made best friends with Bob's bad-tempered Amazon Green parrot, who will let him, and only him, parade him around on his shoulder like Long John Silver.

The conversation turned to recipes, and how to spread the news of the party. We had decided it should be in medieval dress, to get the atmosphere going, but feeding the multitudes required careful planning. We would hire a spit roast, but they are tricky things, always too fast or too slow, so we also needed a dish which could be pre-cooked then carved up more manageably. Without a recipe book we would have been at a loss, but an instinct had made me delve into *Apicius*, the only surviving collection of recipes from the ancient world. It included one for a kind of part-boiled, part-roasted boar joint, flavoured with all sorts of exciting herbs. Along with the spit roast and boar sausages it would have to do, after a little modification in the way of modern ingredients. Dean hit on the idea of replacing 'Liquamen', the pungent fish sauce the Romans added to all their dishes, with Worcestershire Sauce.

A fair amount of drink had been taken by this point, so we got sidetracked into a naming contest. The spit roast was, obviously, 'Boarbecue', and the sausages in bread 'Hot Hogs', but the contribution from Apicius baffled us for a bit, before Dean produced 'Boarabaisse'.

The evening of the great medieval boar feast was mild and clear. The spit roast started turning, the barbecue was lit for the sausages, Dean had fallen in love with Apicius, and the wine was mulling away wickedly in a great black cauldron. It was time for the guests. The citizens of Rye had risen to the occasion, and the costumes were excellent. For the home side, Bob had chosen to appear as Merlin, spangled hat and all, and Morgan was of course Morgan le Fey. Bob's French wife Raphaele completed the Arthurian trio with an elegant Guinevere. The Bounder's build best suited Friar Tuck, his ecclesiastical status somewhat spoilt by the words 'Triar F**k' which he had magic-markered onto the back of his thick leather belt. It proved a surprisingly effective chat-up line. I had rather fancied the idea of going as Merlin myself, but Bob's white beard made him the obvious choice, so I went as a dancing bear. Stuart 'the Bus' and Jack were, of course, Long John Silver and friend.

Of the guests, my favourites were the local historian and well-known cross-dresser who came as Boudicca, and the local sporting club who all came as medieval knights with a banner saying 'Once a king, always a king, but once a knight's enough'. The music was provided by Louis Turpin, brilliant local artist and musician, but after it was stopped to appease the neighbours our historian proposed a poetry competition as more appropriate. The Bounder led off with 'Eskimo Nell', which in his more penurious days he had recorded, leaving copies behind the bar of every local pub, to be turned into beer money by the barman; the historian declaimed an interminable Celtic fable, which was shouted down half way through and got him rechristened 'Boardicca'. Appropriately – and to great acclaim – Bob won with Rudyard Kipling's 'If':

> If you can talk with crowds and keep your virtue,
> Or walk with kings – nor lose the common touch;
> If neither foes nor loving friends can hurt you;
> If all men count with you, but none too much;
> If you can fill the unforgiving minute
> With sixty seconds' worth of distance run –
> Yours is the Earth and everything that's in it,
> And – which is more – you'll be a Man, my son!

As an encore, a local Amateur Belly Dancing Club (average age over seventy) gave us an unforgettable demonstration of their art.

I laughed so much that Bob threatened to call in his paramedic friend, Alan the Ambulance, and have me carted off. Happily for me, Alan the Ambulance, who had become a very regular regular at the pub since Bob's near brush with death, was in no condition even to recognise an ambulance, let alone drive one.

Once I'd recovered from the belly-dancing I calmed down a little, and sat quietly with the Bounder to reminisce about the more madcap episodes of our Rye youth. Our favourite character back then had been Victor, an ebullient Russian who was a manager for Hoverspeed. He managed to bring back the most amazing quantities of cheap booze from France, and used to entertain all and sundry to wild parties (the Bounder, who is somewhat of an expert, says he feels these could properly be termed 'orgies') in his crumbling Georgian rectory. Victor claimed the place was deeply haunted, and I well remember one night persuading the Bounder's extraordinarily attractive then-sister-in-law 'Pussycat' that the only way to survive until dawn was to build a dense nest of cushions in front of the fire and hug a lot. (As they say in the old jokes, 'This concludes the case for the defence, Your Honour.')

Victor's drink bills soon 'exceeded his pay', as Noël Coward would have put it, and he had to sell up. Desperately sad at losing his house, he put a clause in the deeds that meant he could buy it back if he was ever in funds again. Alas, it was not to be. A few years later he decided to prune the top-most branches of a tall tree in the garden of his new house. He had enjoyed his customary very heavy Guinness lunch. The resulting thump could be heard in Moscow.

The evening was drawing to a close. A few fools, the historian included, tried to jump the dying embers of the fire and had to be put out with the dregs of the punch, but all in all it had been a great success, and a fitting tribute to 'Lazarus'.

As we sat licking our lips after the feast, my feelings were with the boar, a truly wild animal that seemed unlikely ever to be domesticated by the warm and fluffy animal-loving brigade. And it still seemed incredible to me that it had re-adapted to nature in modern England. I particularly liked a description of a boar that the Bounder found in a children's book, *Meet Wild Boars* by Meg Rosoff and Sophie Blackall. He quoted the following lines with relish: 'He'll sneer and he'll scratch, stick his snout up your jumper, then eat all your chocolate and give you his fleas.'

'Sounds just like you, old friend,' I said.

Boar *à la* Epicius

INGREDIENTS:

- 4lbs rolled boar shoulder
- rich meat stock to cover
- 3 oz pork dripping
- 5 tablespoons honey
- 1 teaspoon English mustard
- 2 desert spoons Worcestershire sauce
- salt, pepper
- chopped onion
- cornflour
- olive oil
- herbs to taste, such as juniper, coriander, mint, cloves, what have you

Simmer the joint in a large pan for an hour in the stock, then spread with dripping, honey, mustard, salt and pepper and roast for 1½ hours at 180°C (350°F/gas mark 4). Baste occasionally. Make up the sauce by frying the onions with a little olive oil, then adding the herbs, a thickening of cornflour, then stock. Simmer gently. Sweeten with more honey to taste and add some of the roasting juices. Lie on a couch and eat grapes before serving the meat in slices, and drink lots of wine. Enjoy yourself, and spare a thought for the boar!

4
April

IRELAND

'Oh the French are on the sea', says the Sean Bhean Bhocht,
'And will Ireland soon be free?' says the Sean Bhean Bhocht.
'Yes, old Ireland will be free from the centre to the sea,
And hurrah! For liberty,' says the Sean Bhean Bhocht.

Old Irish Poem

THE BART . . .

Last year my teenage son Freddie, obsessed with Charley Boorman and Ewan McGregor's enchanting tale of motorbiking, *The Long Way Round*, persuaded his ageing father to attempt the same trick on a slightly smaller scale – a ride around Ireland. I hadn't been on a bike for more than twenty years, so my initial attempts were harrowing and the spate of 'old fool' comments by my wife a little hard to bear. The Bounder's remarks are unprintable. However, I persevered, and one June day we set off. It was an extraordinary experience, sleeping on camp sites, in remote B&Bs and in guesthouses ruled by powerful landladies with embroidered covers over everything, including their husbands.

Yet at the end of it, I had a strong feeling that something was missing. In pursuit of the mighty Euro, had Ireland itself and its famous charm become an endangered species? Was some of the prettiest landscape in the world now spoiled by the rash of ugly new bungalows, a phenomenon the Irish call 'Bungalow Blitz'? Was the original and independent spirit of the Irish themselves under threat? The Bounder and I both have Irish blood and a special love for the place, so we decided to give it another try. We chose Connemara and especially Lough Corrib as our proving ground, as they hold a particularly special place in both our hearts.

*

Connemara is one of the most magical places in all the West of Ireland. Its wild landscape seems to be reflected in the pattern of endless battles – all of them heroic, many of them farcical – that has characterised its history and is still present in the many castles, battle sites, places of legend, and weird and wonderful stories that haunt the place. From Normans to Elizabethans the land saw invaders arrive and settle, and as alliances and inter-marriages shifted power almost daily, the distinctions between the 'English' and the 'Irish' became blurred. It took the tragedy of the Great Famine, which affected Connemara with its poor soil so badly, to draw the battle lines clearly again. The hated English absentee landowners must bear the blame for the famine graves that still litter the land, but some of the local gentry did what they could to feed their tenants. In Connemara the most famous of the popular landowners was a man known as 'Hair Trigger' Dick Martin, a deadly duellist. One of my favourite stories about him concerns an aspiring Continental duellist who tried to fool Dick by wearing special protective chain mail under his clothing. Dick's servant spotted the trick and whispered in his master's ear: 'Hit him where the Connemara man kills a pig . . .' A neat shot behind the ear despatched the unsporting foreigner.

In fact, one of the Bounder's ancestors made duelling history in 1822 not just by being killed in the last-ever duel to take place on Irish soil, but by being despatched on the *third* exchange of fire. Somehow, it all rings true . . .

The dispute was over – what else? – a woman, a neighbour's wife. Nothing changes in the Daunt family. The Bounder of the day met his opponent at dawn. History does not relate who his second was, but the neighbour's second was a man called Beamish, a member of the brewing family. When Daunt saw this man his heart must have sunk, for he had also been having an affair with Beamish's wife. The two duellists cocked their pistols, turned their backs on each other, walked the usual ten paces, wheeled about, pointed their weapons, and fired. Both missed. This should have been enough to settle an affair of honour, but duelling tradition accords such decision to the seconds – and Beamish insisted that they fire again. Again they missed, but again the cuckolded Beamish insisted they fire – and this time Daunt was drilled straight through the centre of the forehead. The Bounder always maintains that no ancestor of his would have missed three times, and raises the suspicion that the Mrs Daunt of the time may have been involved in her own dalliance. I stand by my original point: the family resemblance is just too strong.

There's an ironic and very Irish postscript to all this. The neighbour escaped to France, but eventually decided to return to Ireland to face the music. Arrested for murder as soon as he landed, he none the less managed to persuade the jury at his trial that he bitterly regretted the death of his friend, despite his affair with his wife. The unfortunate Beamish was hanged.

The days of squires and carefree country adventures ended with the Troubles: Ireland became an increasingly dangerous place for the absentee landowners, fishing rights closed, and many a land agent stood in fear of his life. Since then a new generation of land-owning incomers has arrived, people such as His Highness Kumar Shra Ranjitsinhji, Jam Saheb of Nawanagar, who restored the magnificent Ballynahinch castle and fishery. They do not share memories of Ireland's painful past, and the old tensions have been eased. Then, of course, came the EEC, bringing new wealth and a new Ireland in which making money is the order of the day, and it sometimes seems that the past is all but forgotten – until a new round of Guinness brings out the old stories and the rebel songs. But although I come from the northern Protestant landowning class and the Bounder claims to have true

Irish blood, both of us feel totally at home in this wild and lovely country.

We had decided to start our investigation at Currarevagh House Hotel on the shores of Lough Corrib. As is the case with many of the larger houses in Ireland, its owner Harry Hodgson and his wife June have turned their lovely lakeside home into a relaxed and welcoming hotel. Rooms have no locks, TV or mini-bars. Harry himself serves drinks before dinner in front of real peat fires and the guests, wonder of wonders, even speak to each other.

The charm of the hotel remains in full force, although I could sense that the EEC and its ponderous regulations had become more than an irritant. We had been surprised, on arriving, not to be greeted by Harry's black Labrador Sabby, who used to welcome every guest and beg actively for scraps at breakfast.

'There's some stupid bye-law which bans animals in hotels now,' Harry told us in disgust. But then – as ever – he launched straight into a story. 'Did you hear the one about the two old colonels and the food bowl?'

'Go on!' we said, being suckers for Irish stories of any kind.

'A couple of very obviously English colonels were over here for the fishing,' said Harry, as he ushered us inside. 'They wore the usual uniform of heavy tweed jacket, cavalry twill trousers and a regimental tie, topped with a red face and a moustache. As they were eating their soup the hotel mongrel, a dog of very indeterminate breeding, began to scratch at one of the colonel's legs. It seemed to be trying to jump up into his lap. Eventually, driven to distraction, he called over the waitress.

'"Kindly remove this animal," he said testily. "It's making a demmed nuisance of itself." "Well, sir," said the waitress, smiling sweetly, "you must try and be a little kind to him because we've had a small accident in the kitchen with the crockery and it's his bowl you've got!"'

We were truly back in Ireland.

The hotel had its usual complement of eccentric guests. We rapidly became new best friends with an eclectic mix of nationalities – Udo, a cultured Swiss-German, Anne-Marie, an equally sophisticated Parisian, and Sandy, a dry-witted Scottish doctor who could have stepped straight out of *Dr Finlay's Casebook*. As so often, jokes at other people's expense sealed the bond. I had been hailed at the reception desk by an English couple who insisted on introducing their elderly parents as Lord and Lady Something. At dinner that night they made such a quacking fuss over the meal that they were immediately rechristened the 'Ducks' or, according to Anne-Marie, *Le Comte et Madame le Comtesse Magrit de Canard*.

One of the Ducks rashly asked the Bounder and me if we were 'collaborating' in our writing. Mindful of the *Fawlty Towers* advice not to talk about the war, I nevertheless couldn't resist telling Udo of my father's 1934 tour through Hitler's Germany in his old MG, and the day he attached a Nazi flag to the bumper and found himself driving the most saluted vehicle in the country. Udo was leaving the next day for Donegal, where it turned out we had several old friends in common, including Henry P. McIlhinney, whose family had made millions from tabasco sauce. On the back of tabasco Henry had bought Glenveagh, a massive Victorian castle with a drive that takes more than forty minutes to journey, and filled it with lots of his international gay friends, presided over by Patrick, the demon butler. It was Patrick, I told Udo, who had returned from a package holiday in Austria with a new costume design for the half-dozen or more extremely good-looking young men who made up Henry's indoor servants. Patrick decreed that they would henceforth be dressed in *lederhosen*, those short leather trousers the Austrians wear for their knee-slapping dances. Udo was entranced by the vision of an Irish castle inhabited by a troupe of knee-slappers, and at once got up to demonstrate the finer points of the art. Dr Sandy followed up with an enthusiastic Scottish version, which made me wonder if Patrick might not have got more mileage out of issuing a set of kilts. At this point the Ducks sailed off to bed, looking very bad-tempered. It was a typical evening at Harry's.

Currarevagh may have passed from its life as a family home to a new existence as an hotel, but Ireland still has its fair share of grand country houses and of lives lived in them that seem completely removed from the modern world. One of the grandest of all is Luggala, the romantic house in the beautiful Wicklow Hills converted by my friend Garech Browne's mother Oonagh, one of the 'Golden Guinness Girls' who made a splash in the between-the-wars social scene that makes the antics of modern celebrities pale into insignificance. Life at Luggala harks back to an older, more leisurely Ireland. The first time my then wife and I were invited to stay I discovered that the day started at around noon, with a massive jug of strong Bloody Marys and a lot of chat about the night before and the entertainments to come. On our first morning Nicholas Gormanstown, Ireland's premier viscount and a regular house-guest, asked my wife where I was. I was working for the business magnate Tony O'Reilly at the time, so my wife replied that I had gone to work.

There was a long reflective silence as Nicholas digested the news. This was not normal guest behaviour. The next day the same thing happened, and Nicholas got the same answer to his question. This time he obviously felt compelled to say something.

'But Richard went to work yesterday,' he complained.

Nicholas is a successful art dealer, no doubt as a result of his childhood, when so many of the treasures in his family's rambling mansion were sold for a pittance. He told me once about finding an original auction catalogue which contained a notice that a 'Painting of a Horse – signed G. Stubbs' had been marked down for the princely sum of £1.

Nicholas also told me a lovely story of Oonagh's days at Luggala, when in the big drawing room hung three magnificent Magritte paintings of rocks hung suspended beneath a starry sky. Oonagh took her Irish maid May everywhere, and also used to bring her French gardener Yves back with her to Ireland from her house in the South of France. Although May had never learnt a word of French, this did not stop her having long and involved conversations with Yves, and these were to have serious consequences for Oonagh's art collection. One day May decided to dust the three magnificent Magrittes in the Luggala drawing room. Her conversation with Yves had gone something like this:

May: 'There's a little bit of the dost here, I cannot quite reach.'

Yves: '*C'est une étoile, certainement.*'

May: 'Dost, you say, Yves? I'll just give it a good hard rub with this rag here.'

Even the great Magritte was speechless when the 'dusted' masterpiece was returned to his studio for urgent repairs.

The morning after our impromptu knees-up with Udo, Anne-Marie and Sandy, we set off for what I told the Bounder would be some serious research. He grumbled a fair bit, but at last I unstuck him from his crossword with a promise of a pint of good Guinness and we motored a couple of miles to Oughterard, the nearby fishing town on the banks of the Corrib. My favourite bar here is at the Corrib Hotel where they serve the best pint of Guinness I have ever had – cool, smooth, creamy, and deeply satisfying. If you close your eyes, I swear you can hear the angels singing. The bar then, as now, is propped up from opening time onwards by a fine trio of resident drunks. I had once organised a conference for my software company at the hotel to give them a taste of something unusual, and the leader of the trio would enliven our proceedings at odd moments during the day by wandering into our room, pointing at some computer or other and saying: 'Dat looks interesting. Would you tell me about dat?'

Today they were there as usual. We bought them a pint each for old time's sake and after we had drunk our own, we headed off down the narrow mountain road which winds around the north of the lough and makes for Mayo, the wildest lands of western Ireland.

We passed Mam Ean, the Holy Hill, where you can still take a pilgrimage up the rocky and winding track to the top – and do it in bare feet if your sins are many. I suggested a quick trip up to the Bounder, but he refused, saying he was much maligned and was keeping his socks on. I was pleased to see a few cars parked and empty at the foot of it, a good sign that not all the country's legends are forgotten. On we drove, through James Joyce country, until at last we reached the softer fields and loughs of Mayo. This is the land where Yeats lived and produced his best poetry. I defy anyone to come here in spring and not feel the extraordinary natural magnetism of the place. You might even try a poem or two. It is never too late.

On we rumbled down to the shores of Lough Arrow, a great

mayfly fishing spot – but the object of our excursion today was not fishing. A long line of boats for hire were pulled up on the bank and a gnarled old man who looked at least a hundred was sitting beside them, gazing out across the water.

'You'll be Paddy, I suppose?' I said, as I introduced myself. It was a safe bet.

'I am indeed,' he acknowledged. 'And what would you be wanting?'

What I was in fact wanting were some directions, but I know that if you are not careful a simple question in Ireland can lead you through every subject from George Bush to the Resurrection, before ending with a 'Weeeell, if I was going to there, I wouldn't start from here'. I did my best to cut things short. 'I'm looking for Michael. Is he still living in the caravan back of the hills here?'

Paddy gave me a reproachful look and heaved a heavy sigh. It was clear he thought that spoiling his half-hour of conversation was typical of the younger generation. He took his revenge by giving us at least six alternate routes, which I had to pencil in on the detailed walking map I had brought specially. I knew satellite navigation would not get us back to the Stone Age, and that was where we were going.

It was a bumpy ride up a long unmade track, but at last we spotted Michael's caravan, parked in a sheltered dell with extraordinary views across the landscape clear to Croagh Patrick, Mayo's most sacred mountain. And – yes! There was a car parked outside and a wisp of smoke coming from the chimney. Our Irish luck was holding. I had promised the Bounder a remarkable encounter, and I was about to deliver it to him.

Michael Poynder is tall, balding, about our age (i.e. old) and possessed of an extraordinary calmness. He began his career conventionally as a cavalry officer in a smart regiment, and is a truly endangered species, being a much-travelled, well-bred Englishman perpetually in search of eternal truth. John Buchan would have loved him. He was in no way fazed by our unexpected arrival – indeed, he almost seemed to have been expecting it, and just to accept the fact that I had not seen him for a good five years yet had come all the way to this remote spot purely on spec.

Michael originally came to Lough Arrow for the fishing, built a small hotel which he ran for a while, then became totally obsessed with the remnants of Stone Age Ireland he found in the area. We were ushered into his caravan and were no sooner seated than he started on his latest theory. Michael believes that what he calls 'the sacred geometry' of ley lines and other sources of the earth's energy that he can trace through dowsing predict major world change before too long, and that this has long been foreseen by the Knights Templar and those since who have secretly followed the movement's principles.

This clearly has great resonance for anyone obsessed with Dan Brown's bestseller *The Da Vinci Code*, but I knew it was not the Bounder's cup of tea, so I suggested Michael gave him a little demonstration of his dowsing skills. We went outside and Michael took an old piece of stone marked with concentric swirling circles from his pocket. It was, he told us, probably more than five thousand years old. He then attached it to a short leather string and offered it to the Bounder.

'Just hold it naturally,' he said. 'Anyone can dowse if they can open their mind.'

'My mind's as open as the next man's,' the Bounder asserted stoutly, and rather gingerly took hold of the string. Sure enough, the little stone began to wobble a bit, then it began to swing backwards and forwards. Michael marked our start point with a stake, and we then followed the direction of the stone's swing and repeated the process. In no time we had a set of about ten stakes in an absolutely straight line.

'Now, look forward about a mile or so,' said Michael. Directly ahead of us we could see a large stone-age cairn; but, most extraordinarily, when we looked back along the row of stakes we had driven into the ground, they were pointing exactly towards the monument.

The Bounder was astonished. 'How on earth did you do that?' he asked, always keen to add another party trick to his repertoire.

'I didn't do it,' Michael said, and went on to explain. 'In Stone Age times the animals followed the smells of underground water courses, so regularly that they made natural paths across the countryside. You can still see them today. Stone Age man as a hunter followed these paths, and erected great stones to mark where they crossed, as here springs were often to be found, with energy-giving or healing properties. The medicine men of the tribe soon discovered that these properties were influenced by conjunctions with the sun and the moon, and became adept astronomers as they worked out when and where these events might happen. While doing this they realised that the "geometry" of these forces could also be used for predicting where to build, where to worship, even where to graze the flocks. Over the millennia many adepts, from the ancient Egyptians to the Templars to the handful of people who still believe in these mysteries today, have further developed the art.

'No one has yet worked out the source of Ireland's extraordinary spiritualism, which provided the foundation for the missionaries who converted Europe back to Christianity after the Dark Ages. My Stone Age magicians had the time to understand great secrets – secrets that have been long lost in centuries of fighting, and now in making money. You talk about endangered species,' said Michael, 'and I guess I must be one myself. I was never very interested in fighting, and I'm not interested in making money, but I do want to understand these real mysteries.'

The Bounder and I sat fascinated as the afternoon wore on,

listening to Michael's quiet voice as he talked of his discoveries; then, as the great red orb of the sun sank exactly over the stone cairn we had dowsed, it was time to go.

The Bounder was uncharacteristically quiet on the drive home. At length he spoke. 'I have to confess, Bart,' he said, 'I understood about one word in ten of what that chap talked about – but you know, there's something there. In fact,' he went on, 'I'm so convinced, I think I have divined the need to stop and have a drink.'

On the way back to Currarevagh we stopped at one of those long low pubs – in fact just a small bar tacked onto the side of the landlord's house – which are so typical of the West of Ireland. There seemed to be signs of activity from within, but the door was firmly locked. The Bounder, who lets nothing stand in his way when drink is needed, went round to the house next door and peered through the window.

'There's someone there,' he harrumphed with all the enthusiasm of a camel finding an oasis after a long, dry day. 'I'll knock them up.'

I peered over his shoulder. All I could see inside the room was wall-to-wall children, watching TV and eating pizza. None the less, we persisted with our urgent rapping on the door. We were about to give up when it suddenly opened and a smiling woman in a cotton dress stood in the doorway.

'Now, is it a drink you're after, boys?' she asked.

We nodded enthusiastically, and were led down a dark corridor, though an old store room littered with empty bottles, under the drinks counter, and into a brightly lit bar packed with locals, including two Gardaí in full uniform.

I waited until we had our first pints served before asking the obvious question. Why was the bar door locked?

The landlady looked at us both in astonishment. 'But it's Sunday,' she said, as if addressing a mental defective. 'The pub's shut!' she said. The Bounder and I were delighted. The Irish have always had their own eccentric way of ignoring the law, and clearly nothing had changed.

The next morning we were in for a treat. We had booked Harry Hodgson's eighty-year-old ghillie 'Pa', and the old wooden fishing boat he prefers. The lunch was loaded up: sandwiches and two bottles of excellent Chablis for us, bread, cheese and two bottles of his favourite Guinness for Pa. I had also brought along my portable Abu fish smoker. Hot-smoked, pink-fleshed trout straight from the lake makes an epicurean feast fit for Lucullus.

Pa was taking us 'dapping'. This is the easiest and one of the nicest forms of fishing, designed for those like me who prefer quiet contemplation to all the drama and the paraphernalia of the right fly, the right rod, et cetera. It consists of attaching a live insect – usually a mayfly or a grasshopper or 'Daddy' as the Irish call them – onto a hook, then onto a long floss line which can blow in the breeze. Using a very long rod allows you to let the insect dance over the water by changing its angle. For me, the quiet lapping of the waves against the boat, the constant sparkle of the sun on the ripples and the cries of the birds beat any relaxation therapy – and a wild brown trout or two for the smoker is a bonus.

We were lucky that day, and had landed three trout by the time Pa steered us to a small island for lunch. The water was clear but slightly peaty-coloured and we dipped our Chablis bottles in it to cool perfectly. Pa built a small fire, and once he had his Guinness in his hand we got him talking about Ireland and how it has changed. As always in Ireland, it was not what we had expected.

'It was best before the cinema and the telly,' said Pa, settling back in expansive mood. 'We had our own dance every Saturday night; we had our own dances and our own songs. But, you know, when the emigration took its toll and the young women went to America, the dancing had to stop.' He paused and gave a long sigh. The Bounder and I exchanged puzzled glances – which century was Pa talking about?

'And then,' he went on, 'the older women gave up the spinning, and people bought their clothes off the peg. The farmers let the fields go to weeds. When the young girls left off the shawl and put on the pants and took to the bicycle, the bottom fell out of the place.'

This long speech from the normally taciturn Pa left even the Bounder completely silenced, although I could see that he was interested in the implication that local morals had collapsed with the casting-off of shawls. But clearly for Pa this was indicative of the passing of a way of life he had grown up with, and so we sat quietly with our thoughts through the second bottle of Chablis, until I could hang on no longer. The call of nature beckoned and I had to break the spell.

'There's a grave up yonder, where people say that Saint Patrick himself is buried,' said Pa. 'Don't go pissing on his remains,' he warned as we scrambled to our feet, 'or he'll be after cursing you something terrible.'

The Bounder and I picked our way gingerly over the rocks, and there indeed was a very old tomb standing in a small clearing. On the top we could just discern the faint outline of a figure and a strange runic decoration that I thought I had seen before. This was a Viking burial, not a Celtic one, and it seemed to be a woman at that, maybe a princess. Then we noticed the tree. It was quite dead, but forced into the peeling bark were all manner of coins and handkerchiefs, some clearly marked with messages. This was a place for asking the spirits for help, and not to be disturbed. Suddenly, it fell silent. The constant wash of the waves on the stony shore behind us, the cries of the birds above, all were gone. That quiet seemed to stretch back to eternity, and I swear the hairs on the back of my neck were standing up like soldiers. The Bounder felt it too. Without speaking we moved out of the clearing, finished our business, returned to the beach, packed up, and went back to the dapping. There was not a word from Pa, but he clearly knew what we'd seen. I wouldn't have been surprised if he hadn't planned the whole thing.

That evening, back at Currarevagh, Harry proposed a traditional Connemara way to celebrate our catch – a bottle of poteen. I claimed immediate familiarity with the stuff from my time living in the north of Ireland.

'Hold your nose, and throw it over the tongue,' I said bossily, and suited my actions to the words.

Harry and the Bounder exchanged glances. 'Didn't quite catch that,' said the Bounder. 'Just show us one more time.'

Idiots, I thought; but then, drinking poteen is quite a knack. I showed them again. This time my glass missed the table on the way back. My audience fell about. It was going to be one of those evenings.

Over dinner we got talking to a pair of young American honeymooners full of questions about Ireland and Connemara. Eased by the poteen in my case we were getting on famously, so Harry suggested we all go into Oughterard to visit the music pubs where lively rebel songs were a speciality.

'Traditional folk songs, I suppose?' asked the newlyweds.

'Traditional rebel,' said the Bounder, who has an enormous repertoire of IRA songs. 'Absolutely authentic.'

I don't think our American friends quite heard what had been said. They had already shown extreme nervousness at our stories of wild Connemara, but they gamely came along anyway.

The local pub was filled with noise, smoke and locals. As promised, the music was duly rebellious, and we all joined in. Even the Americans couldn't ignore some of the more extremist

Republican verses, such as this gem to which the Bounder gave his remarkable all:

On the 28th day of September, the Tans were leaving Macroom.
Off in their big Crossley tenders, motoring off to the Dune.
But the boys in the column were waiting, their hand grenades
    primed for the spot.
And the Irish Republican Army, they shite on the whole
    feckin' lot.

Our friends managed to contain their understandable nervousness until the very end of the evening, when the band signalled closing time by playing the Irish national anthem.

'What's that tune?' the husband asked me. They had both steered well clear of the Bounder after his solo, and were clinging to me under the misapprehension that I was a man of sense.

But the poteen had taken its fatal hold. 'It means death to foreigners!' I shouted into one of those sudden silences that always open up for truly memorable gaffes. 'And I love dancing to it!' As the band got into its swing I took to my heels in an awful imitation of Michael Flatley.

It was too much for the honeymooners, who fled out of the back door. The Bounder and I staggered, giggling helplessly, all the way down the road back to the hotel, where another poteen or two were called for. I eventually made my way up the stairs, while the Bounder, who had sensibly – for once in his life – foresworn the poteen – finished a last whiskey with Harry. They found me later, or so they claimed, half-way up, flat on my back, talking to Harry's stuffed tiger. 'You seem a friendly chap,' I was mumbling, apparently. 'Take me to your leader.'

*

Next morning was a little difficult to face. We packed up and made our thanks (and apologies) to Harry and his tolerant and ever-patient wife June. Surviving the two-mile trip into Oughterard was a close-run thing, but at last the Guinness sign over the Corrib Hotel hove into sight. As the Irish say, 'When it's a hangover you've got, a pint of Guinness is your only man.'

Half-way down that said pint, my mobile phone rang. I extracted it from my pocket and held it carefully, a few inches from my ear. One of the resident drunks spotted it immediately.

'Dat looks interesting,' he said. 'Would you tell me about dat?'

From the depths of my hangover I heaved a great sigh of relief. Despite bungalows, the Euro and the new prosperity of the Celtic Tiger, at heart I felt that nothing would ever diminish the Irish spirit.

5

May

DUFFERS' FORTNIGHT

I went out to the hazel wood,
Because a fire was in my head,
And cut and peeled a hazel wand,
And hooked a berry to a thread;
And when white moths were on the wing,
And moth-like stars were flickering out,
I dropped the berry in a stream
And caught a little silver trout.

WILLIAM BUTLER YEATS, 'The Song of Wandering Aengus'

I t was a huge trout, one of the biggest I had ever seen, and it was feeding with wonderful regularity, sipping mayfly from the surface. I had stopped in a small lay-by to look with longing at the hallowed waters of the Test, and here their incomparable worth was being demonstrated right in front of my eyes. I was nineteen at the time, and had driven down to Hampshire on a fishing pilgrimage to visit places I had only read about.

The waters I was now staring at so enviously belonged to the Houghton Club, founded in 1822 and still the most prestigious and sacred trout fishery in the world. There was only one problem: no one was fishing. This seemed to me to be complete sacrilege: any member worth his salt ought to have been casting for a trout as large and wonderful as this, I thought. I sat and watched it for another five minutes, then I could bear it no longer. In the back of my old and decrepit Mini van I always kept a fly rod, 'just in case'. I got it out and looked up and down the bank. There was no one about. I climbed the fence and went down to the river. To be fishing this piece of water was the stuff of dreams; the fact that it was completely illegal was beside the point. I knelt down and cast to the still-rising trout. It took immediately and, after an immense battle, it was safely landed. I looked at the fish in awe. It was certainly the biggest that I had ever caught or, indeed, ever seen.

I knocked it on the head, and then again peered to see if anyone was about. Suddenly, in the distance, I spotted the unmistakeable figure of a river keeper approaching. The temptation to run was enormous, but somehow I controlled my panic and, with a nonchalance I certainly didn't feel, strolled back towards my car. But the God who sometimes smiles on sinners was beaming down on me. A brand new and beautiful Mercedes had parked beside my rusty old banger. Casually I leant against it and, with shaking hands, lit a cigarette. The only answer was to bluff it out.

The keeper climbed the fence and approached me. 'Are you a member of the Houghton Club?' he enquired, rather aggressively, I thought.

'Of course I am,' I said.

'Well, what's your name?' he demanded.

'You should jolly well know,' I replied. 'Don't you know your members?'

'Yes I do,' he replied, 'and I'm sure you're not one of them. Anyway,' he continued, 'I've got the number of your car and if I find out you've been poaching I'll have you prosecuted.' And with great care he wrote down the number of the Mercedes.

Since that far-off day when the world was young and innocent I have caught literally thousands of trout (although I have still never fished the Houghton Club legally). Each year I look forward to the hatching of the mayfly. It is called 'Duffers' Fortnight' (although it is actually more like three weeks) because the trout go mad for the fly and are very easy to catch. I love everything about our rivers and their inhabitants at this time. There is a passion in the world as the earth throws away her winter chill, everything awakens anew, and nature begins to appear in all her fertile splendour. To me, now, there is nowhere more beautiful than the English countryside – a cornucopia of green, but a pristine green that is never seen the rest of the year. The beech woods in particular, which are beautiful in any season, are especially lovely now. Their fresh leaves have an ethereal, lime-coloured sheen against the new season's sun, and underfoot there is often a cerulean sea of bluebells. But it is the flower of the hawthorn that is the true signal that summer has begun. Its white blossom, or may blossom to give it its country name, is spread like snow upon the hedgerows and its pungent smell lingers on the sweet air.

The rivers too have a new and untouched look. Marsh marigolds line the banks and the streams have shrugged off the dank greyness of winter and taken on the shimmering sparkle of incipient summer. High in a sapphire sky above the water meadows skylarks sing their piercing, restless song of springtime welcome. A shimmering shot of azure blue streaks down the stream as a kingfisher searches for minnows. And the spreading rings upon a glass-like glide in the stream announce the presence of a feeding trout – for when the may is in full blossom, then is the time for the greatest feast in the fish's calendar.

The mayfly generally appear in our rivers on approximately 10 May and last for about three weeks, although this varies from river to river. Not all are blessed with this beautiful insect, and indeed sometimes only parts of a river will have them. Our largest water-fly, they are of an incomparable beauty, lace-winged, delicate and exquisitely speckled, with three ebony tails. To trout and to many other fish they are the height of gourmet food, and for three weeks the fish gorge themselves upon their succulence.

The life-cycle of the mayfly is fascinating. It is born from an egg that has been dormant on the river bed for roughly six weeks. At the end of this time the egg hatches into a nymph, a small, dragon-like creature that crawls around on the bottom for anything up to three years. During this time it feeds on vegetable matter from which it extracts nourishment before ejecting the waste through its gills. When the time comes for the amazing metamorphosis to take place the gills close and the nymph inflates itself with oxygen, making its way to the surface in a series of jerky movements. At the same time the wing cases are filling hugely, and on reaching the air they burst open. Now the wings unfold and the new insect takes to the skies in an upstream direction, leaving the old casing or shuck behind to be carried downstream like a little boat. If the mayfly now mates it has a life of only five hours – which is not so awful, as during this time it does nothing but bonk. Because its life is so ephemeral it has no mouth or stomach, for it does not need to feed. When the moment comes, mating is done communally, and on the wing. The mating dance is one of the loveliest in nature as in the late afternoon thousands of mayflies swoop and swirl among the branches of riverside trees, the sun glinting off their iridescent bodies.

Towards evening the dance is finished and the males, exhausted from their courtship, flutter onto the water, their wings flat upon the surface in death. But the most important moment for the females has arrived, and they settle upon the surface and lay their eggs. This is done in a series of fluttering, upstream move-ments as the precious eggs, thousands at a time, sink to the bottom, to begin the whole miraculous process again. Then, her job done, the female's wings fall flat and she too dies. All water-flies follow the same pattern, but the mayfly has the shortest above-water life of them all.

(While on the subject of entomology, the Bart alerted me to the habits of the male *Empid* fly called *Hilara*, which he claims shows particularly 'Bounder'-like qualities during mating. Having cap-tured a small insect the male fly binds it with a few strands of silk to prevent it struggling, and presents it to his chosen female.

While he is pleasuring her, she complacently eats it. Sometimes, however, he cannot find a choice morsel to give her; he therefore wraps a bit of twig or something equally inedible in his silk, gives it to her, quickly has his oats, and does a runner before she has time to unwrap it and discover that she has been conned.)

The mayfly is mainly confined to the south of England, and particularly the chalk streams of Hampshire, Wiltshire and Berkshire. The most famous of these are the Test, Itchen and Kennet, all of which have a prolific mayfly population on parts of their systems. The trout-fishing on these rivers is among the most expensive and exclusive on earth. Someone once wrote that the water is 'as clear as gin and twice as expensive' and, particularly during the time of the mayfly hatch, this is essentially true. There is so much food about at this time that the trout are spoilt for choice. They may pick the nymph as it rises to the surface, or they may only eat it as it is metamorphosing. Sometimes they will take the fly with its wings upright, and sometimes only the dead or spent fly with its wings flat on the surface. There are times when an over-excited angler cannot catch trout despite the feeding frenzy, and becomes very frustrated. This is because he is doing a 'Dr Watson'. Sherlock Holmes once said to the duller Watson: 'You see, but you do not observe.' The same criticism may be made of many a fisherman.

Corporate hospitality takes over many beats at this time, and what more beautiful setting could there be to further trade than these rivers in May with the trout rising? The perfect spot to encourage that multi-million-pound deal. But of course, nowadays the streams have become totally unnatural. No river could begin to cope with the pressure placed upon it if it were not for the introduction of artificially reared trout in their thousands. For every five-pound fish which is caught, another is put in to replace it. Size matters, too. To the financiers, stockbrokers and other City types who fish these waters the need to boast about their catch is inherent, and thus the fish are bred bigger and bigger every year.

On the other hand, on some badly managed beats the fish are often small and in poor condition, but to some undiscerning anglers the fact that they have broken fins and pot bellies does not seem to matter. In fact, size is *not* always everything: the Bart and I would far rather catch a wild half-pound fish and eat it for breakfast than any six-pound monstrosity. The pink salmon-coloured flesh of the six-pound fish *looks* delicious, but it often tastes of mud. The wild fish, on the other hand, will generally be white-fleshed but delicious to eat. The reason for this is that the bigger fish will have been out of its stew pond for only a short time, and its flesh is pink because it has been fed on pellets that contain cochineal. The small fish has fed on nymphs and flies, and its fresh will only be pink if it has eaten freshwater shrimp.

There is, incidentally, no such fish known to science or nature as the 'salmon trout'. Invented by the restaurant and the fish-mongering trade, the name fools most people into thinking that it is sea trout. It is, of course, nothing of the kind. It is usually cochineal-fed rainbow trout, bought at a quarter of the price of that other, more noble, fish – and it, too, will taste of mud unless it is cleverly disguised by a strong sauce.

The Test is historically and traditionally the most famous trout stream of all. There is a real cachet in fishing the Test, and it attracts the rich and famous from all over the world: kings and princes, pop stars and actors, entrepreneurs and tycoons walk its hallowed banks, optimistically and often ineptly casting their flies at the aristocratic trout. Apart from the Houghton Club water, one of the most famous beats of all is Compton. It is four and a half miles long, but because of the various feeder streams it has six

miles of banks, and its clientele reads like a fishing equivalent of
Who's Who.

The keeper who looks after this large stretch of river is Phil
Walford, a forty-five-year-old countryman who employs his
'retired' seventy-year-old father as under-keeper. It matters not a
jot to Phil who anybody is: prince or pop star, billionaire or
buffoon, Phil treats everyone in the same straightforward – and
sometimes blunt – manner. We had arranged to meet at his fishing
hut, and after he had made coffee and laced it with a good tot of
whisky, I asked him about his job. In river-keeping terms, it is the
equivalent of winning the lottery. 'I quite often wake up in the
morning and kick myself to make sure that I'm not dreaming,' he
said to me. 'I reckon I'm the luckiest man in the world. Mind you,'
he went on, 'the fishing isn't as good as it once was. There are
nowhere near as many water flies as there used to be. It's all the
women's fault.' He glared at me as if I was somehow complicit. 'It's
all to do with the Pill,' he said. 'The oestrogen gets into the water
through the sewage system and decreases the fertility of the male
flies.' He looked at me and winked. 'I'm told it's the same with us
men too. *We're* none of us as fruitful as we used to be, either.'

'And then,' he went on, apparently growing gloomier by the
minute, 'water extraction's a problem, too. One of the most
important growths in a chalk stream is ranunculus, that beautiful
dark green streaming weed that you see in the fast runs, which is
the best environment for water flies. Because of excessive water
extraction and drier winters the streams are lower and slower and
there's less ranunculus. Ranunculus is the sign of healthy water,
and there is far less about nowadays.'

We left the hut and walked beside the renowned river. As I
looked at the pure and clear waters beside me and trod the pristine paths I thought about where I was. There is a mystique about
fishing the Test. It is generally agreed to be the home of purist

angling where only the driest of dry flies are used and where the anglers epitomise all that is best in piscatorial sportsmanship. I asked Phil if this were still true. He shook his head.

'Those days are long gone,' he said. 'You wouldn't believe what some of them corporate fishermen will stoop to.' He stopped and pulled an erring branch out of the water. 'Look at that,' he said. 'It's just bloody typical.' I stared at where his finger pointed. There, securely embedded where some cheating and incompetent fisherman had left it, was a gaudy reservoir lure, banned from most rivers in the country but definitely illegal on the cherished Test. As we walked on back to the hut, Phil pointed to a large, flat stone on the bank. 'You see that?' he asked. 'At one time fishermen were always lifting it to try and find worms underneath. I got so fed up with them that I put a child's spring with a Punch's head on the end underneath it. I'll bet that made some bugger jump! But the worst I've ever seen is when one angler attached rabbit droppings to the hook to look like fish pellets – call that sport?'

Back in the hut Phil sat in gloomy silence for a moment. 'And then there's the greed of them!' he suddenly exploded in outrage. 'They're only supposed to kill four fish per day, but of course during the mayfly it's easy to catch five times that number.' He snorted in disgust and then looked around and lowered his voice. 'There was one particular gentleman,' he said, 'a seventy-year-old knight of the realm no less, who I knew was taking more than he should, so I waited in some undergrowth and watched him. The old devil was hiding little bags of fish all over the river under bushes, and then when he thought the coast was clear he was smuggling them to his car. All was going fine – until I sneezed and he jumped a mile in the air and started haring off through the nettles and scrub, hoping to reach his car and leave before he was caught. I tell you, for a seventy-year-old he couldn't half move – but the nettles held him up . . .' Phil rubbed his hands with glee at the memory. 'Do you know, he had eleven fish in his car besides the four he was carrying! When I finally got hold of him, he had the cheek to complain that he was badly stung because I hadn't done my job and cut the nettles back!'

As we were talking I had been watching fish moving in the pool below the hut. This was the famous Hatch Pool, renowned throughout the Test valley. I pointed over to it. 'That looks full of fish,' I said.

'It is,' replied Phil. 'It's got brown trout in it up to twenty-five pounds. It's a perfect place for them, deep and well oxygenated. I feed it every day during the winter and it keeps the fish in perfect order. During the summer they still stay there until the last glimmer of daylight, and then I see their dorsal fins going over the gravel bar at the head of the pool as they make their way upstream in search of fly life. No one is allowed to fish it except little girls and lady beginners, but you'd be amazed the number of rods I've caught trying to poach it when they thought I wasn't looking. All they have to do is wait until the witching hour when the fish have moved out of the Hatch Pool on their short migration, and then they have every chance of catching them. Trouble is that by that time they've either gone home or they're sitting pissed in the fishing hut!'

My ears had pricked up. 'My eight-year-old daughter Tara would love to have a go in the Hatch Pool. I don't suppose I could possibly bring her here one day to see if she can catch her first trout?'

'Course you can!' said Phil.

'And', I went on while the going was good, 'I'm afraid she's got a ten-year-old brother, Hugh, who's mad about fishing . . . I can't just bring her along by herself because I think that he would probably kill her.'

'All right, all right,' said Phil resignedly. 'Bring him along, too.'

On the appointed day we arrived at Compton and Phil was there to greet us. It was pouring with rain and the leaden sky looked as if it were set for the day.

'I thought you would ring and call it off with this weather,' said Phil.

'I wouldn't let him,' piped up Tara. 'I want to catch a trout!'

By now we were in Phil's hut and having a warming cup of coffee into which Phil and I had poured the usual helpful and nourishing measure of whisky.

'If I were you,' said Phil to Tara, 'I'd put a pellet on the hook. That should guarantee you a trout because I feed them every day – but I hope you've got a strong cast 'cos otherwise you'll be broken.'

I put a salmon hook on salmon nylon and attached a pellet. Tara was pink with excitement and jumping about like Tigger. Her brother was looking miserable.

'Why didn't you bring two rods, Dad?' he asked resentfully.

'Because', I replied, 'I can only concentrate on one of you at a time, and anyway *you* are going to learn how to land a trout – *if* we catch one.'

'Come on,' said Phil, standing up and downing his coffee in one gulp. He was looking a bit warmer. 'Let's get the fish stirred up!'

We went outside into the rain and Phil threw a handful of pellets into the water. It boiled, and I could see that some of the trout were enormous. I held Tara round her waist and helped her to cast into the pool. Instantly her bait was grabbed by a trout – I was pleased to see it was one of the smaller ones. I helped her to pull line off the reel so that the fish had the bait well into its mouth. 'Strike!' I shouted when I thought the time was ripe, and she did, nearly pulling the fish out of the water. Then it ran – and I had to prise Tara's hand off the line, which she was holding so tightly that I thought it would break. 'Wind in!' I shouted, and her small fingers turned the handle as fast as possible. At last the trout began to tire, and now Hugh had to land it. Tara brought the fish to him and he made a hopeful stab at it with the net. The trout didn't like this at all and disappeared into the depths again with Hugh in hot pursuit. I shouted at him to come back, but by this time his boots were full of water.

'Remember what I told you,' I said. 'The trout comes to the net and not the other way round.'

He nodded, small face screwed up in concentration as he manoeuvred the net – and then – 'I've got him!' he shouted excitedly, looking very pleased with himself. It was a beautiful brown trout of about four pounds.

Tara was jumping up and down with excitement. 'Let me bash it on the head, Daddy, please, please,' she shouted. I felt that any future boyfriend who didn't behave himself could be in deep trouble. After she had killed it, I got hold of it and blooded her on both cheeks.

'Thank you, Daddy!' she said. 'I won't ever wash again.' I had visions of what her politically correct teacher might say if she appeared at school proudly wearing the emblem of a kill.

Not wanting to be left out, Hugh grabbed the rod from Tara's hand. 'I want to do this all by myself,' he said. 'Leave me alone Dad,' and then, grudgingly, 'please?' He cast into the pool but nothing happened, and after six more tries with no result I began to suspect that the fish had learnt a lesson.

'Let's try somewhere else,' I said. 'Read the water and cast where you think the trout will lie.'

This time when he made the throw, it was instantly grabbed by a fish. I saw it swirl on the surface, and realised that it was huge. It fought like a badger and took him well into the backing, but he didn't panic, and at last it was wallowing in the shallows. It was almost too big for my net but I finally managed to scoop it up, and it lay on the bank. We weighed it in the net, and it turned the scales at fifteen pounds.

'That's by far the biggest brown trout I've ever seen in my life,' I said, turning to Phil.

'There's bigger than that in there,' he replied, 'but that's pretty good.' He turned to Hugh. 'You can keep it if you want.'

'No,' said Hugh. 'It gave me a great fight and it's so beautiful; I'd like to put it back, Dad.'

I have seldom been more proud of my son.

After the excitement of the children's day at Compton I was hungry for some fishing myself and so I was thrilled when my old friend Daniel Busk rang up to invite the Bart and me over for a day. Daniel owns a mile of the River Test, much of it opposite the Houghton Club. A large man in every sense of that word, kindness, personality and intelligence are written in each crease of his usually smiling face. Daniel is that rare animal in Hampshire, the latest in a long line of country squires who still works his own land and has a genuine love of the countryside. Most of his neighbours are technology million-aires with mobile phone implants, even during the shooting season.

Daniel is also a genuine eccentric, the sort of warm and lovable character that only England can produce. He keeps a grumpy set of Vietnamese pot-bellied pigs in his garden to help weed out vis-itors, and down by the riverbank he has a bush cut into the shape of a dragon. When anyone approaches it, a cunning electronic device emits a great puff of smoke and a baleful bellow. Daniel, with his wit as dry as fine sherry, would not be out of place in one of R. S. Surtees' nineteenth-century novels – he's an endangered species all on his own.

I remember one dinner party we went to together, when Daniel was seated next to a very obvious 'townie' lady who was rhapsodising about Hampshire and how she would love to move there if only she could afford it. 'Tell me, Mr Busk,' she enthused breathily, laying a hand on his arm, 'wouldn't owning five hundred acres of Hampshire be wonderful?'

Daniel, who farms more than a thousand, thought for a moment. 'Well,' he said, 'it would certainly make life easier!'

Daniel also adores his fishing, but with the refined enthusiasm of a dedicated expert in his understanding of the nuances of the river, its fly life and its fish, worthy of one of the great late-nineteenth-century naturalists such as Sir Henry Halford or G. E. M. Skues. Not for him the endless pursuit of quantity or poundage above everything else which so dominates today's sport.

'It's all in the experience,' he says. 'I know that the mayfly season is supposed to be the peak of fly-fishing, but it's either too easy to catch fish then or too difficult, because the river is covered in great rafts of fly and the trout are totally stuffed. I'd much rather slip down of a September evening, when you have to work out exactly what the trout are feeding on, then choose a fly to match.'

Daniel has little time for the know-alls who have elevated fishing into a science and come down to the river with hundreds of specimen flies and equipped with riverside tying gear. 'About a dozen favourites is all you need,' he says. 'And then you must know exactly how and where the fish are feeding. I've no time for all these fellows who keep changing flies faster than a three-card trick. There was one chap on the river last year who spent hours trying to imitate a Caenis, those tiny white jobs that drive trout mad and fisherman insane. After he had produced a minute object, just about big enough to catch a minnow, he asked me over for a look. "What would you do, Daniel?" he asked. "I'd go home for a large vodka and come back tomorrow," I told him!'

Daniel is also a massive storehouse of history about the Test and how it got its reputation of being 'clear as gin and twice as expensive'. According to him, dry-fly fishing started because it was easier than the old wet-fly game of dragging large lures downstream across the current, as you would for a salmon. As he explained, 'The rivers were full of weed after May, as the landowners didn't rate the sport too highly and anyone could fish by checking in at the local pub and sending their card up to the big house. The streams were surrounded by water meadows which flooded the land through an intricate system of channels and helped force on early crops. The farmers were called "drowners" and would release all sorts of stuff into the water, which made wet-fly or bait fishing impossible. Then came the great agricultural crash of the late 1900s when cheap food imports destroyed the profit from farming and a whole generation of countrymen with it. Wages, if you could get them, were only nine shillings and sixpence a week then, so many left the land. The estate owners soon realised that their angling could be sold for more than their wheat, and the whole system of smart clubs, syndicates and gentry with country property grew up, which has hardly changed to this day. I regret it – in Regency times you could take your greenheart rod down to the bank for a few hours and catch twenty brace or more, all fighting wild fish. Those were the days!'

The Bart was still curious about the Houghton Club. 'Is it as exclusive as ever?'

'Dead men's shoes only,' said Daniel. 'There are about eighty members and none are allowed who live locally, so they can't over-fish. They are a good bunch – and they like their dining as much as their fishing. I recently came across a letter, written in 1875 by the naturalist Halford when he was a member of the club.

Thought you might like it, Bounder!' Dan fished in his coat pocket and pulled out a scrappy piece of paper. He held it out in front of him, coughed, and intoned: ' "Houghton is one of the most picturesque little villages that I have seen. Every cottage is smothered in honeysuckle and roses. Most of them have capital gardens, and in the bettermost, the anglers find lodgings; and here, with home-brewed beer and home-baked bread, home-cured bacon, fresh eggs, home-made butter and cream, eels from the weir and magnificent trout from the river – he must be a dainty angler indeed who cannot contrive to live with these luxuries, so freely available." ' He looked round at us for approval and we both nodded. I found that I was feeling ravenous.

'Do they still fish for pike and coarse fish?' asked the Bart, who must have had a full English breakfast as he seemed inclined to carry on talking. He gets very bored with stew-fed trout, and has the same enthusiasm for meddling about with floats as he did when we were children.

'Doubt it!' said Daniel. 'I've always found pike fishing boring as sin.'

The Bart, who has never found sin boring, grew argumenta-tive, and from the debate came a great idea. We would set up two 'traditional' days on the bank, for both 'coarse' and game fishing. Points would be awarded not just for the catch, but for the setting, the people, the chat – everything in fact which makes fishing so special to us. Daniel would hear our stories and judge.

It was decided to have a day's coarse fishing on the River Frome and a day's mayfly fishing on Daniel's stretch of the Test. We set a date in late May for Daniel's beat and a day in mid June for the Frome.

The day of the mayfly fishing dawned warm and clear. It was a morning when the English countryside could not have looked lovelier. Arriving at the water at 10 a.m. we were pleased to see empty nymph cases drifting down with the current, which showed that there was already a hatch of mayfly. As if to prove the point, a fish immediately rose opposite us. 'About three and a half pounds,' said Daniel. 'You'll find it almost impossible to catch with a conventional mayfly. I'd wait until we see one behaving in a more reasonable fashion.'

We sat on a bench and watched the river. 'Now *that's* a proper rise,' said Daniel suddenly, 'and a big fish too; probably about six pounds.'

The Bart cast at it and it took his fly immediately – and duly weighed in at exactly six pounds!

By now the river was dimpled everywhere with feeding fish. The conditions were perfect. By 4 p.m. the Bart and I had caught twenty-two trout between us, all of which we had returned, including one monster of just under ten pounds. It was one of the best day's trout fishing that I had ever had, and I said so enthusiastically.

'Yes, well,' said Daniel. 'Let's not make any comments until you've done your beastly coarse fishing.'

The day of the coarse fishing could not have been more different from our time on the Test. We arrived at the Frome in pouring rain with a strong north-east wind blowing. It was bitterly cold. I reckoned that our chances of catching anything were extremely slim. None the less, we started to put up our rods and the Bart foolishly leaned his against the car. I was already in a bad mood, and stupidly slammed the door on it, shattering it in three places. 'We'll just have to share one rod,' I said crossly.

Things went from bad to worse. As we were walking along the bank I slipped on the sodden ground and fell headlong into the river. Of course it wasn't a nice shallow spot, where I would merely have filled my boots. Oh, no! It was a ten-foot-deep hole I had to swim out of. At least the sight of me standing there dripping with pond weed cheered the Bart up – that and the thought of Daniel's derisory comments seemed to keep him going. As I stripped naked and started wringing out my clothes, I heard a torrent of obscene comments and ribald comparison coming from the house opposite, which in my haste I had failed to notice. Quickly I covered myself with a tackle bag, emptied half the river from my boots, and re-dressed.

At last we reached a promising-looking place, and the Bart cast out his bait. Two hours and four different places later we had had not a single nibble. I was frozen to the bone and my teeth were chattering. The Bart, too, was looking thoroughly miserable. 'Come on,' he said, 'let's pack it in.'

Just at that moment I saw a swirl under the alders on the opposite bank. 'Look!' I said. 'I think there's a chub!' The chub obligingly confirmed its identity by striking on the surface again.

The Bart threw his lobworm at it. Nothing happened, although he tried with two other different baits as well. 'That fish has seen it all before,' he said resignedly. 'It's too clever and too wise.'

Suddenly I became aware of a small movement at my feet. Looking closer, I saw that it was a tiny frog. I grabbed it, found some thin nylon, and bound it loosely to a stripped-down salmon-fly hook. 'Throw that out above the chub,' I said. 'They love frogs, and it can still swim easily.'

The Bart made the throw, and the frog swam jerkily towards the opposite bank. Nothing happened. Then, just as it was about to reach dry land, there was a huge swirl and the Bart's rod bent over hard. He hustled the fish away from any tree roots into mid-stream and proceeded to fight it. The chub spat out the frog, which had managed to escape from the hook and now continued unperturbed on its journey. The Bart had a good hook hold, and shortly afterwards we landed the biggest chub that I had ever seen. It weighed just under eight pounds. Tired, wet and cold as we were, we danced a jig in celebration.

We met Daniel for lunch the next day, with my two children, Hugh and Tara, in tow.

'Well,' said Daniel, sitting back in a rather superior fashion, 'did you catch any of those ghastly fish?'

'Yes, we did,' said the Bart proudly. 'We caught a near-record chub!'

'Ah, yes,' said Daniel, looking down his nose. 'The chevender or chub. A particularly nasty creature which displays all the fighting spirit of the Italians. I gather that if you want to eat it you bury it in newspaper for three weeks, dig it up, and then eat the newspaper.'

We ordered our lunch and as I was enjoying a glass of wine Daniel asked us what had happened.

The Bart told him the tale, including, in my view, an unnecessarily detailed description of my ducking which had the children rolling about on the floor, and at the end declared himself the winner with his fine chub.

Keen to put the memory of the day's soaking behind me, I argued strongly for the wonderful mayfly day. We all sat back and waited Daniel's summing-up.

'On the day's mayfly fishing,' he said, glaring at both of us, 'you demonstrated the skill, intelligence and cunning of a pair of backward warthogs. Anyone could have achieved what you two did. But let us consider your skirmish with the chevender. I am going to deduct marks for catching such an unpleasant example of the fishy race, but I will add marks for size and for Bounder's use of an unusual bait. Therefore I declare the competition a draw.'

'Not possible!' cried the Bart.

'A fix!' I shouted. I was now well into the third bottle.

'Well, then,' said Daniel, with an air of Solomon making a momentous judgement. 'How about if the children decide?'

They went into a huddle, shrieking excitedly, which made me suspect that they had been at my glass when I wasn't looking. Eventually Hugh stood up. 'We definitely think the chub wins,' he said. 'It took far more skill to catch it – and anyway, *we* like catching chub.'

And so it was decided. But on the way back to the car I couldn't help noticing the Bart giving my boy a secret wink, and although my eyesight was a bit blurred by this stage, I thought I caught sight of something being slipped between them.

In fact, for the Bart and me, nothing compares with the catching of completely wild fish, be they the aristocratic salmon or the plebeian chub.

We grew up as coarse fishermen, he fishing the mill at Welford-on-Avon and I my uncle's lake at Pyrton in Oxfordshire. The grounding in coarse fishing we received as children has hugely helped our fly-fishing skills, and anyway both of us love any type of angling. We each caught our first fish, a small roach, at the age of four. I caught mine on a piece of dough, and can remember every moment of it – the trembling of the porcupine quill float prior to its dipping under the surface, the excessively strong strike, and the searching in the nettles where the fish had flown over my head are recollections which remain vivid to this day. I took it to the kitchen and insisted that it be cooked for my supper. It tasted disgusting, but I pronounced it delicious and ate it with pride.

We both put down our early enthusiasm for fishing to the influence of one man. Our two nannies read the *Daily Mirror*, and would share a copy, clucking over its pages as they knitted away during the long summer afternoons. Ada, the cheerful, red-faced cook, square and comfortable as the white Aga she tended day and night in the big kitchen, had her own copy. I can still see her reading it now, turning the pages over slowly with stubby, flour encrusted fingers. Jack Gardner, the aptly named handyman, had yet another copy, which he usually read in his tool shed, another paradise, hung with streams of raffia for tying up the beans and redolent with the heavy smell of old oil and damp soil.

We knew that Jack brought his copy to work, along with his lunch, in an old canvas satchel marked 'MOD Property'. The Bart and I were at war with Jack, ever since he reported us for stealing the strawberries, which grew lush, red and totally irresistible in a patch to the side of the big vegetable garden. Our campaign of revenge was simple. Jack loved his marrows and desperately wanted to win a prize at the annual Harvest Festival. This much we had learnt from his son, a spotty youth, older than the pair of us, who would sometimes deign to part with snippets of information. The marrows were carefully nurtured on big pieces of slate to keep them free of bugs, and watered regularly from the ancient, wheeled tub that Jack would take on his rounds. The Bart and I had carefully lifted each marrow and scratched 'Jack is a fool' on their bottoms. We knew that when fully grown, the letters would be enormous and scarred right into the tough green skin. What a shock he'd have! We couldn't wait.

Our family referred to the *Mirror* as 'that left-wing rag', but as both of us spent more time with our nannies than with our parents, we were desperate to get our hands on one. The nannies guarded their copy jealously, so we came up with a plan to steal Jack's instead. The start of the grass mowing season gave us a chance. Jack would push the old manual mower back and forth across the lawn, pausing every now and then to lean on the handle and get his breath back. We devised a cunning plan of attack. I would engage Jack in conversation while he was resting, and the Bart would nip into the tool shed and steal his *Mirror*. We got away with it. Retreating to our hideout, we opened the pages one by one, but could see nothing to explain the adults' fascination – until we came across a cartoon showing a man catching an enormous fish. Slowly we spelt out the title of the mystery: 'Mr Crabtree goes Fishing' it said, by Bernard Venables. The pictures of Mr Crabtree teaching his son Peter to catch huge fish were inspiring. He always seemed such a wonderfully kind man to his son, with endless patience, whereas we had been mainly self-taught. Strangely, I didn't seem able to catch fish with the same regularity as Peter, nor were they as large, but I put this down to personal ineptitude and I decided that I liked the *Mirror* better than *Woman's Weekly*, Nanny's other read, if only because I preferred fishing to knitting.

I have always thought it ridiculous that our freshwater fish are divided into two types: salmon, sea trout, trout and grayling are referred to as 'game' fish while all the others are described as 'coarse', with all the connotations that that word implies. To me the pike is just as sporting a quarry as the salmon, and equally beautiful, and the barbel offers just as much of a challenge as the brown trout. There is a terrible snobbery attached to the names as well. I have often heard people talking along these lines: 'Of course, I'm purely a game fisherman, y'know. Wouldn't know what to do under a green umbrella, ha! ha! Anyway, those other fish are nasty and slimy and you can't eat them.' This attitude is typical of the sort of person who has taken up fly-fishing because he thinks it will advance his social standing, and when country sports are under threat it is divisive, and extremely dangerous. We need to be 'brothers of the angle' as Isaak Walton so succinctly described it in his seventeenth-century masterpiece on the joys of fishing, *The Compleat Angler*.

Our interest rekindled by the competition and the early lessons learnt from the *Daily Mirror* revived, the Bart and I determined to try to do more coarse fishing and thus, in the following winter, we went pike fishing on the Hampshire Avon with another master of his craft, the illustrator John Searl. He is eloquent on the absurd distinction between coarse and game fishing.

'It's ridiculous,' he said, 'and even more so because those so-called game fish are the most stupid freshwater fish of all, and by far the easiest to catch. I mean, if you think about it,' he continued, 'the game-fishing fraternity have to handicap themselves by contriving rules for themselves which make the sport as difficult as possible. If they fished for salmon with worm and shrimp and if they allowed the use of a float and bait on those hallowed chalk streams, the salmon and trout would fall over themselves to be caught. But the coarse fish – now, they have a natural cunning, and they're rightly suspicious of our baits.'

John had booked us into The Royalty Fishery on the River Avon. This, for fishermen, was the stuff of dreams. It's the best coarse fishery in Britain. We arrived at the river with the autumn trees a riot of titian and henna colours. Clouds dappled a winter sky, belts of rain occasionally misted the landscape, and no birds sang. We were fishing the Parlour Pool which looked promisingly 'pikey', with plenty of Norfolk reeds in the margins of the river and backwaters where pike could lurk in ambush for their prey.

We were both angling with a dead bait on the bottom and a float on the surface, and while we were waiting John told us how he had started fishing. 'I was born in the East End of London,' he said, 'and there wasn't much fishing there, but I read the *Daily Mirror* and I was completely hooked on a cartoon strip by a man called Bernard Venables.'

'Mr Crabtree!' the Bart and I chorused.

'Did you know,' said John, 'that the book of the cartoon strip *Mr Crabtree goes Fishing* sold two million copies? I got to know Bernard later on, and was always surprised that he wasn't a rich man. But you see, he was an employee of the Mirror Group, and all the profits went into their pockets. When he stopped working for the *Mirror* Bernard fell on hard times financially, but a fan organised a collection of memorable fishing stories and put them into an anthology called *Red Letter Days*, which he published, and gave the proceeds to Bernard. I did the illustrations, and that was how I met him. By this time,' John went on, 'Bernard was getting very old, but he lasted another seven years and died in 2001 at the fine age of ninety-four. His wishes for his funeral were explicit, and he was buried in a field at St Bourne wrapped in a wicker basket like an old-fashioned fisherman's creel.'

It seemed to me, as we stood on the riverbank watching the water for signs of movement, that Bernard's funeral was a wonderful way to go. But my reverie was short-lived. Just then I noticed that my float was moving over the surface and, grabbing the rod, I struck, and after a short battle landed a beautiful ten-pound pike. Mr Crabtree would have been proud of me.

We moved downstream and on the main weir we found a man lying back in a reclining armchair covered in a sleeping bag and with two rods on rests fishing the pool.

'He's fishing for barbel,' John said, 'but the way he's fishing is the classic modern lazy man's method. He merely baits up the swim, casts out, attaches a bite detector to his line and goes to sleep until the alarm goes off.'

I looked at the fisherman, and did indeed think I could detect a gentle snore. 'You see,' John continued, 'I only like to fish with the old-fashioned tackle. It's simple and very direct and you can feel every touch on the bait. Look – ' he showed us his rod – 'this is an Alcock's Ariel centre-pin reel. It was made in the 1920s – and I'll bet that I catch just as much as someone with all the fancy state-of-the-art tackle. And I'll tell you something else,' John went on. 'I knew a man who wanted to catch a record barbel. So he fed a piece of river for months with specially made-up bait. Must have cost him a fortune! Of course, by the time he eventually fished for them, the barbel were virtually tame, and very fat. He caught them in huge numbers, but I'm glad to say none of them was a record. Imagine what Mr Crabtree would have said!'

To me the fish, be it salmon or roach, has always offered sanctuary, shelter and peace of mind from a madly spinning world. I have lived in days of gales and rain on a Scottish spate river, and times of lazy warmth in May at the king-cup-bordered waterside of an English chalk stream. I have watched the gentle bobbing of a float on the quiet waters of a reed-girt Norfolk broad, with the curlews crying and the wind rustling in the withies. I have stood in the clamouring torrent of a mountain river and cast my fly for the salmon's elusive silver with another fisherman, the osprey, waiting overhead. The fish has taken me to a different place where the spirit is freshened and in which truth is found. When I have been happy it has made me euphoric, and when I have been in despair it has lifted me from my misery and placed me in a kinder world. Now it seemed that the circle of life had come full turn. Because of 'Mr Crabtree' I had been given a supreme gift, and now I had willed it to my children. I can only hope that it will give them the joy and contentment it has to me, and that when the time comes, they too will pass it on.

6

June

THE MIGHTY TWEED

The rich man in his castle,
The poor man at his gate.
God made them high and lowly,
And ordered their estate.

A verse from the English hymn 'All Things Bright and
Beautiful'. This politically incorrect verse, now seldom
used, to me describes the immutable hierarchies of that
endangered species, the English class system, alive and
well in the Borders.

The mighty River Tweed, one of the most prolific salmon rivers in Europe, dominates the Scottish Borders with more than two thousand miles of waterways. Over the last two centuries it has struggled for existence against both man-made and god-given enemies. In the Industrial Revolution the abundance of mills built along its banks took much of its waters through great stone-built dams before returning them so polluted that almost all fish life was destroyed. Then, after the mills closed, a massive clean-up restored the fish, only for ulcerative dermal necrosis (UDN), the dreaded salmon disease, to strike in the 1960s and 1970s, leaving the giant fish scabbed and dying with ugly white patches down their sides. The salmon eventually developed immunity to UDN, but then came mass industrial farming, which poured pesticides into the water and reduced the precious 'redds', the nests of gravel which the salmon need to spawn properly, by extensive drainage schemes. Now, with new understanding of the impact of modern farming methods on the environment, the Tweed is once more restored to its rightful position as the sporting and economic powerhouse of the region – although salmon stocks are yet again under threat, this time from destruction by *Gyrodactylius Salaris*, a tiny deadly parasite, a quarter the size of my fingernail. This is the story of the Tweed and its people, and of how they have learned to live with themselves and their giant friend.

The Bounder and I first visited Floors Castle in Kelso, the heart of the Tweed salmon fishery, in the 1970s. We were broke as usual, but had managed to save enough money for an out-of-season beat and a local bed-and-breakfast. We headed north one Saturday morning in February in my old Mini, which rattled at every joint and was blessed with a heater that gave out a noise like a demented wasp but little warmth. By the time night fell we were glad to find sanctuary with the Bounder's friend Ian, a career bachelor who lived in Spartan splendour in his old family farmhouse in Northumberland. A large whisky or two restored the circulation, but Ian's offer of supper was politely refused.

The Bounder had warned me. Scorning the delights of Elizabeth David et al., Ian cooked every meal in the black dirt-encrusted frying pan which occupied the only working ring of his ancient gas stove. The fat in the pan had not been changed for generations.

'But what's the point?' asked Ian, apparently surprised to be challenged about this. 'One lot of fat is as good as another, and the stuff in there now has history.'

I came as near to the stove as I dared. 'Look!' I said, and pointed out that its 'history' included the tiny paw tracks of a kitchen mouse, delicately etched in the congealed mess. Worse, closer inspection revealed that the mouse had stopped for a poop half-way through his journey, leaving a few tiny pellets for the cognoscenti.

Ian seemed unfazed by this. 'It'll all taste the same fried up,' he said, encouragingly.

The Bounder and I thanked him, but declined the invitation. We dined instead off a plate of cold baked beans.

We were glad at first that our B&B booking gave us an excuse to turn down Ian's invitation to stay the night. I suspected the energetic mouse might well have needed a lie down in the beds upstairs after its meal. But it soon appeared that our visit to Kelso could have been better timed. The owner's wife had just run off with the roofing contractor, and there was no one to do the cooking. We had been looking forward to dinner after our culinary experience at Ian's, so our hearts lifted when our host said that he had rollmops on the menu. I am partial to herring in any disguise, and also reasoned that the serving instructions ('Remove from jar, place on plate and serve') would not be beyond an amateur chef, even one traumatised by his wife's abandonment. I was wrong. He boiled them.

Were we downcast? We were on holiday! We were in Scotland. We immediately took refuge in that infallible Scottish remedy 'a wee dram' in the next-door pub. It worked a treat. Closing time involved shutting us in, not out. I recall a great deal of singing, but not much else.

The next morning dawned bright and clear, but bitterly cold. As so often in Scotland, the clean air swept away any lingering fumes of drink, and we were both keen to have a crack at the salmon. Donald, our ghillie, was hedging his bets, however.

'Aye!' he said, with well-judged pessimism. 'There's a few aboot!' Whether they could be caught in sub-zero conditions, and by us, was clearly debatable.

We tackled up, and I stood for a time watching the Bounder as he cast a beautiful Devon Minnow clear across the wide river. Poetry in motion he is as a fisherman, and I shall never be his equal. But, as Napoleon said of his favourite generals, I have luck . . .

By midday I was frozen to the bone and could not feel the rod, my feet, or any other part of my anatomy. The frost still glittered harsh and white on the fields and even the birds seemed to be giving the day a miss. Donald had lit the stove in the bothy, his little wooden fishing hut, and the pillar of white smoke drew me to it like a drowning man in a storm. The survival instinct is a funny thing. Inside there was another pleasant surprise: a bottle of the finest McCallan malt whisky.

Just one little sip, I reasoned, but one thing led to another, and the level had, mysteriously, sunk almost half-way down the bottle before the Bounder returned, stamping his feet against the cold and moaning about the lack of fish. He seemed rather put out by my behaviour, but there was little to be done, and by now everything seemed vastly amusing to me. In revenge, that afternoon he relegated me to a seat in the flat-bottomed boat which the phlegmatic Donald anchored safely in mid-stream. I suppose he thought that at least I might get a cast out without doing myself or anyone else an injury.

Donald and I got on splendidly, helped by the last of the malt, and soon settled to swapping fishing stories. As usual my casting was terrible, not helped by the cold or the whisky. As I finished one story with an expansive gesture, the Minnow flew backwards over my shoulder and landed with a splash behind the boat. Reeling it in, I caught the only salmon of the week. The Bounder was furious.

I had my first experience with *Salmo Salar*, the wily Atlantic salmon, at Bellarena, our family estate in Northern Ireland. The family had held salmon-netting rights since James II's time, when my ancestors were first 'planted' in the area, and these now helped eke out the tiny income on which my father attempted to run the estate and pay the wages of our little team of workers. The ancient draught net that we used needed all hands to get it working right.

Our team leader was a dour Scot named McCunn – if he had a Christian name I never knew it – who had been the land steward since my great-uncle Frederick's time. Great-uncle Fred was a six-foot four-inch martinet of a man, with no sense of humour and much given to barking instructions at the servants at every opportunity. McCunn was responsible for the outdoor jobs at Bellarena, which included the never-ending task of fixing leaks in the acres of roof over the big house. 'McCunn! The roof's leaking again!' great-uncle Fred would bellow down the phone. A sullen McCunn would appear, disappear up the servants' staircase to the attic, thump around a bit, then reappear once more. 'All done, your Lordship,' he would mutter before skulking off across the court-yard back home. When my father inherited Bellarena the roof was still leaking, and when we investigated we discovered McCunn's magic solution to the problem. The attic contained a number of rusty old hip baths, and McCunn would simply move one of these under the latest leak and report that all was well. Ingenious!

Two wonderful old countrymen made up the rest of the fishing crew. Johnny Stewart, who was 'on the disability' and limped badly, got the easy job of 'trail rope', and my father's favourite, Joe Docherty, nicknamed 'The Horse' because of his enormous strength, had the important job of closing the draught.

The salmon-netting is one of my favourite memories from my Bellarena childhood. As the tide ebbed and the first salmon jumped in front of us – a bar of silver catching the last golden light – the crew would launch the flat-bottomed punt which held the net, and we were in business. Fishing was a simple matter. The lead rope (Father) pulled the net off the boat and along one side of the river; Johnny on the trail rope kept the back end hard against the opposite shore; at the end of the pool, Father would drop his rope and Joe would haul the closing net fast across the river, to be pulled in a great loop onto the shore. We children would help Father, then row across to watch the action in *Tar*, our old tin boat, named after the three rivers – Thames, Avon, Roe – on which it had seen action. McCunn would growl at us all, whatever happened.

On one memorable night, it was as dark as pitch. Only the last closing moments of the net would reveal whether or not we had a salmon, marked by a sudden thrashing and splashing, then the dull thud of McCunn's killing stick. Tonight there was a bigger than usual splash.

'Good fish?' we called out.

'Indeed!' grunted McCunn heavily. 'Yer feyther's fallen in the water.' Clearly, drink had been taken.

McCunn not only enjoyed himself at my family's expense, he also delighted in keeping the Bellarena guests in their place. On one evening at the netting, as we waited for the tide to turn, my father's greatest friend, Henry 'Tarka the Otter' Williamson, attempted to impress us all with a display of fly casting, until he got tangled in the trees. McCunn was delighted.

'Ye'll not catch one up there, your worship!' he chortled, to our secret delight. Williamson left in a huff.

But it was Joe who was Father's favourite conversational partner on the estate, although a more unlikely combination it would be hard to imagine. I once found them both leaning over a fence in the pouring rain.

'It's wet, Joe,' I said.

He looked at me for a moment without reply. Then, 'Just dry spitting,' he replied dourly.

'But what are you both looking at?' I asked.

Again a silence. Eventually, 'It's a great evening for growing,' he told me, and my father nodded sagely.

They were as happy as Larry, the pair of them, and now lie

buried side by side in the little mountain church yard, able to chatter for all eternity.

Over the years my fishing expeditions to Scotland with the Bounder have been irregular, but all enormous fun. Between his several marriages, my role was to deliver his actress mistress to wherever he was staying. On one occasion we arrived just as he was landing a salmon. A keen fisherwoman herself, she rushed down to share in his success. I still have a photo of the Bounder, woman in one hand, salmon in the other – his two great pleasures in life – caught in a single moment.

Now, in pursuit of Endangered Species, we were once more on the way to Scotland, courtesy of Great North Eastern Railways and their excellent dining car. Fully refreshed all the way, we arrived in Berwick-on-Tweed station exactly on time, and picked up the 'wee car' I had hired for the trip.

The Bounder eyed the wee car with great disfavour before somehow squeezing his bulk into the front seat, like a disgruntled haggis, along with much huffing and puffing. I took the wheel, forgot that the wee car was not automatic, and stalled it with a jerk.

'You'll need to use the wee gears,' advised the Bounder grumpily.

We were staying in a small estate cottage right by the Tweed itself, lent to us by a friend whose family has owned land around Coldstream for generations. Her instructions had been charming: 'Turn right past the graveyard and waterworks. Continue for about a mile up the curly-whirly, uppy-downy narrow road. After a dip, you'll see a signpost on the right – cross the cattle grid and follow the steep (poorly) gravelled road down to the river. Your cottage is the second one by the woods.'

The (poorly) gravelled drive was just as described, and I got stuck in my first ascent and had to knock at the ghillie Dougie's cottage. 'Aye! It's a wee bit tricky at first,' he conceded. 'Jump in and I'll show you how.' Gunning the wee motor, we roared off up the track, like doing the Cresta Run in reverse, leapt the cattle grid at the end with, I swear, all four wheels off the ground, and made it to the road. More than a wee McCallan was needed to calm the shaking nerves, but the cottage was as warm and comfortable as Candy had promised, the view down to one of the best beats on the river was spectacular, and Dougie was already a friend. It felt good to be back in the Borders.

Floors Castle was our first port of call. It is an impressive sight – the largest inhabited castle in Scotland, according to the guide book. Given my experience of Scottish central heating systems, I am not sure this is an advantage. The Duke of Roxburgh had a bad cold (maybe proving my point), but made the effort to see us anyway.

'I caught my first salmon on a trout rod when I was eight,' he said when I asked him how fishing had changed in his lifetime. 'In my father's time, in the 1960s and 1970s, we shared the sport with our friends and rarely let anything, so there was a completely different feel to the river. Now it's all focused on how many fish you catch, although the beats are usually let to the same people year after year.'

'I can't stand the notion that fishing pleasure is tied to how many fish you catch,' the Bounder said stoutly. It is one of his hobby-horses, and there was every chance that he'd mount it and go charging off into the distance.

The duke did not seem to realise the danger he was in. 'You can't spend all your time looking back,' he said. 'People have less time, and they want results more quickly. Fishing has also become much more popular, with all the corporates involved, and it means that you have to put on a better show, which makes it more expensive. It's all much more commercial these days, and we have to be forward-thinking to protect the assets.'

The Bounder and I had done some research to find out just what such assets might be worth. An average beat, say half a mile of single bank on the Tweed, catching about three hundred fish a year, would cost around £12,000 a fish to buy – nearly £4 million. Prime beats, like the Junction Pool, would be worth three times that. A day's fishing on a good beat would cost between £50 and £1,000, averaging about £250 – so we could see why one would not want to give something so valuable away to mates who dropped round for a fish now and then!

We could see that the duke's cold was getting worse, so we cut short the meeting and headed off to see the people most closely involved in the changes in river management.

In Kelso we decided to stop for a bar lunch at the Ednam House Hotel, scene of many fond memories. The Bounder, with a sigh of nostalgia, reminded me of his fortieth birthday party: distrustful of the hotel's cooking, his glamorous actress mistress, who was organising the event, brought a massive sirloin of beef up from London and cooked it herself in the kitchens. It was magnificent, and was received with rapturous applause by the guests (as an actress, she liked a curtain call now and then), and we were all eager for seconds. The waiters, however, had inexplicably vanished, and when we went to ferret them out from the kitchens we found the entire staff of the hotel, including the gardeners, seated around the kitchen table, just polishing off the last of our beef. The head waiter wiped his mouth, summoned his dignity and quoted some ancient Scottish precedent about 'the Master's Leavings'. We could willingly have strangled him.

One story led to another, and I reminisced about the time the Bounder and I had stayed at a small fishing lodge near Aberdeen. The food was inedible, but we were eagerly awaiting Saturday, when we had been promised a 'joint'. We sat there in the formal dining room, gastric juices primed, to be greeted by a pale, wizened white object, brought to the table with much ceremony. It had, the housekeeper assured us with some satisfaction, been 'biled' for an hour or so, and the juices used to make soup. We left that afternoon . . . Just as we were settling up my Siamese cat, which used to travel with me everywhere, crapped on the carpet to show his disfavour.

'Ahm *verra* disappointed in the cat,' said the housekeeper, severely.

'And we're *verra* disappointed in the joint,' chorused the pair of us. No tip was left.

Scotland's culinary skills have improved since those days and now, replete with some rare roast beef sandwiches (to make up for the lost sirloin) and a bottle of claret, we headed off to see the Tweed Commission. We were welcomed by Nick and Ronald in their offices in the stable block of a big country house a bit further upstream. Nick is an enthusiastic former fish farmer who was brought up in the Devon countryside but left when he felt it had been ruined. His colleague Ronald is a biologist whose professionalism and sense of humour seem an echo of those admirably competent Scottish engineers and scientists who helped Britain forge its Industrial Revolution.

Nick explained that the Tweed Commission is an independently financed organisation. 'We raise our money by a tax per fish on everything caught in the river, which we charge the beat owners. It varies between £40 and £60, dependent on what we need. It was highest when we bought out the draught netsmen, who were taking at least 20,000 fish a year out of the river.' (Later we were to meet a single netsman who, operating exactly the same draught nets that my father had used to much less effect in Ireland, had regularly caught 15,000 fish each year by fair means and foul. Multiply this by the almost sixty netting stations, and it is clear that someone had been telling porky pies.)

'Don't some of the proprietors object to forking out such big sums?' asked the Bounder.

'Strangely enough, no,' Nick replied. 'The value of lettings is now very high, and we have just done a survey that shows that every fish caught adds over £1,000 into the local economy, so it is in all our interests to work together. The great thing about the Commission is its democracy. It has 81 members, of which only 38 are proprietors, the rest being angling associations, district council appointees, and so on. The proprietors, who are still mostly "Old Nobs" – I use the term loosely,' he giggled, '– but it is a fact that the gentry seem to have hung on longer in the Borders than in most places, and they're part of the community. Everyone – including the duke – regularly attends meetings. It's much better than some other Scottish rivers I could mention, when the only time the committees meet is after a long lunch at Boodle's.'

'That's the Commission,' said Ronald, 'but its scientific arm is known as The Tweed Foundation, and it's the driving force behind our efforts to get the river working properly again.'

Ronald has a historical perspective way beyond the twenty-first century. 'The big problems for the Tweed came with the Industrial Revolution in the 1850s,' he said, 'when all the mills were built along the bank. They needed huge amounts of water to drive the machinery, and diverted the river with great stone-built dams and sluices. Worse, after almost draining the river during the day, at night they'd throw all the refuse out and wash it downstream from the sluices. For a time the river was deemed incapable of supporting animal life. Even after the mills shut, the dams stopped salmon running up to spawn and made fishing near-impossible.

'There was a splendid river manager before Nick and I arrived,' continued Ronald, 'who was determined to tackle the problem. He was an old colonel, and he used to load up his boat with every sort of high explosive, then just blow up the dams one by one. The townspeople hated it, as they liked the beautiful stonework, and they would throw rocks at him from every bridge. In the end he had to make himself a suit of leather armour. Look!' Ronald left us and returned wearing an extraordinary leather helmet, with great bars across the mouth and eyes, which made him look like Hannibal Lecter's twin brother. His voice echoed eerily from inside: 'Do you know my secret weapon?' he rasped.

The Bounder and I shook our heads, wondering what on earth was coming next.

'Gin . . .' he whispered, then roared with laughter and took off the helmet. 'When the old man retired, we found enough empty bottles outside his office to build the great pyramid!'

Once Nick and Ronald had got started on stories of their conservation work to 'get the river working for itself', as they described it, there was no stopping them, even when we had to break for tea and cakes. But the mood became more sombre as they talked about the small parasite *Gyrodactylius Salaris*. The parasite is rife in Norway, and attaches itself also to trout. A single diseased specimen imported will spread it quickly through the country and could wipe out the whole salmon population, so you can see why they are worried.

'They seem to have done an extraordinary job,' I said to the Bounder, as the wee car lurched towards our next appointment. 'The last time I went fishing with you in Scotland, the river was differently-coloured every time the local paper mill started making a new order of bog roll, and it stank to high heaven. Don't you remember? We caught nothing but condoms which had floated down from the student Halls of Residence. I seem to remember a fishing competition won by the Chief Constable with three pink ones.'

The Bounder reminded me that on that occasion we'd had far more fun catching worms late at night after a visit to the pub. They came out on the guesthouse lawn, but vanished back into their holes quick as snakes. You had to switch on a powerful torch, and then jam your finger where worm and hole met. Great sport after a few pints!

Our next appointment was with Andrew Douglas-Home, chairman of the Tweed Commission and nephew of former prime minister Sir Alec. Andrew is a local, born and bred, and a keen fisherman with an excellent beat of the Tweed at the bottom of the garden. He has been involved with the Commission since its earliest days in the 1980s.

'The heart of it is how we all work together,' he said. 'Most river bodies fight like cats and dogs. We are the only one that is totally democratic, and we also raise twice as much money – around £600,000 a year – as any other. It's not just a matter of the individual wealth of our proprietors – there are plenty of wealthy beat owners in Scotland – but ours dig deeper into their pockets, and back it with time and effort. Then, there are the new people the river brings to the Borders. One of our biggest employers is now a pharmaceutical company, which is only here because the founder loves fishing. Everyone sees the value of what we are doing for the local economy: fishing alone brings nearly £120 million into Scotland – more even than golf – so it's not just blood sports for the upper classes. Mind you, there is still a bit of poaching, and one persistent fellow who leaves rude messages on the Duke's fishing hut . . .'

The next morning I left the Bounder with Gerry, our hostess Candy's affable Irish husband who is mustard-keen on every sort of sport, and set off on my own. I had told the Bounder that I was going to potter around some old ruined castles, something I know bores him witless, but I had fibbed: I had planned a day with two extraordinary women, and I wanted to keep them to myself.

Both women live in Traquair, a pretty hill village about an hour's drive up the Tweed valley from Coldstream, and a journey worth making for the view alone. Fiona (Fi) Martynoga, my first port of call, lives in an eighteenth-century manse to which she and her doctor husband moved from Bath. Sadly, he died unexpectedly, leaving her to cope with life alone in the Borders. Many incomers would have headed straight back where they came from, but Fi is made of sterner stuff and was determined to get to grips with living in a less crowded, more self-sufficient world. We chatted in her book-lined kitchen, warm up against the Aga, Fi tatting away at a rag rug.

'The reason we moved here', she said, 'was that the country was big and the telephone directory small. It's a tiny population for a big tract of land. My husband was a doctor who really wanted to be a farmer, so we soon started keeping chickens and sheep – all that backyard stuff that few people can be bothered with now, but we loved it. Learning how country people ate in the old days – I mean in the late eighteenth century, when this house was built – made me realise how well-off we all were before the dictatorship of supermarkets began, so a year ago I decided to recreate the experience.'

'Tell me more!' I demanded, rubbing my hands. It was getting near to lunchtime, and I've always been rather attracted by the idea of eighteenth-century fare.

'I already had a full garden of vegetables,' Fi continued, 'and knew I could be self-sufficient in them. But I wanted *really* to experience what life was like then. Among the outbuildings were the remains of an old cottage – it was pretty rough really: my family christened it 'the Hovel'. And I had also been collecting old artefacts, like this griddle.' At this point, Fi broke off to show me a circular metal disk on chains, which she later put to good use to cook me up a home-made barley bannock – simple to do and really delicious! 'Then,' she went on, 'all I needed to do was clear the place out, put in an old range and a sleeping platform for myself, and I was back two hundred years.'

'But what about things you couldn't grow yourself?' I asked, thinking nostalgically of that sirloin. 'What about milk and meat?'

'I had to set myself a standard of living,' Fi explained, 'so I decided to be a Domini's – a schoolmaster's – wife. This meant I couldn't have servants, and would have to live on a stipend of £20 a year – about £25 a week these days – plus an allowance of grain.'

'And was that enough?' I asked.

'Just about,' said Fi. 'The local farm labourers, who at that time had not had a pay rise for a hundred years, had to make do on something similar. I wasn't going to cheat, so I paid out for bus travel, stamps and so on, but I made do. I should have kept a goat, but instead bought milk from a local farmer, and made my own cheese and butter. Then there was the occasional gift of a deer from one of the big estates for salting or smoking, and Paddy, an itinerant Irish poacher from Edinburgh, would often leave a rabbit or a pheasant out on my doorstep.'

I told Fi about the gypsy way of catching rabbits by blocking up most of their holes, which causes a sort of motorway pile-up. All you need to do is reach in and grab the last one by its back legs – no snares, no guns, no anything. She laughed, and I asked about cooking.

'Lots of porridge, stews, and fresh vegetables, of course,' said Fi, 'filled out with home-made bread and bannocks, as well as apples, both fresh and stored.'

For a second I had the sense of an evocative odour right out of my past: the sour, perfumed smell of my grandmother's old apple house.

'I became an expert in wild herbs and vegetables,' Fi went on. 'Wild garlic in the spring, sprigs of ground elder, Good King Henry, which is much nicer than spinach. It was a huge joy to experiment. I even started using natural remedies, like comfrey for sprains. In the seventeenth century, I am sure I would have been burnt as a witch!'

'I'll bet you got lonely in the evenings,' I said. 'I remember visiting cottages just like yours with my father when I was growing up in Ireland. Calling on neighbours was the great evening entertainment before telly. Everyone would sit in circles around a great, glowing peat fire, the old folk nearest and the children whispering and giggling back in the shadows. It was always a bit embarrassing, when we dropped in, to be offered the best seat, displacing some aged matriarch, but once Father got onto his stories, everyone relaxed and we all felt at home.

'And when Father's eyes gave out' – I was surprised to find that even now, thirty years later in Fi's warm kitchen, my eyes began to prick – 'and he couldn't drive any more to visit his friends, he found life was no longer worth living and he shot himself. They all came to the funeral and sang the fishing hymns that Father had chosen so joyously. He had written them down for me on the back of an old bill – the last thing he ever did. The tears ran down my face in torrents. When we came out of the church, we found over a hundred more locals, including the Catholics and those too shy to come inside. Everyone helped with "lifting" the coffin – the further you were carried, the more popular you were, and Father went a good mile. I shared my turn with Malcolm Mullan, the local purveyor of both funeral services and sporting goods. Half-way down the road, it occurred to me that Malcolm had done pretty well out of the family, selling us both the coffin and the gun that helped fill it, and I asked for a discount. I got a wry smile from Malcom, but I could hear Father laughing a last time from his cloud.'

'I was lonely,' admitted Fi. 'I had lots of visitors during the day, but the evenings around here are reserved for the soaps and the pub. I desperately missed my radio.'

'So what did you learn from the experiment?' I asked.

'I learned the joy of walking,' said Fi, 'that – and, of course, a whole new recipe book. I think the locals thought I was interesting but a bit dotty, to make myself so uncomfortable – maybe, here in the Borders, the bad days of country poverty are still too close. But above all I ended up much closer to the land. The great empty hills around here may seem picturesque, but they are actually quite threatening to someone who comes from a more tamed part of the country.'

What Fi said made sense. You cannot forever keep the country at bay through the car windscreen and the double glazing. I made my goodbyes and headed off to my next date – not this time an incomer, but a woman whose family has had twenty-three generations in which to become comfortable with life in the Borders.

Catherine Maxwell-Stuart lives in Traquair House – the oldest

continuously-inhabited house in Scotland. Her family enter-
tained Bonnie Prince Charlie on his way south to Derby, and
swore never to open the 'Bear Gates' at the top of the drive until
Charlie or one of his successors became King of England. Even if
the Windsors were thinking of handing over in favour of a quieter
life, the present Stuart heir is a Bavarian Prince who is not mad
keen to press his claim, so the gates stay shut, the drive stays
grassed over, and the wee car and I had to use the tourist entrance.

Although born at Traquair, Catherine got itchy feet when she
was fifteen, moved away to the city life, and only returned when
she was twenty-five. 'I am an only child,' she said, 'and when my
father died, I had to take over. It's in my blood. All the time I was
in London or abroad, I always felt something missing: a hanker-
ing for the countryside.'

Traquair, Catherine told me, had been open to tourists since
1958. 'It was a hunting lodge when this area was all forest; then it
was fortified as one in a line of "peel" towers to keep the English
out. My family converted it into a home between 1500 and 1700 and
it has survived intact since then, which is amazing considering that
the family were Catholics and the whole Border was continuously
fought over from one side or the other. Maybe it's been saved from
"improvement" because we lost much of our fortune by always
picking the wrong side – and by endless unwise speculation, like
gold-mining in Spain!'

'But the house is so old,' I said. 'Aren't the repair bills horren-
dous?' I was thinking of how hard it had been trying to keep
Bellarena leak-proof.

Catherine nodded. 'Soon after I took it over, we discovered
a massive crack in the roof which took £250,000 to fix. We
couldn't work out what we could sell to finance it, and then I
thought of making the brewery a commercial proposition.'

She showed me a line of prettily-labelled bottles: *Traquair*

House Ales – 10% proof. Absolute rocket-fuel! My conscience was pricked: I should have brought the Bounder after all.

Like many old houses, Catherine explained, Traquair had had a small brewery in the courtyard since the eighteenth century, to brew beer 'for the master's consumption'. Her father had turned the original equipment, slumbering but still amazingly complete at the back of a junk room, into a tourist attraction, But it was Catherine who had upped production without changing the classic oak maturation process that gives the beer its genuine flavour. She is now in the microbrewery business, with a thriving export market.

Catherine showed me around the house, which gives a remarkable picture of life in the seventeenth century. Pictures of Bonnie Prince Charlie gaze smugly down from the walls, but I liked the way he only got a corridor slot in the house's painting hierarchy – serve him right! I thought. He may have been 'bonnie' to some, but he wasted a lot of gallant lives along the way, all for nothing, and ended his life a miserable old has-been. But it was the old brewery I liked best, with its wonderful oak vats and copper tubing. I could see it was Catherine's favourite part of the house too, and suddenly I realised that what she had created and rescued from oblivion was another Endangered Species – the working manor house at the centre of its community, as it was before the gentry all got posh, built enormous mansions and buggered off to London to spend their money on dressing up.

There was a lesson here, I realised. Just like Fi, Catherine had seen right to the heart of what makes living in the country worthwhile – creating something unique and beautiful in a crowded world. As I bumped down the back drive in the wee car, I reflected that it was time she opened up the main gates. The women of Traquair had no need of a twerp like Bonnie Prince Charlie!

I headed back to our cottage to pick up the Bounder, who I found still debating the finer points of lurcher hunting – a very popular Border sport – with Gerry, and we drove back up the Tweed to Kelso. That evening, we were after a humbler quarry than the noble salmon – wild brown trout – and on Dougie's recommendation, we stopped on the way at Tweedside Tackle. Despite a beautifully presented shop, trading is tough for Tim and Caroline, as for so many small country retailers in the world of Google, but they are fighting back with their own website. We were met in the shop by Ronnie and Bert, both long-serving leaders of the trout-fishing community and expert anglers, and we couldn't have been in better hands. As we drove to the river, they both filled us in on how they managed to enjoy excellent sport without having to pay the eye-watering amounts charged for the salmon beats.

'The angling clubs are well represented on the Tweed Commission and we know all the proprietors well,' Bert explained. 'We've managed to convince them that responsible anglers act as unpaid bailiffs for their waters and, just as importantly, won't get in the way of the salmon boys. So they let us fish for "peppercorn rents" – one charges a single old penny per year, which is returned afterwards.'

'But what about the anglers who aren't responsible?' asked the Bounder.

'Ah, well,' said Bert, 'we've worked out some codes of conduct . . . We caught some lads claiming to be fishing for winter grayling, but they were using hooks and bunches of worms like boa constrictors that only a salmon could get its mouth around – they won't do that again!'

On the river bank it was champion Ronnie who showed us how to do it. He has eyes like lasers and the stealth of a Big White Hunter. Even the Bounder took a while to see the little sipping trout rises that Ronnie cast to, and like Daniel Busk, our friend in Hampshire, he was truly an expert at matching his fly to the natural insect life around him.

'Blue-winged Olives are best at this time of year,' he said, 'but you have to be quick. The feeding rise here may be ten minutes or less, and you'll only get one cast at a good fish.'

He easily beat the Bounder four to two in a little competition for the evening's score. I was content to watch the two experts, their lines so perfectly cast that they made hardly a ripple on the darkening water, while the last swifts of the evening whirled and swooped about them. This is what I truly love about fishing, I thought, the soothing magic of the art – a fish for tea is just a bonus.

The Bounder and I took two of the larger trout, gold- and red-flecked wild brownies, to my mind one of the most beautiful of Nature's creatures, and packed up for the evening. On the way home Ronnie told us about his latest venture, teaching the kids to share his love of the sport.

'Fishing is an ageing sport,' he said. 'When I joined the club, I was the youngest member, and over twenty years later I'm still almost the youngest. At a recent meeting someone said we shouldn't charge OAPs, until we realised that we'd hardly take a penny in subscriptions if we didn't. My father taught me to fish and his father taught him, but somehow we've missed a generation, and we need to find new ways of interesting the kids if the sport is to survive.'

Ronnie talked about his initiative 'Tweed Start', which works directly with the schools. 'We don't teach fishing as such,' he said. 'We're more interested in making the kids interested in the natural environment to start with. I take them bug-hunting in rivers and a special pond, where they may even catch the odd rainbow trout and feel the excitement of fishing. I show them how to match the bugs to an artificial fly and give them a go at tying a fly themselves, and then show them how to cast. They ask what the point of the sport is, and whether it's just for old people, so I always tell them that angling benefits everyone – from the visitor buying his petrol in the Borders to the people who set up businesses here. When I talk about jobs, they are interested well enough. We don't expect them to take it up immediately, but when they grow up and want to get out of the house into the fresh air for a moment, perhaps they'll remember and mebbe give it a wee try.'

That night we barbecued the trout outside our little cottage, and sat listening to the quiet bubbling of the mighty Tweed, arguing and fussing around the old mill channels and dams in front of us (or those somehow missed by the explosive colonel) as it had for more than two hundred years. A last McCallan, and it was time for bed.

It rained heavily that night, the comfortable pattering of water on the cottage roof keeping the Bounder and me longer in our beds than usual. When we finally emerged, the Tweed had risen a good foot and the water was coloured and angry-looking.

'It would be a good day to spend with the ghillies,' the Bounder announced with authority. 'It'll be damn' nigh impossible to catch a fish and they'll be prime for a chat. With any luck we'll get all the local scandal, and find out about this famous poacher who leaves rude messages on the duke's fishing hut.'

He was right, of course. The syndicate members were already out flogging the waters, but with no success. The ghillies stood around, shaking their heads and occasionally managing a 'Weel, there might be a fish . . .' We started by talking to Andrew Douglas-Home's ghillie, Malcolm, a veteran of the river.

'Has the job changed much in the last twenty years?' I asked.

Malcolm thought for a moment. 'The people are different,' he said. 'Most of the fishermen used to be the Big House crowd, lords, ladies, colonels and the like, but now it could be anybody. Today I've got a joiner, a caravan-site owner, and an insurance broker. And now everyone expects to catch a fish for the money – but that's not right. They pay the money for the *right* to fish only, and if there's only a wee chance of a salmon, ye'll often work all day with nothing at the end.'

'What are the new owners like?' asked the Bounder. 'Any real bastards?' he enquired, keen for gossip and scandal.

'Och! There are a few fellows that make themselves unpopular when they first come,' said Malcolm. 'There was one who cut down all the trees and threw out the trout club, but he soon changed his tune.'

By now it had started to rain again, so we went back to the cottage and stoked up the fire. Dougie joined us later, wet and cold, but soon thawed out with the help of a wee dram. He proved a mine of stories, many of them too scurrilous to repeat, but here's a taste.

'Did you ask the duke about the writings on his fishing hut?' he asked.

'I didn't dare!' I said. 'Were they funny?'

'Aye,' said Dougie. 'One said "Duke of Roxburgh 0, me 56". Then there was another after the duke's divorce: "No Wife, No Fish, Back Soon." '

Dougie had slowly worked his way up from 'kennel boy' at a local hunt to ghillie. It had been a long apprenticeship. 'The modern generation wouldn't have the same patience,' he said. 'I had one young lad who tried it, then came in and told me that he was no' going to play nursemaid to a lot of old farts, and he was away!'

'And so where will the next generation of ghillies come from?' I asked.

'There are local men coming back to the area,' said Dougie, 'and you even get some interesting people looking for a quieter life. There's a new ghillie starting on this beat who was an international salesman for a big fishing company, but is fed up with too much travel and never seeing his family.'

I don't think I'd have the patience for the job, but I suspected that if things had turned out differently the Bounder could have made his life here, fishing all day and swapping stories with the lads in the pub. He certainly seemed interested in the author of the graffiti in the duke's fishing hut.

'So, who is this famous poacher, then?' he asked.

'He's known around here as "the Weasel", because he's a shifty little f***er,' said Dougie. 'He'll tip the bailiffs off about poaching somewhere on the river, then go somewhere quite different and clean up.'

'And how does he do it?' I asked.

'Usually by what we call a "chucky-in",' said Dougie. 'That's about ten yards of gill net with a brick on one end. I'm not in favour of it myself, as the net will kill everything which touches it. The salmon drown once they can't move. I found one net, which had caught on a rock, with thirty-six dead salmon – the biggest nearly twenty pounds.'

'And what would you use yourself?' enquired the Bounder, all innocence.

'Weel . . .' said Dougie, with a wink, 'I wouldn't know anything about that, but there's a retired netsman hereabouts, called Hamish, who is a real craftsmen, so they say. He might talk to you.'

It wasn't as difficult as we thought. We hared off to the local pub and the barman pointed out a tall, weatherbeaten, grey-haired man with a set of those piercing blue countrymen's eyes that look as if they could see for ever. Mention of Dougie's name proved the Open Sesame to getting Hamish talking, although we did have to do it in the pub car park.

'If it's poaching ye want to know about,' he said, looking around him rather nervously, 'weel, you've come to the right man. It's a craft to do it the old ways, and I don't hold with all this murdering using the modern nets.'

'How do you do it, then?' I asked.

'Pouting's the best,' said Hamish. 'Ye need a fair bit of flow and colour in the river to drive the salmon in to the bank. Then come the real skills. You take a long net with a handle, a landing net will do as it'll give you an excuse if you get caught, then watch for a fish moving up-river.'

'But how can you spot it in the coloured water?' asked the Bounder, expert knowledge to the fore.

'It's experience that does it,' said Hamish. 'The fish makes a bow wave, what we call a "drought", and if you know what you are doing, you can even tell how big it is. Then you have to bring the mouth of the net down to the fish so carefully that it doesn't touch the sides, or it'll be off, quick as a flash. Once it's in the net, you turn the front over and there you are.'

'Do you still do it?' I asked.

'Aye' said Hamish, with a wink, 'but it's just for the fun and keeping my hand in now. The keepers know what I'm at, but I'm doing no real harm. Usually I'll put the fish back too, but it's grand sport.'

'Probably the keepers are not averse to a spot of pouting them-selves, when they'd like a fish on the table,' said the Bounder.

'Ye're right!' said Hamish. 'I can even tell you a wee tale of a duke going pouting with his keeper – but I'm not telling you which duke, mind you.' He paused, looked each of us in the eye, summed us up, and then made the offer we'd been hoping for: 'Would you two boys like to try a hand at it? The river's in just the right condition.'

Next morning, at 5 a.m., the Bounder and I met Hamish underneath one of the big Tweed bridges. For the sake of our reputations we'll tell you no more, but we will say that everything Hamish said is true, and although for the life of us we couldn't tell a drought from a downpour, it was the most enormous fun.

On our last day on the Tweed we had planned to meet two old friends of the Bounder's. They had forked out the astronomical sum needed to fish the famous Junction Pool, where the Tweed and the Teviot meet. It is one of the most famous and prolific pools on the river, but on this occasion the poor water conditions were against our little party, and by late afternoon we had caught absolutely nothing.

One of our friends said that he'd give it one more shot, and after a minute or so the two of us wandered down to watch him at it. As we rounded the corner of the bank, the Bounder was horrified to find that he had pulled out from his waders a short, stubby spinning rod and was trotting a shrimp under a pike float down the most sacred water in Scotland.

'You can't do that!' I said, equally horrified. 'It's not just the law of the beat, there's an Act of Parliament which says you can't.'

'If you think I've come all this way and spent all this money not to catch salmon,' he said, 'you can feck off!' He was a big bloke, so we did.

Downstream, however, the ghillie had spotted the float bobbing gaily down the hallowed water.

'What's that?' he demanded angrily of our other friend. He stared at it long and thoughtfully.

'I think,' he replied eventually, 'it's an apple.'

Suddenly and mysteriously, the 'apple' went backwards upstream . . .

The next morning, the Bounder and I dropped in on Dougie to say goodbye. The story of the 'apple' was by now famous.

'You're all very naughty boys,' said Dougie with a twinkle, and wished us Godspeed.

The Bounder was unusually quiet as the wee car purred down the empty roads towards Berwick. Eventually he turned to me.

'Tell me, old friend,' he said. 'Would you rather be Dougie or a duke?'

7

July

CORACLES

Then good-bye to the fishermanned
Boat with its anchor free and fast
As a bird hooking over the sea,
High and dry by the top of the mast.

Sails drank the wind, and white as milk
He sped into the drinking dark;
The sun shipwrecked west on a pearl
And the moon swam out of its hulk.

DYLAN THOMAS, 'Ballad of the Long-Legged Bait'

There is nothing lovelier than the smells and sounds of a river at the witching hour. It's that moment of half light when bats skim over the water and the world is at peace with itself. It was on just such a June night that the Bart and I were fishing for sewin (as sea trout are known in Wales) on the Bathing Pool of the River Towy. The sun had sunk below an indigo horizon and cast its last, long shadows from the trees as the 'V' of a grass snake swimming to the opposite bank moved gently across the ebony stream. In the distance I could hear a fox barking and in front of me a sea trout splashed, sending ripples spreading across the silver surface to lap against the shore.

The Bart and I were sharing a rod but wading down the river side by side so as to enjoy the night to its utmost. We had been taking it in turns to cast for ten minutes each before handing over the rod. I had caught a small fish of about 1 lb and now it was the Bart's turn.

'The fish that splashed just now sounded a fair size,' I said encouragingly 'You should cover him this cast.'

At that moment the rod arched and the reel screamed. But we'd missed the big one and this one was about the same size as mine. Just as we landed and released it the glorious peace of the night was ruined by the wailing of ambulances and the sirens of police cars on the opposite bank. Lights flashed and voices shouted. Sound carries easily across water, especially at night, so we could hear a great deal of what was said.

'Get a stretcher!' someone commanded.

'I don't know what was going on!' said a male voice querulously. 'He just collapsed on top of me all of a sudden.'

'Well, help me get his trousers up,' said the first voice with infinite patience. 'We can't take him to the 'ospital like that!'

Next day all was explained to us by Cyril Fox, the ghillie for the beat. 'Just opposite where you were fish-ing,' he said in the beautiful local lilting accent, 'is a public toi-let. Every night they're at it!' He rolled the words round his tongue with relish. 'And last night,' he dropped his voice to a whisper, 'someone 'ad an 'eart attack whilst he was on the job, like! Don't know who it was, mind, but there are all sorts of rumours . . .'

I had had a yearning to fish the Towy for many years. It is regarded as some of the best sea-trout fishing in England. It is also one of the last rivers on which coracles are used to net the fish and I badly wanted to see how this ancient art, which pre-dates Roman times, was practiced. I am very against all forms of netting on our rivers, as both the salmon and the sea-trout are an endangered species, but netting with coracles is so highly skilled and takes relatively so few fish that the coracle men are really an endangered species in their own right. Eventually I managed to wangle an invitation to fish the Abercothi beat of the river from Sir Edward Dashwood, a shooting friend of mine. His estate at Slebech (pronounced 'Slebidge') in Pembrokeshire consists of 20,000 acres of some of the best wild shooting in Britain. Woodcock, snipe and teal are mostly migratory birds and they seek good habitat, food and safety, all of which Slebech has in abundance. Under Ed Dashwood's care, wet grasslands have been allowed to revert to rough pasture grazed by cattle, the ideal combination for snipe. Scrub and forestry have been encouraged where it was sparse, and thinned where it was too thick to make a perfect habitat for woodcock. Ed himself has excavated extensive ponds, which are quiet, sheltered and well fed to attract the teal. No ducks are put down and vermin is vigorously controlled, especially foxes. As a result of the twenty years Ed has spent creating and maintaining this remarkable habitat, a great variety of plants and insects flourish there, including the rare Marsh Fritillary. It offers what many feel is shooting at its best: a combination of field craft and hard walking, good gundogs and challenging quarry, rather than the ritual slaughter of huge numbers of semi-tame birds.

It was on one of Ed Dashwood's shoots that I first met Gareth Edwards, the hero of Wales who, with fifty-three caps, is arguably the greatest scrum half that the game of rugger has ever known. The Bart and I had decided to drop in on Gareth on our way down to the Towy as we knew that he fished it too and we wanted to ask him where the best spots were. We arrived to find that poor Gareth had had a nightmare flight from France where he had been commentating on the France v Wales match for the BBC. As the plane was about to take off British Airways had discovered that the number of items of luggage and the number of passengers did not tally. There were some four hundred people on board including the Welsh team and their supporters. The aircraft was bound for Cardiff. 'Is there anyone here called Jones?' asked the stewardess brightly.

Despite this and the fact that Wales had lost, Gareth welcomed us and settled down with a drink. I asked him what he thought about the coracle netting on the Towy.

'There are of course seine nets as well,' he replied, 'and in fact

I gather that the average catch for both coracle netting and seine netting is a total of about eighty salmon between them, which is not going to harm any river. Of course that's the *reported* total. There are usually three sets of figures for the nets: the official public figure, the figure that is told to the taxman and the real figure. But whichever set is taken, I don't think it's enough to be harmful.' Gareth took a long draught of wine and then continued. 'The coracles are really a hobby and a tradition and it would be sad to see them go. I think they'll fade naturally as the old men die off – the young don't seem very interested – but, on the other hand, there's some real passion in the community for the way of life the coracles represent. Not long ago, I was stuck in a traffic jam leaving Twickenham and a woman approached the car. "Are you Gareth Edwards?" she asked, as I wound down the window. I was expecting her to ask for an autograph and instead I got this great harangue – "You should be bloody ashamed of yourself," she said. "You leave our coracle nets alone!" She was really telling me!'

As we were driving from Gareth's to the Towy and Abercothi, I received a text message asking me to telephone Garth Roberts, secretary of the Towy Anglers Association, the angling club with the most water on the river and therefore the most influential. 'I hear,' he said, when I rang back, 'that you are going to see the spokesman for the coracle fishermen.'

I admitted that we had an appointment for the following day.

'Don't believe a word of it,' he said.

I mumbled a non-committal answer and rang off. I turned to the Bart. 'I can't believe that,' I said. 'We haven't even got there and they're playing politics already!'

The Bart, wise in all things, looked unsurprised.

After a blissfully unhealthy breakfast the next morning at Ed Dashwood's Abercothi farmhouse, we were met by Cyril Fox, the ghillie. A very young looking seventy-year-old, Cyril's eyes are full of laughter and he has the true countryman's tanned face. He claims the secret of his youth is down to the exercise he has by the river and because he takes life '*un dydd ur y tro*' or one day at a time. ('It doesn't seem to have worked for you, Bounder,' muttered the Bart a little unkindly.)

Cyril took us across to his fishing hut which is something akin to the Ritz in comfort and size. Here, over more coffee, I expounded my favourite theory that every true fisherman is a poacher at heart. Cyril agreed.

'I was born only five miles from here,' he said, 'and when I was a teenager I rode a motor bike. Sometimes of a summer evening I used to go torching the salmon – you know, shining a light into the water to attract the fish and then gaffing them. I only did it for the pot and it was great fun.'

'Weren't you ever caught?' asked the Bart, who tends to be more law-abiding than me.

'No!' Cyril laughed. 'But I came very near to it at one time. I was cycling back at about 2 a.m. one summer morning with a salmon of about 17 lbs. I had hidden it with its head in my underpants and its body under my shirt. The problem was that it was so big that its tail stuck out under my chin. Suddenly the village policeman came out of nowhere and held up his hand for me to stop.

'"What you doin' out at this time of night, boyo?" he demanded.

'"Just come back from visiting Jones, baker's son," I said to him, certain the game was up.

'Well – he looked at me very suspiciously and shone his torch on me, but for some reason he never raised that beam any higher than my waist so he never saw that fishy tail sticking out of the top of my shirt, nearly tickling my nose.'

Cyril thought that the netting with the coracles did no harm, but pointed out that while the rod anglers returned 50 per cent of the fish they caught, the coracle men returned nothing. We asked him if there was much poaching of the river.

'Not nowadays,' he replied. 'The value of the salmon is now so low because of the farmed fish. These days, people go after the sea bass which is far more valuable. But in the old days, the poaching was terrible! I used to look for a glove on the bank and then I knew that a pool had been done because the poachers would use the glove to hold the fish's tail. Do you know? I regularly caught poachers swimming, too.' The Bart and I looked properly outraged. Cyril went on: ' "What are you doing?" I'd ask them. "Just swimming," they'd reply. "Well, let me smell your hands," I'd say and of course they'd nearly always smell of fish. Hah!' Cyril appeared to brighten at the next thought. 'And if I still wasn't sure, I'd make them pull down their swimming trunks because that's where they kept their snares!'

The Bart and I had done our research on coracle fishing and discovered that as well as their ancient history in the British Isles, coracles have also been used all over the world – even Wellington employed them during his campaigns in India. The earliest coracles were covered in animal skin which must have weighed a fair amount when wet and made them difficult to carry. They would probably only have been used for crossing rivers and not for fishing. The traditional coracle is made of willow or ash laths which are covered with calico or canvas impregnated with pitch and tar or, more recently, bitumastic paint. They weigh between 25 and 40 pounds and so can be carried on the shoulders. In the old days the fishermen would sometimes walk 5–10 miles to the river. There they would fish the coracles in pairs, drifting down with the current with the net strung out between them. Nowadays they are to be found in working use on only three rivers in the world: the Towy, the Teifi and the Taf in South Wales. All these coracles, however, have to be licensed and their numbers are dwindling rapidly. There are now only twenty-five left in the world licensed for fishing. They are indeed an endangered species.

On the Towy the method of fishing has not changed in centuries and the coracles there still drift down in pairs on the current taking salmon or sewin at restricted times of the year. They are propelled with a single paddle held in two hands over the stern, moving in a figure of eight. When one hand is fishing the net this same movement can be executed with the other, but it requires great skill.

Coracle licences come up for renewal every ten years and were due for review that August. There was a rumour that the environment agency wanted to reduce the river Towy's allocation of licences from twelve to eight. We met the self-appointed leader and shop steward of the Towy Coracle Men's Association, Mike Elias, in the local car park. 'Do you realise,' he said, 'that in 1800 there were four hundred licensed coracle boats and now there are only twelve? In those days we could fish the whole river and now we are restricted to only fishing in the estuary in the months of June and July. They say it's about conservation, but we disagree. Coracle fishing has been here since the time of the Celts. It was mentioned in the Domesday book as part of the town's income.'

'So what does a coracle licence cost?' I asked.

'Each license for a pair of coracles costs £525,' Mike replied.

'So why do you do it?' I asked. 'There doesn't seem to

be much money in it.' The Bart had done a bit of totting up on the back of an envelope and we reckoned it was barely profitable.

Mike Elias clearly felt passionately about it. 'It's our tradition,' he said, 'and we're not having it stopped by anyone. We're being regulated out of existence! It may no longer be a living, but it can maintain your standard of living.'

Later, we spoke to Garth Roberts, the secretary of the Towy Anglers Association. 'So what do you feel about the coracle fishermen, then?' I asked.

Garth Roberts seemed unfazed by the issue. 'Look,' he said, 'I don't think they do much damage and I don't think that they should be banned. Tell you what,' he went on. 'Why don't you go and see Raymond Rees – or "Dazzler" as he's known round here? He makes coracles and what he doesn't know about them isn't worth knowing.'

Raymond's wife Linda gave us tea and biscuits. Raymond was another sprightly seventy-year-old with intelligent, piercing eyes. Maybe there was something in Cyril's recipe for a young old age. I wondered where I'd gone wrong. Actually, I knew only too well . . .

I asked Raymond how he had begun with the coracles. 'My grandfather got me started just after the war,' he said. 'All the poor families who lived in the slums by the docks were moved onto a new housing estate, and our whole family found ourselves together, all coracle men, and this was a big influence on me. My brother and I were endorsees on Grandfather's licence and he taught us all he knew. In the '30s all of us fishermen formed ourselves into an association with our own bye laws. We had something very precious that even the King of England did not have – the right to catch salmon in a net. So if anyone broke our laws, there was summary justice amongst us.'

'And how much skill is there to the fishing?' I asked.

'Ah!' Dazzler's face lit up at the very thought of it. 'It's an art. You have to make sure the bottom of the net is on the river bed, but it also has to be very light, so it can be carried on the coracle. You can't buy a coracle net – you have to make it up yourself. Back in the '70s I redesigned the net, because it was actually illegal. You have a piece of large net, then a bag of smaller mesh underneath and above it to trap the fish. The secret is adding or subtracting tiny pieces of lead to keep it on the bottom of the river. You can either do it or you can't.'

'So what happens in the future?' I asked. 'Are there any young to take over from the present generation?'

A look of sadness spread over Raymond's face. 'The older families have all packed it in,' he said. 'New people, who are taking out licenses now, have no previous association with the river. They have very steep learning curves to make. Take the paddle for instance. You control the net with one hand and the coracle with the other. You have to be ambidextrous as it is different for each one of the pair. The new boys cannot do this, but I was taught left handed, so can do it both ways. Most of them come to me for help and I can show them all I know but the only thing that I cannot teach them is how to fish.'

'And what about your children?' I asked.

'My son is a broker with a bank. He doesn't have the time – or the patience,' replied Raymond.

'Grandchildren?' I enquired hopefully.

'Four granddaughters,' he said with a rueful smile.

'So when you die,' I continued, 'all your priceless knowledge will die with you.'

Raymond nodded. 'I've made videos of everything,' he said. 'But I still can't teach people how to fish.'

We sat in thoughtful silence.

'I am 73,' Raymond said at last. 'Fishing is a way of life, see. All my life I have tried to preserve the old ways. I still like tradition. I used to make all the main lines for the net ropes out of the hairs from cow's tails. I would take scissors down to the slaughter houses and gather them up. The first thing we used the baths for in the new council houses was to wash the shit off these tails.' He paused and went to a drawer out of which he took a cow's horn. 'Here's another use for the cow,' he said. 'I get these from the slaughter house too and bury them for a year in quick lime. When I dig them up the inside falls out and I can saw the horn into rings for the nets. Nowadays I use bits of polythene piping sawn up but I always put in a ring of cow's horn as well just to keep up the tradition. But all these skills are lost now. It's been my life's work. I've caught the biggest salmon – 43 lbs – ever taken with a coracle, but all my skills will die with me.'

'And how long does a traditionally made fishing coracle last?' I asked.

'A fishing coracle has a maximum life of three seasons,' Raymond replied. 'When it is finished, only the seat is re-usable – but you burn this as well as the rest. Someone once told me that this was an offering to the river gods. Over twenty years I had emptied my grandfather's brain of everything he knew, except this one thing. When I asked him about the gods, he shut his eyes for a long time and I thought I had offended him. Then he said: "There's no such thing as river gods, but you had better keep on burning the seats, just in case." '

I thought about the days when the catching of a salmon or a sewin meant the difference between a full belly and an empty one for an entire family. The same pressures no longer exist but it would be a tragedy if the skills and the traditions died out. I thought about this man, Raymond Rees, who had given his life, with very small financial reward, to preserving those skills and inventing new ones.

'Wasn't it you who first used fibreglass as a medium for building coracles?' I asked

'I may be a traditionalist,' said Raymond, 'but I became more and more interested in extending the life of the working coracles and making them simpler for the new generation to build and repair. I saw a programme on television which featured an expert in canoe construction called Alan Byde, and he was saying that coracles should have been made out of fibreglass. I got in touch with him, and he couldn't come here quickly enough. He looked at our coracles and came up with a new trick. He covered the coracle with a plastic sheet, then plaster of paris, then smoothed it over and made a fibreglass mould. When the first new coracle made of fibreglass appeared it was a day for celebration. The only thing I didn't like was the top, but I redesigned it by fixing it between two lathes of ash and this was the birth of the fibreglass coracle.'

'I much prefer the old ones and the old materials,' said the Bart sentimentally.

Raymond looked at him sharply. 'You don't go to the toilet at the bottom of the garden anymore, do you?' he asked severely. 'This is a proper fishing boat, and it has to be made in the best way possible using today's materials. The people of Carmarthen have been very innovative in the use of materials. During the war we tried aluminium strips from aircraft, but they dented easily so we made layered wood gunwales instead, which helped with the nets. The next step was fibreglass, so you have had four generations of coracles – basket work, aluminium, new gunwales and fibreglass.'

'I want to buy a coracle to go fyke-netting for eels,' I said, suddenly filled with enthusiasm. 'They seem to be ideal for the job.'

'You wouldn't be the first,' said Raymond indulgently.

'What would a new one cost?' I asked.

'£250,' said Raymond promptly. It seemed incredibly cheap to me. Had we had a bit more room in Old Cow I'd have bought one there and then.

'And what of the future of salmon and sea trout?' I asked 'They're very close to my heart as I am sure they are to yours.'

'A fish will only come into the river to spawn,' said Raymond. 'The only thing which sustains that river is the quality of the water from its tributaries. The main stream of the Towy has too high a ph now, it's too acidic, and this will kill the eggs. Not only that, but the whole ecology is changing and floods now only last two days and not the two weeks as they used to. But as long as the water is right, a river will recover very quickly. For instance if there are fewer redds, or spawning areas, there will be much more efficient spawning. Historically the coracle fishermen have always been the guardians of the river, watching it and reporting quickly if they see anything wrong.'

'It seems to me such a shame,' I said, 'that the anglers and the coracle fishermen cannot work together. They both have the future of the river in common, after all.' Then, anxious to show off a bit of book-learning, I tried some mild provocation: 'I think it was Gerald the Welshman, an advisor on Welsh matters to Henry II,' I said, 'who wrote in his "Itinerary through Wales" in 1188: "The best way to conquer the Welsh is to let them fight amongst themselves."'

Raymond chose to ignore this completely. 'At one time,' he said, as if I had not spoken, 'we decided to form a new association and met the anglers in a pub. The netsmen have no quarrel with anglers, but if a river is extensively fished it is survival of the fittest.

The anglers wanted us to join their association. I wanted us all to become one. It was easy enough to convince individuals but convincing groups was much harder. But you ask me whether the salmon and sea trout will survive? Yes, I believe that they will because there are now huge financial interests to assist them.'

All the while we had been talking I had become increasingly gripped by the notion of owning a coracle of my own. I wanted one very badly. In my mind's eye, I saw myself on various friends' lakes, skilfully working the paddle with one hand and setting the fyke net with the other. There would be a small, admiring crowd on the bank watching the silhouette of the coracle against the amber rushes of the lake as a gallant figure manoeuvred in the pale autumn sunlight. Two pretty girls would be chatting. 'Isn't he *wonderful?*' they would be saying to each other.

Suddenly overwhelmed by the possibilities this picture presented, I could contain myself no longer. 'Raymond,' I burst out, 'I'd like to buy one of your coracles!' Raymond blinked. The Bart rolled his eyes. I sighed. I should, I supposed, show some small degree of caution. 'Before I do,' I hastily amended, 'can I try one out and see if I can do it?'

Raymond seemed delighted – and somewhat relieved. 'Course you can,' he replied. 'I've got one in my shed. We'll use that.'

When we got down to the river, I was still in the middle of my day dream and not inclined to pay much attention to Raymond's instructions on how to work the paddle at the same time as keeping the coracle afloat. After what seemed to me to be an unnecessarily long lecture, we finally put it into the water and I stood poised on the bank with the rope in one hand and a paddle in the other.

'Don't forget to step into the middle,' said Raymond, as I put my foot on the side. I wasn't listening: the pretty girls were still singing my praises. Alas, they abruptly disappeared in a wave of cold river water as the coracle tipped up and deposited me in the reeds by the bank. Soaked through, I clambered ashore and, to the howls of mocking laughter from the Bart, tried again. This time I did as I had been told and managed to position myself centrally in the coracle. I pushed off from the bank with the paddle and as I reached midstream without mishap, the pretty girls swam back into my day dream. 'This is easy!' I thought, amidst the admiring cheers of my imaginary crowd as I laid the last of the fyke net. With consummate skill I worked the coracle towards the bank to where the prettier of the two girls now stood with open arms to greet me. It was too perfect. I collided with a rock in mid-stream, the coracle turned over again and once more I was deposited in the river. Miserably I began to swim towards the shore.

'Don't forget the bloody coracle!' shouted Raymond, who was making a poor show of hiding his delight at my ducking.

I grabbed the rope and towed it to the bank where no cheering crowd and no pretty girls awaited me. Just the Bart, convulsed with laughter.

Afterwards, when I had changed out of my wet clothes, thanked Raymond but said that I would not, after all, be putting one of his coracles on my Christmas list, we got back into the car and set off out of Wales. After our various encounters in the past few days it seemed to us that neither the coracle fishermen nor the anglers had very much to fear from each other and it suddenly struck both of us that Gerald the Welshman might have had a point about the self-inflicted wounds of the Welsh. The Bart waited until we were safely over the border and then turned to me. He seemed very pleased with himself. He'd obviously been saving this up. 'Bounder,' he said, 'I've got the most perfect quote. In *A Horse Under Water* Len Deighton wrote: "The Welsh are gourmets at the feast of insults."'

8

August

WHO LOVES LYME REGIS?

Lyme, although a little place,
I think it wondrous pretty;
If 'tis my fate to wear a crown,
I'll make of it a city.

Attributed to the ill-fated DUKE OF MONMOUTH

THE BART . . .

Many of my best childhood memories come from the little seaside town of Lyme Regis, where my mother bought a house after the war and I first went to school. The Bounder would often join me on holidays, and we'd spend long sunlit days shrimping and crabbing around the Cobb, Lyme's famous harbour wall. I have even earlier memories of being taken out after lobster and mackerel by the local fishermen, whose families had supplied the town with fresh fish for generations from their sturdy timber-built boats. The skippers' names – Holmier, Crabbe(!) and others – are now mostly to be found in the churchyard, and their boats, *Sunbeam* and *Condor*, have long since vanished – or so I thought, until I chanced to walk down to the Cobb on a hot August day.

I must have been daydreaming, because I suddenly received a heart-stopping jolt. There, right in front of me, was the *Sunbeam* of my boyhood, wood gleaming with fresh varnish, mackerel lines laid out for a day's fishing, swinging at anchor. For a moment I thought I was imagining it, but the boat was real enough. The only thing that had changed from the *Sunbeam* I remembered was the Jolly Roger flag, flapping jauntily at the mast, and the name of the owner, Ian Gillam, burnt into the stern seat. 'That's a funny coincidence,' mused my wife Susie, obviously enjoying her own memories, of the 1970s in her case. 'I'm sure Ian Gillam was the lead singer of Deep Purple.'

'It's the same guy!' said a voice from behind us, and we turned round to find a tall, sunburnt man with long hair and a cheerful smile sitting on the harbour wall. 'I'm Mike Curle,' he said. 'Fancy an hour's mackereling?' We did – but what I couldn't have known then was that Mike would become a great friend and would introduce me to a new and fascinating side of life in Lyme – a life I had assumed was fast becoming an endangered species itself under the dead weight of second homes, holiday lets and retirees. How wrong I was . . .

Lyme is almost *too* perfect. It is beloved by all film-makers, and not just the directors of *The French Lieutenant's Woman*, because if the TV aerials are removed, it looks exactly as it did two hundred years ago. This is due not so much to the foresight of town planners as to the Blue Lias clay which forms a thick and highly unstable layer, just under the topsoil. Put too much weight on the Lias and the whole layer will slip, and your shiny new building will end up on the beach. Even the Duke of Monmouth, Lyme's most famous visitor, would still recognise the place.

Monmouth was the illegitimate son of Charles II and endlessly given to plotting to ensure his succession. Eventually exiled to Holland, he attempted to invade England, landing at Lyme Bay with one small frigate, three tenders and enough arms for some two thousand troops. The farcical invasion went from bad to worse and Monmouth's rag-tag army of up to five thousand old soldiers, ill-armed peasants and tradesmen wandered aimlessly for some days around the West Country before being soundly beaten by the royal cavalry at the Battle of Sedgemoor.

The Monmouth rebellion was soon overturned by the Glorious Revolution of 1688 that put William of Orange on the throne. Lyme's brief moment at the epicentre of British political life was over, and it relapsed into becoming the popular seaside resort and fishing town that it still remains.

Aware of the threat our once-great British fishing fleet is under, as fish stocks dwindle and ecological pressures mount, the Bounder and I had decided that there would be no better place to find out just how endangered communities survive than the Lyme of our childhood. We began our quest – as in fact I realise we have begun *all* our quests for endangered species – in a pub, in the garden of the Royal Standard, to be precise. The sun was shining, seagulls were swooping and crying to order, we could hear children shrieking with excitement on the recently restored beach (imported, rather like Monmouth, from mainland Europe), grockles were grockling and the Bounder, Mike Curle and I were swapping stories like proper old-timers. If I smoked a pipe, I would probably have been tamping it. Naturally, the flow of conversation moved to the fisher-men we could see touting for business down on the harbour wall below, and to how things had changed since we were boys.

'How did you get into the Lyme fishing game?' I asked Mike. 'I thought it was a closed shop for locals – it always was in my day.'

'Coincidence, really,' said Mike, 'like all the best things in life. I used to skipper a tug for the Thames Conservancy, when a bunch of friends who were living on a commune near Branscombe asked me to join them.'

The Bounder sat up. 'A commune?' he said, with great inter-est. 'Lots of free love and substances, I suppose?'

'Something like that,' replied Mike rather enigmatically. The Bounder resumed his slumped position. 'But it was a much tougher life than we had expected, especially in the winter. The following spring I moved to Lyme where I met Victor Holmier,

who ran his own boat, crabbing and lobstering, and taking trippers out in the summer. He still had the original old clinker-built
Sunbeam' – Mike turned to me – 'You remember it, Richard? She
could sail as well as use the motor, but he had also just built
Sunbeam 2, a newer version, but still all wood. He needed some
help with the two boats, so took me on. We'd be out at 7 a.m.
summer and winter, back at 10, and then we'd cook up the crabs
in an old laundry copper in the watch house on the Cobb and sell
them where we could.'

The Bounder, used to fishing on a small scale, has always been
fascinated by the world of the deep-sea fishermen, and is fond of
recounting their taller tales. He was clearly in search of new
material. 'What were the local fishermen like in those days?' he
asked. 'I bet there were some real characters!'

'Victor was the best,' said Mike, 'a real traditionalist. Used to
make all his own lobster pots out of hazel wood. And there'd be
others you'd remember – Ron Crabb and "Mr F.", whose language
was especially salty after his daily crate of brown Guinness – he
never quite got the knack of attracting custom. "Like a boat trip?"
he'd say, lurching up to some harmless tourist. And if they dithered
– as you would with "Mr F." swaying unsteadily in front of you –
"Well, are you effing going or what?" He wasn't the only one – most
of the fishermen drank heavily in those days. There was one man
who swore by brandy-and-lovage as his tipple and sometimes, after
he'd had too much, he'd sleep through a tide or two, right out there
on the slipway, and be none the wiser when he woke up. One time
when he was drunk we sneaked a chicken into one of his pots. Well
– when he went out next morning, he pulled it in and couldn't
believe his eyes. He spent the next few years touring the pubs of
Lyme and telling anyone who would listen about his extraordinary
catch. No one ever told him the truth . . .'

'So what did you do in the winter?' I asked.

'Starve!' said Mike succinctly. 'There was a little building work about, but not much else to do except make the pots for the next season. Occasionally I'd get work on a boat out fishing for queen scallops, and if all else failed there was always pebble-picking on the beach. 'Course, the year they made *The French Lieutenant's Woman* was a real bonus. They laid cobbles all over the town, and there were all sorts of jobs as extras for us locals pretending to be poor fishermen – we didn't even have to try that hard to look the part!'

'What about that scene with Meryl Streep standing on the end of the Cobb?' asked the Bounder. He's always had a soft spot for actresses. Many would call it a weakness. 'Did they really shoot that down there?'

Mike laughed. 'No way,' he said. 'It was blowing a real gale that day – far too dangerous. You know who that vulnerable little creature is you see standing there? It's my mate Terry, the great black-bearded locations manager, wrapped in a cloak and then strapped to a ring bolt on the wall in case the wind was too strong even for him.'

'And how did Ian Gillam become part of things?' I asked.

'Eventually Victor got too old to go out fishing,' Mike went on, 'and when Ian moved down here fifteen or so years ago he used to come out with me on the *Sunbeam*. They were great days – we always had parties on board. A case of champagne and a bit of music as we drifted down the coast were what Ian enjoyed most, and he eventually decided to buy the boat and employ me as skipper.'

'So what about the future, then?' asked the Bounder, who seemed rather struck by the idea of drifting down the coast with a case of champagne. I wondered if he was going to offer himself as crew.

'Lyme's future as a fishing port is secure for the moment,' said

Mike. 'One of the local families, the Watsons, runs three proper trawlers out of the harbour, mainly scallops, which they sell down in Brixham market, but it's tough work, often seven days a week, and terrible on the back, with all that hauling. I'm not sure the next generation will want to do it.'

'And if they don't?' I asked. 'For me, it's always been the fishing community that's made Lyme. I'd hate to see it turn into a ghost town full of second homes and retired people.' I thought for a minute. 'Mind you, retired rock stars are a different matter – they'd shake things up a bit!'

Mike grinned. 'Look – I'll take you out on the boat tomorrow and you can experience the fishing at first hand. That's the easy bit – but if you really want to hear how Lyme's adapting, you ought to talk to some locals.'

'Where will I find them?' I asked. 'My mum always used to say that she'd have to be dead before the locals accepted her.'

'How about a pub crawl?' said Mike.

The Bounder was out of his seat before the words were out of Mike's mouth.

We made our way down the picturesque main street towards The Volunteer. Joe, who runs it, originally came to Lyme with the RAF thirty years ago, but married a local girl and stayed on. I asked him what he thought had changed in the town.

'Lyme's problem has always been that there are only about 3,500 locals, but a floating population of three times as many,' he said. 'The houses in the old centre were so dilapidated that they built the new estates up the hill – and then of course the new-comers converted the picturesque ruins and made them very valuable. It gives the town a bit of an "us and them" feeling, but the nice thing about the visitors is that they keep coming back. There's something special about Lyme.'

A holiday-maker from the caravan park agreed. 'It's my twelfth summer here,' he said. 'The kids just adore it and won't go anywhere else.'

The beer in The Volunteer was excellent, all locally brewed and drawn straight from the barrel. We stayed for another round then headed down the hill again for the Old Town. The streets are narrow here, and the swift-flowing River Lym bustles past the cramped houses and tiny gardens on its way to the sea, smelling, I am glad to say, a lot better than it did when I was a boy. There is still a traditional butcher's shop, and an excellent chippie that draws the locals down the hill from the estates. There is also The Ship, the nicest pub in town.

Dave, the landlord, could have walked straight out of *East Enders*. He is the perfect publican: one 'That's enough' from Dave – and that is certainly enough. On this particular evening, the pub was bursting with locals. The juke box was belting out rock 'n' roll, a couple were jiving as if there was no tomorrow, the thump of wooden balls from the skittle alley in the back added to the din, and even Dave's infamous bicycle-hating dog looked in a good mood.

The Bounder and I set ourselves up with a pint each of Palmer's and got stuck in. It was a very friendly crowd, although not above attempting a leg-pull or two on a pair of daft old strangers. One couple tried to persuade us that they had caught two pheasants on the wing while casting off the Cobb, but having been tipped off by Mike's story of the chicken in the lobster pot, we weren't about to be fooled. We waited until the local rat catcher fell off his stool – a nightly occurrence, we assumed – and took it as our cue to leave. We had some serious music to listen to.

To get to The Nag's Head, a popular music venue, we had to

make a near-vertical climb up the aptly named Hill Road. By this stage we were a little the worse for wear and it was quite a daunting prospect, so we decided to optimise our chances by refuelling at The Angel, Lyme's most haunted pub, before setting out. Oddly enough, another pint did seem to help the Bounder, who true to at least one version of his name bounded up the slope like a mountain goat.

Last time I had been in Lyme I had been lucky enough to hear Lyme's very own music legend Steve Black and the Elderly Brothers. They had been a real eye-opener. As a rock band they did not fill one with confidence at first sight, for it looked as if just unpacking their instruments was giving them terminal exhaustion, but the first chord had sent the tingles right up my spine. It was pure 1960s rock of a sort I had not heard since the heady days of my first faltering career as a motor trader in Hackney. After yet another fruitless day in search of punters who didn't have to 'ask the wife first' I used to frequent the best of the East End gangster pubs, where I heard the likes of Spencer Davis – and Steve and the Elderlies were every bit as good.

Tonight, top of the bill at The Nag's Head were Karl and Willie, two American Country 'n' Westerners who were raising the roof with a good thumping R&B rhythm.

'I love this little coastline,' Karl told me in the break. 'It's prettier than New Hampshire, and better weather. And I can get just enough gigs together to make a living, and if you are doing what y'all love doing, that's all you need.'

We walked home – downhill all the way – with the last 'Yee-hah!' ringing in our ears and a sense of great achievement. In fact that pub crawl has proved close to a personal best for the Bounder and me – five pubs in one night and not a trace of a hangover, due, we think, either to the sea air or the number of 'Yee-hahs!' we belted out.

The next day dawned bright and clear with just a hint of mist. As they say in Lyme, 'If you see France before breakfast, it'll rain before lunch.' The Bounder and I, feeling as fresh as newborn babes, took ourselves down to the Cobb, where three of the squarest men we had ever seen were engaged in loading endless gallon-sized plastic jugs off the back of a rusting red pickup into *Sunbeam* 2. We got there just in time to help with the last jug or two of what turned out to be scrumpy cider from the farm just up the hill, but whether it was to keep us in refreshment or power the diesel, we weren't quite sure. A quick set of introductions – 'This 'ere's William and this is Ted. The dangerous-looking booger at the back is Damian. T'ain't his real name of course, but he's got the devil inside him' – and we were away, chugging sweetly out of the little harbour before the first trippers had arrived to claim the boat.

As we cleared the harbour wall Mike put out a few mackerel lures for bait, while Damian filled the first in an endless series of plastic cups with scrumpy. The Bounder lectured us all on the fun to be had from catching mackerel on fly rods, but surpassed even his own personal best by catching a seagull. It wasn't as difficult as you might think. He had just caught a small mackerel that was breaking the surface half-way to the boat when a flash of wings and a splash took the fish and the line a good fifty feet up into the sky, the bird bucking and screaming behind us.

Damian seemed to know what he was doing. 'Wind the booger in, hard as you go,' he shouted. 'Watch them wings as he comes over the side – a good swipe with them and they'll break a man's arm!'

Bravely we flung ourselves to the deck. The crew were

doubled up. 'It's not a fookin' eagle!' yelled one of them as I gingerly got to my feet.

'Grab his beak, while I hold his wings!' Damian roared. All very well, I thought, as I tried to follow his instructions, but I was at the sharp end.

'Easy does it. Now – turn the hook with the tweezers, and out it comes. Off she goes!' The seagull took off, did a victory circuit round the boat, making a beeline for the Bounder's flat cap, and then flapped off, none the worst for its adventure.

Excitement over and a few more easily caught mackerel later, we wound in the lines and enjoyed a quiet smoke as *Sunbeam* headed for the old Second World War wreck where we were to spend the day fishing.

Mike cut the diesel and *Sunbeam* swung slowly around to drag against the anchor. We baited up and let the big lead weights carry the lines down to the wreck below. Again, it was the Bounder who scored first. His rod tip bent right down, there was a brief struggle, and the winged shape of a big skate was in the boat.

The next bite was mine, and after a short pull on the line, it felt as if I'd hooked the *QE2*. There was nothing I could do: the reel unwound, then went dead in the water.

'Conger eel, I reckon,' said Damian. 'And the booger's got his tail around a rock. You've got to be quicker than that.'

It was all right for him to say that, but it was no easy job. Strike too fast, and you pulled the bait out of the conger's mouth and ended up tumbling arse over tit in the boat; strike too slow, and you'd never shift him. At last I felt I was getting it right, and slowly and steadily reeled the eel in. I could not believe the hideous immense shape, thick as an Atlantic liner's cable, that slithered reluctantly over the stern of the boat. For a time all was chaos, the air blue with 'Take that, you booger!' and 'Mind me legs, you wanker!' until at last the great conger was subdued. It weighed over a hundred pounds on Mike's scales, and was a huge cause for celebration.

There were many more triumphs that day, all duly celebrated with scrumpy, and as the cider sank in the jugs and the sun in the sky, we eventually set off back to harbour, the Bounder and I we had had a unique taste of Lyme life.

It was just as well that we had both been too exhausted by our respective wrestles with a seagull and an eel to go on much of a bender that night. We needed to be on our best behaviour the next morning because we had secured an audience with Lyme's most Senior Local.

We were summoned to his semi-detatched house up on the hill. Rather surprisingly, there was a mermaid outside. The Senior Local – 'Don't call me anything else,' he warned us. 'I'm keeping a low profile' – was a big man in every sense of the word. He had 'served his bones' in the community at everything from skippering trawlers to being on the council. He knew everything and everybody. There was no escaping him.

'So.' He gave me a glare that reminded me of my first prep-school headmaster. 'Ask your questions.'

As the Bounder had gone unaccountably quiet on me, I cleared my throat to ask my usual penetrating question about changes in the town. The Senior Local completely ignored it. He was not to be hurried. He would tell his story his way, or not at all.

'Like many Lyme kids, my mother didn't want us to be fishermen. She didn't want us to have the insecurity of that life. But somehow we couldn't keep away, and after she died, my brother and I came back, took over the trip boats and had a real trawler built. For most of the year we were the only proper fishermen in the harbour. It was a mixed bag: skate, plaice and Dover sole in the winter, potting and trippers in the summer. We reckoned that we'd either starve or make a lot of money; more often than not, we starved.

'The town probably thought we'd go bust, but slowly other people joined in and started finding better-priced catches – like scallops, along with the occasional potting for squid. There's big money in scallops, but it's hard work and you have to put in the hours. For thirty years, all I had off was Saturday afternoons – and my brother had Sunday mornings. That was it.'

Listening to the Senior Local, I caught more than a hint of pride in how tough life had been. Here, as the Bounder and I had found in Yorkshire among the miners, a hard life breeds a strong sense of community.

'Will there be another generation of fishermen to follow you?' I asked.

The Senior Local shook his head. 'I don't think so,' he said. 'There's only one of us who's got a son fishing at the moment. I reckon the red tape and regulations will kill it all off in fifteen years' time.'

'So what work is there for locals?' asked the Bounder.

'A lot of people have made good in the holiday trade,' said the Senior Local. 'Anything from cleaning toilets to running coach tours – and we've all done Bed and Breakfast. But I reckon there are no more than a dozen of us who go back more than three generations in Lyme.'

'What about all the people who come here to retire?' I asked. I must say it had occurred to me a few times, but I didn't dare run that idea past our friend.

'There's some who've just arrived who are great,' said the Senior Local, and then added darkly, 'and some who have been here twenty years I wouldn't pass the time of day with . . .'

Anxious to keep things pleasant, the Bounder jumped in with one of his favourite gripes. 'What about the newcomers who get on the council and spend their time bringing in bloody stupid regulations?' he asked.

The Senior Local cast him a slightly friendlier look. Perhaps he thought we were not quite the buffoons we appeared to be. 'We've got a few of those,' he acknowledged. 'But the trouble is that most Lyme people here want to get on with their football, golf, beer and skittles and just aren't interested in local politics. Anyone can come in here and if they can be bothered, they can be on the council in no time.'

It's not just Lyme, I thought. If country people are an endangered species, sometimes they have only themselves to blame. But I didn't venture the comment out loud. We were far from home and dry.

'It's not all bad,' conceded the Senior Local. 'There are almost seventy clubs and associations in Lyme, mostly run by people who have retired here – photographic, croquet and so on – and they make a fair show of breathing new life into the town. After all, retirees have been settling here since Jane Austen's time.'

'It all sounds a bit gloomy to me,' said the Bounder as we made our way to our next appointment. 'Fishing is dying, red tape is rampant, and the only action round here is the croquet club. No wonder the locals get pissed in The Ship!'

But David, our next interviewee, who runs the town's holiday letting business, had a much more positive view of what was happening to Lyme. Like many others we were to meet, he was a refugee from London, although he was far from being retired. An inherently modest man, he had escaped from a life as an 'Empty

Suit', as he put it, and had made his lettings business a huge success.

He refused to be gloomy. 'Yes, the town has its problems,' he said. 'For instance, the average age of the members of Lyme's Development Trust was 79 when I arrived. But we're livening the place up, and although you'll hear some mutterings from the locals, I suggest that you meet a few more newcomers before you make your mind up.'

David passed us on to his friend Marcus, who now runs the Development Trust. Marcus grew up in Lyme, then went to work in London, and has returned to the town to run the Trust. We quickly got talking about endangered communities.

'A community is a kind of delicate equation,' said Marcus. 'If you mess it up, it starts to melt down in a way that you can just feel in everyday life. I was in a town not far from here recently and came across a back-street Co-Op. When I asked about it I was told, "This is where ordinary people shop." You see? "Us" and "Them" – very bad for a community.'

'But how can you stop this happening in Lyme?' asked the Bounder.

'I call myself a Social Entrepreneur,' said Marcus. 'Just like any business, we have a plan to find work, rebuild skills, finance low-cost housing, and so on. If you let market forces make the running, and with property prices as high as they are, you'll end up with all the hotels turned into apartment blocks, with a consequent impact on local employment and the undermining of the whole economics of the town. Do you know that Lyme ranks in the bottom ten out of one hundred local areas in terms of child poverty, despite the fact that house prices are ranked second only to London? I love what I'm doing, although it can be very frustrating at times because we have limited money and it's often an agonisingly slow process to agree investments. But there is something special about Lyme . . .'

'Well,' I said, 'a sense of history is a great starting-point for a community – but how do you encourage that?'

'In all sorts of ways,' Marcus said, brimful of infectious enthusiasm. 'The coast here has just been named as a World Heritage site and we've started up the most fantastic Fossil Festival. Then we've turned the theatre into an exhibition centre part-time, which gives it new life. We've got Arts and Music festivals as well, and even a web cam on the end of the Cobb that has already had 50,000 visits. They're all helping to extend the tourist season beyond the summer months and bring Lyme alive.'

Weighed down with brochures and the sheer force of Marcus's enthusiasm, we went on to pay our respects to the Mayor.

Ken is another refugee from London. An ex-cabbie, according to the Senior Local, he is a well-known figure as he strides through Lyme in his signature hat, an Edwardian monstrosity – just like mine. I spruced up the Bounder as best I could and the two of us were ushered into the oak-panelled mayoral chamber. Ken had got into office on a Reform ticket, and was determined to keep Lyme lively.

'There's a huge sense of history here,' he said, leaning back in his mayoral chair. 'We're trying to keep the old traditions alive and give them a modern edge. There are a number of days when the Mayor dresses up in his red hat and coat and walks the streets accompanied by the two silver maces and our town crier, and in my view this is more important today than it has ever been – so last year I even led the jazz festival procession down the main street.'

From Ken we went on to meet Phil, the Town Crier. A local man whose real job is as a Project Manager for a helicopter company, Phil's love of pantomime has helped him win many competitions. His favourite ceremonial is the twinning ceremony with Bermuda, which has a strange history. Sir George Summers, a seventeenth-century Lyme mayor, was shipwrecked on Bermuda and opportunistically claimed it for the English crown. When he died his body was buried in Lyme but his heart in Bermuda, so this ceremony is the perfect excuse to reunite his various body parts.

At this point the Bounder began to muse on the most effective distribution of his own body parts when the time came, and I felt it prudent to make our excuses and bundle him out and into some fresh Lyme air.

The Bounder's idea of fresh Lyme air seemed to be swapping Irish reminiscences with Joe at The Volunteer, so I parked him on a bar stool there and and walked back down Broad Street. There, a motley assortment of anoraks and backpacks were awaiting the arrival of Dr Colin Dawes, the town's fossil expert. I was just in time to catch the man himself, a trim enthusiastic figure in a battered bush hat and enormous side-whiskers. Colin shepherded his little flock together, a mixture of dedicated regulars, such as Derek 'the Twitcher' plus his mate, a silent chap who carried an enormous bible of fossil law and never said a word, and various families with excited children. The Doctor ('I'm a *real* Doctor, not one of those medical chaps') had that natural gift of treating children like adults, and as we set off on the fossil walk it was they who were finding the fossils. Each 'Look at this one, Dr Dawes!' received the level of congratulation merited by a major discovery for the British Museum, before the precious objects were loaded up into the backpacks of the long-suffering dads.

The walk for me was pure nostalgia. Every part of Lyme holds good memories, and the town's historians are adept at keeping its history alive. We started down Marine Parade, past the site of the old Assembly Rooms, once the heart of Lyme's social life, which were replaced by what John Fowles called 'the ugliest lavatories in England', still there, but locked up in case there is a landslide when someone is in an embarrassing position. The town bands play once again on summer evenings, the soaring brass drowning out the raucous gulls. Further along the parade, we passed the spot where Jane Austen wrote *Persuasion*, then into the narrow alley, heart of the original fishing port, where – had we not had so many enthusiastic young palaeontologists with us – we might have stopped for a pint at The Standard.

Past the pub, we passed the Cobb on our left, and up ahead on the steep hill I could see the windows of the cottage my mother had lived in catching the sun. The Doctor led us down past the immaculate bowling green and hurried us onto the Monmouth Beach. The children were soon shrieking with discovery and excitement while the adults stood watching, trying to retain a little dignity. But fossil-hunting is exciting, especially with a guide as amusing as Colin. My ears pricked up at one particular story of his about a rock-boring mollusc, the piddock, which attaches itself to a large stone, then slowly grinds itself a deep hole, using its sandpaper-like front end. The piddock was a favourite delicacy in Roman times, said Colin, but was now an endangered species. It made me think of the conversations we had been having about some of those incoming Lyme dwellers, those who never leave their smart cottages except for their weekly shop, and put nothing back into the community. They were a bunch of piddocks I thought, rather pleased with myself.

I had an opportunity to share my insight with the Bounder that evening. The two of us had dinner with David and Marcus in the pretty Alexander Arms Hotel, with its wonderful views over

Langmoor Gardens and the coastline. That night the evening was clear and still pleasantly warm, and the lights of the Cobb were reflected in the gently rippled water of the little harbour. Down below, the last of the Waysons' trawlers was tying up to unload its precious cargo of scallops into the back of the family truck, and we could hear the relieved shouts of a fishing crew, after a long day, floating up to us on our terrace.

As the darkness gathered my attention started to drift and, as always in Lyme, I began thinking about my mother, Gwiffy, whom I missed very much. I still have a favourite photograph of us all, comfortably spread out on the beach with Gwiffy stretching out an elegant arm towards the last bottle of wine as a drowning sailor reaches for a lifebelt. When she had the stroke that was to prove fatal, I would sit beside her in the hospital and read to her from *Brideshead Revisited*. At her funeral service, I chose to read her favourite scene, the one where Charles and Sebastian are enjoying what proves to be their last truly happy moment together and Sebastian says:

> I should like to bury something precious in every place where I've been happy and then, when I was old and ugly and miserable, I could come back and dig it up and remember.

In her will Gwiffy asked for her ashes to be scattered from the Cobb wall. One summer's evening I loaded up the car with the children and a last picnic. My mother's ashes I decanted into a fruit jug, then (as per instructions) mixed them with a full bottle of her favourite whiskey and poured the mixture into the sparkling waves beneath us. It was a good send-off, and shortly afterward, when the Bounder's mother Elspeth died, I organised a bench for them in the very best corner of Langmore Gardens, from which they had an excellent view of the Cobb and of Theo's

Cottage, where they had shared such happy times. On the back is carved the words: 'For Gwyneth and Elspeth, who loved Lyme'.

'Our' bench soon became a popular venue for courting couples – both straight and gay. The sisters would not have minded. Both actresses, they had always been very liberal for their age, and had in fact shared the favours of many famous English actors. I remember them once discussing Robert Newton, one of the most charismatic actors of his generation and a lover of the Bounder's mother. My aunt Elspeth once turned to my mother in the pub and asked her a question which had obviously been brewing in her mind for half a lifetime. 'Did you ever . . . with Bobby . . . well, *you* know?' She hesitated, out of embarrassment. 'Yes, I did,' was Gwiffy's reply. The subject was never mentioned again.

Now I realised that the bench and its inscription exactly summed up my feelings about Lyme. As in my favourite 'Never-ending Story', it is a place of extraordinary magic – and if a human child (and here I mean anyone between 2 and 98 who still enjoys life) believes in it, then it will survive. But if it becomes full of piddocks, then it will die.

9
September

THE ISLAND

I shall sail across the Sound,
I shall sail across the ferry,
To my native Isle I'm bound,
Braving wind and wave and skerry.

Soon I'll cross to Jura isle
Where my dearest ones are dwelling,
Mother waits to welcome me,
Mine's a joy beyond all telling.

NEIL SHAW, 'The Bard of Jura'

The Jura ferry was firmly shut and looked most inhospitable. Heavy rain lashed the rusty skips on the wharf, a wild west wind whipped the waters of the sound into a grey froth, and it was only September. It had been a frustrating drive from the airport. The folk in charge of road signs on the Isle of Islay seemed strangely reluctant to indicate the way to the ferry, and the map we had been given by the car-hire people was mainly concerned with distilleries. But somehow we managed to make it to Port Askaig and the ferry with minutes to spare. As it turned out, we need not have hurried. There was no sign of life.

Out of the corner of his eye the Bart spotted a couple of sinister figures swathed in fluorescent yellow waterproofs heading for the nearby pub. He leapt into action. The conversation went something like this:

The Bart: 'Is the ferry running?'

First Yellow Man, over his shoulder, hardly pausing in his stride: 'Ye'll need tae book.'

The Bart (keeping pace with him): 'I rang up yesterday and the man said no problem.'

Second Yellow Man: 'Who did you speak to?'

The Bart (somewhat stiffly): 'We were not formally introduced.'

Both Yellow Men come to a halt. The first one appears to

consider the matter: 'Wheeell . . . It might have been Hamish before he was away to his tea, or it might have been Angus, who was tending to that computer thing, or . . .'

The Bart, now clearly losing his rag: 'So, can we travel or not?'

Second Yellow Man: 'Wheeell . . . I suppose ye can noo you're here.' Stops, scratches his head and makes up his mind: 'But we'll hae to wait to see if any other unexpected travellers turn up, who havena booked like yourselves.'

We drove onto the ferry, and despite the penetrating rain I stood against the rail as we made the short sailing across the Sound of Islay. It was wonderful to be back in the islands. Island folk are completely different from the rest of us, particularly in the north of Scotland. They live by their own rules; there is almost no crime bar the odd punch-up, and even that is usually dealt with by the community and not the police. Children can roam wildly and freely with safety. Doors and cars are never locked and everyone makes their own entertainment. Islanders have an independence of spirit and a wildness about them that has always appealed to me. I've had many happy times as an islander, particularly on South Uist in the Outer Hebrides where I have always felt very much at home. It's a remarkable place. More whisky is consumed per capita on South Uist than anywhere else in Britain, and yet there is almost no sclerosis of the liver. What's more, the islanders all seem to live to a ripe old age with all their faculties intact. I once heard a programme on the local radio in which a certain rather sprightly Miss Morag Mackay was being interviewed on her one hundredth birthday. To me, it summed up the island spirit.

'You look very well for your age, Miss Mackay,' said the presenter. 'Have you ever been ill?'

'Noo! I've ne'er had a day's illness in ma life.'

'Do you mean to say you've never been bed-ridden?'

'Och, don't be so silly, young man! Hundreds of times – and *twice* on the ferry!'

On that particular trip I was staying with a friend who was part of the syndicate that owns the island. All game fishing is banned on the Sabbath, so we had decided to take out the boat and fish for mackerel for the day. For the joy of his company we also decided to invite the island's oldest ghillie, Charlie Maclean, a man of great wit and character, to join us. He was eighty-nine and his wife Elsie was eighty-two, and had only one leg. We could not ring Charlie in his tiny thatched croft because there was no telephone, so we drove to his house and banged on the door. There was no reply. We banged again. After a while, Charlie opened up. He was in his dressing gown, wiry white hair looking a bit wild. In the background we could just see Elsie, leaning on her crutches, wooden leg propped up against the range. She had a contented smile on her face.

Charlie looked none too pleased to see us. 'Ye little buggers!' he said furiously. 'We've been a-pleasuring for the last three-quarters of an hoor and ye've just deprived me of paradise!'

When the Bart first suggested that our quest for Endangered Species should include a trip to the island of Jura, I had to get my schoolboy's atlas out. Jura lies on a latitude with Glasgow and just north that of Londonderry. There is strong historical evidence to suggest that Jura was once 'Hinba', the mythical island of rest and tranquillity associated with Saint Columba, who is believed to have stopped here in AD 563 on his way to restore Christianity to England. Jura, like so much of northern Britain, was captured by the Vikings, and even after they were eventually driven out it continued to be fought over as part of the Kingdom of the Western Isles, which long asserted its claim for independence. A contemporary account of the then king stating that 'three winters he had been out in war-ships, without coming under a sooty rafter' gives an evocative insight into the life led by those tough fighting men. Even when, finally, the islands were brought into greater Scotland, inter-clan battles between the MacDonalds and the Campbells kept the men of Jura in arms. The MacDonalds eventually triumphed, although the Campbells continued to live on the island until 1938 when the last of the family estates was sold. An ancient Jura prophecy that 'the last of the Campbells will be one-eyed – and when he leaves the island all that he will take with him will be carried to the ship in a cart drawn by a white horse' was, remarkably, fulfilled. Charles Campbell did only have one eye, and his few possessions were taken to the ship by a cart drawn by a white horse . . .

Over the last two hundred years Jura's population has shrunk from more than 1300 to fewer than 200. Some were driven out by hunger, others by the infamous Scottish clearances of the eighteenth century which swapped crofters for sheep. Another tale tells of a whole village cleared by the laird's factor because, he claimed, they had been poaching salmon. When it was eventually discovered that it was the estate factor himself who had been doing the poaching and the villagers were invited back, they proudly declined. A local poem describes the emigration ships leaving the island, 'the cries of the islanders at their last sight of their homeland, echoing back from the mountains around the little bay'. The population continued to fall until, five years ago, the community numbered just 160 mainly elderly people, and barely justified the essentials of survival such as a doctor, a school and a store. The people of Jura were truly an endangered species. But then came an extraordinary reversal in the island's fortunes, and it was this that the Bart and I had come to investigate.

Our guide to Jura was Donald Ewen Daroch, a tall man in his fifties with humanity and laughter in his eyes. The Bart's son-in-law, who had stalked on the island with Donald Ewen, had introduced us to him. Rollo had told us that what Donald Ewen didn't know about Jura wasn't worth knowing, and he was absolutely right. The two most famous Jura names are Daroch and Buie, and Donald Ewen was related to at least half the island. We met him the first evening that we arrived, in the dining room of the Jura Hotel in Craighouse, the island's only hotel.

'You know,' said Donald, 'five years ago I might have said the island was dying, but now things have changed very much for the better. The population has climbed back to over two hundred, mainly from islanders returning home, and we have a wonderful community with lots of social life. The problem is that the majority of the new people who come to live here do not last that long. We find that a lot have gone in five years, almost all in a decade.'

I once asked an old ghillie on the island of South Uist what it was like for outsiders to come and live on the island. He thought for a while and then said: 'If ye come here for a week, maybe a month, and touch the stone, ye'll go away refreshed in body and spirit. But if ye try and grasp the stone and stay here, it'll kill ye.'

Donald Ewen continued: 'Some outsiders just have a problem with island life. It's hard to say specifically what it is – but they get upset because they don't get the daily paper on time, or the ferry stops working for a day and they cannot get off the island or get fresh milk.'

'What about the islanders' children?' asked the Bart.

'They stay now, but my generation left,' said Donald Ewen. 'You see, in those days we had to go to secondary school in Oban, which was so far away, and many never returned. They lost the link with island life. Now they only go to Islay, which is a huge difference because they can live at home and just travel on the ferry every day. Many young leave for a short time after they have first left school, but now a lot are returning.'

'What drags them back to the island?' I asked.

'You'll have to ask them that for yourself,' said Donald Ewen. He leaned forward conspiratorially and tapped his jacket pocket. 'I've made up a wee list of people of two types.'

'Two types?' I echoed, perplexed.

Donald Ewen leaned back in his chair and smiled. 'The first,' he said, 'are people you should visit to see how they live. The second –' he paused enigmatically, '– are those *you might meet in your travels*.'

The Bart and I exchanged befuddled glances. The whisky was taking its toll. The roar of voices from the public bar penetrated our fog.

'Ah!' I said, as light dawned. 'You mean the people with whom it's worth sharing a dram!'

The Bart and I love public bars – the rougher, the better. Donald Ewen took us through and introduced us to all and sundry. Maggie Boyle turned out to be pure Irish with a huge sense of fun, and her brother Patrick was the same. Their father had come to work on Jura for five months and had stayed for fifty years. Duncan Buie, the mainstay of the bar along with his ginger cat Tigger, was, like Donald Ewan, from an old island family. He worked at the island's distillery and the islanders had appointed him head of the fire service *and* the coastguard because they always knew where he was: either at work, at home, or in the pub.

The ceilidh is part of every northern island's life and will happen – as it did that evening – completely spontaneously. Suddenly a guitar appeared, and before long we were all singing the old Scottish and Irish folk songs. The Bart and I know them well, and with our tongues now generously lubricated with ten-year-old Jura whisky, we sang along with the best of them. Neither of us is remotely musical, but when drunk, and encouraged by the Bart, I always seem to end up playing the guitar and singing 'Why must I be a teenager in love?' That evening was no exception, and accompanied by the only three chords I know on the guitar, I gave it my all. Coming from a pissed old fool it gave the audience great pleasure – although when, overwhelmed by deafening applause, I offered an encore, they seemed strangely unenthusiastic. The real guitarist and lead singer was Ross Rozga, a tall, good-looking young man descended from a Polish grandfather who had settled in Jura. Ross was one of those who had tried the outside world and come back. We asked him why.

'I hated the hassle,' he said. 'You know, I have a big problem with people telling me what to do. When I was on the mainland it felt like slavery. I'm glad to be home – and I'm not the only one.'

A glass of the Jura ten-year-old was prescribed, and with it a set of questions. Most country people don't trust the media, and I had the feeling that despite Donald Ewen's sponsorship that first night, the Bart and I were definitely on trial. In these situations we have a secret weapon up our sleeves: we tell lots of stories about poaching. It never fails. I described how, in our youth, we used to tickle trout. I turned to Donald Ewen, who as one of the two Jura special constables had his own round of poaching stories. It might have been the drink taking effect, but we began to get confused about who were the poachers, and who were the bailiffs. Was the whole island at it, I asked?

He laughed. 'The whole bloody island!' he replied. 'But only one for the pot.'

The talk of poaching and the singing seemed to mellow the evening, but I still felt we were on trial. Mind you, it took a woman to say what everyone was thinking. As I shouldered my way to the bar for the sixth or seventh refill (I'd lost count, and I certainly didn't care by this stage), Maggie Boyle made her way over.

'Now look here, boys,' she said, turning to look hard at the Bart, who was weaving his way towards me. 'I want to know what you are really up to. Are you on a mission?'

Overcome with emotion, the Bart swept her his best bow. 'We are on a *mission*,' he enunciated carefully, 'to find the *heart* of Jura – and I have, and it's called Maggie Boyle.' He then spoilt it all by tripping over his own shoelaces and cannoning into a bar stool. I smirked, Maggie laughed – and suddenly we were all friends.

From then on, the evening is somewhat confused in my memory. I do remember Maggie talking about her croft, and how we were all welcome to visit her the next day (although for obvious reasons we never quite made it), and the Bart and me singing rebel Irish songs, but eventually it was time for bed and we took affectionate leave of Donald Ewen, who had to make the long trip to the bottom of the island. At least he didn't have to worry about meeting the law: he *was* the law.

As we made our way unsteadily up the stairs we caught sight of a large, totally monosyllabic Scotsman who had said nothing but 'Mphhhm!' all evening, edging his way towards Maggie, who had collected her coat. True to her reputation for frankness she waylaid him. 'You fancy me, you great lump, don't you?' 'Mphhhm!' he replied, rather downcast, as she marched out, head held high.

The next day, it became apparent that the entire island knew how drunk we had been. We had passed the first initiation test.

The island census of 1881 shows the single hotel and pub in Jura to have been in the hands of one John McKechnie – 'Innkeeper, farmer, general merchant and postmaster' – and now his direct descendant Fiona and her husband Steve run it. Fiona's late father Gordon was the island's historian, and his books have been a huge help in writing this chapter. Her mother Carol is still a great influence in the community, and it was to her we turned to find out why the island's recovery now seemed so full of promise.

Carol was a sprightly woman in her seventies with a twinkle in her highly intelligent eyes. She came to the hotel the morning after our performance in the public bar and had obviously heard all about us, but in spite of that seemed very happy to talk to us. 'My grandparents ran the hotel and my grandfather built the shop as well – I remember it so well as a child. My favourite memory was of the bacon-slicing. Before the days of packaging the bacon came in great long sides and was cut up by hand for each customer with a slicer. It was a bit of a tight squeeze in the wee shop, so we used to put one end of the bacon through the window, and sometimes some of the children would sneak out to cut a little off the end, which they'd toast over the open fire in the schoolroom.' She then read out to us the appendix from one of her husband's books about the shop at Christmas. We sat there in the hotel lounge, nursing huge hangovers and gulping endless cups of black coffee, strangely soothed by her comforting tones. Oh God, I thought, please make me feel better, and I promise that I will never drink again.

The little store is full; some of the occupants are waiting hopefully for letters and parcels, others for bread and cookies or sausages, and others just to see what has come by the boat. At the post office end mail bags are being emptied and letters sorted out. Pieces of string and labels are lying on the floor, and in the cramped space, the postmaster, Mr McKechnie, who owns the store, and his assistants keep falling over each other. He has the busiest time of all. One moment he must be at the post office checking the mails, and the next his presence is required at the other end of the shop, where old Neil McLeod is disputing with Annie Darroch over the ownership of the last currant loaf. Mr McKechnie quickly brings the dispute to an end by announcing that it has already been ordered by Dr McAlpine, and he is promptly seized upon by another customer. There is great indignation when it is learnt that no supplies of sweets or chocolate have arrived. 'What! No sweets at Christmas!' is the general cry. Mr McKechnie smiles to himself and surveys the customers over the top of his spectacles. He is prepared for such an emergency and great is the delight when he produces several bottles of 'sweeties' from the back shop.

There was a nostalgic pause, and then the Bart looked over his own spectacles. It was now eleven o'clock, and he had apparently deemed it safe to take off his dark glasses. 'How did you manage for schools and doctors?' he asked.

'Finding a replacement doctor was the biggest drama,' went on Carol. 'When the last one left, the Health Board said that we didn't need a doctor on Jura because we could be served from Islay. But we put our foot down, because when the wind and tide are bad you can be totally cut off from Islay. The Health Board reluctantly agreed to advertise, but told us that no one would want to come to Jura because a doctor would be expected to be available at all times and modern GPs can now opt out of long hours. Anyway, they put a tiny little advertisement in the paper weekly, for a year, and only got one enquiry.'

'I read about it in the *Telegraph*,' I said. 'How did you get your case into a national newspaper?'

'Well, we had another meeting with the powers that be,' said Carol. 'We asked them if they would pay if we did the advertising, and they agreed. By luck the advertisement was picked up by BBC Radio, and then the national newspapers. We got over a hundred enquiries, and thirty-six applications. The result was that we now have not just one doctor, but two!'

'That must have been a real test for the island,' I said. 'If you'd been turned down, the future of the whole place would be in trouble.'

'Och! He wanted a change in lifestyle for himself and his family,' Carol replied. 'He and his wife love the local folk music [I wondered what they would have thought of last night's rendition of 'Teenager in Love'] and they had already been working with the Highlands and Islands Board. But I think the main reason was a chance to do some real doctoring amongst people he knew, and really get to grips with his patients' cases, not just fob them off with yet another pill prescription. As the last doctor used to say, "When the phone goes at night, I don't say, 'Oh God!' but rather, 'This might be something interesting!'" There's also no crime on the island – the last major incident was when someone stole a cooked chicken from the hotel kitchen – so it's a wonderful place to bring up young children.'

'So now you have a new doctor, a school, and a thriving hotel. What about the shop?' I asked, thinking back to the days when her grandparents sliced up the bacon. 'That's always the real, day-to-day heart of the community. Is that under threat?'

'You'd better go and talk to Steve Martin, who runs it,' said Carol. 'I think he might surprise you.'

As she came out to bid us goodbye, Carol was keen to make her point. 'Whatever you write, don't say Jura is a dying community,' she said. 'It's not. It's thriving.' She smiled. 'It's the young people,' she said. 'They're coming home.'

When we reached the shop there was no sign of the owner. Tiny on the outside, it turned out to be an Aladdin's cave of goodies, stocking everything from tinned peaches and waterproof jackets to corned beef and condoms. Fresh vegetables and milk were hidden behind butter and cheese in the crammed refrigerator; day-old newspapers jostled for space with dog leads, brooms with shrimp nets. When we asked for Steve, a loud voice rang out from behind shelves of tea and coffee: 'And what do yer bloody want?'

Steve Martin proved to be a vigorous blast of fresh Yorkshire air. A slightly overweight man in his fifties, he had a shrewd but kindly face, as pink as one of his own hams. He took us outside the shop to talk, leaving the running of it to a pretty young Swede, the girlfriend of one of the newly returned young men.

'People coming back,' he said, 'that's a very recent thing, only the last four or five years, and I reckon it relates to society on the mainland, which is driving both old and new people here. I was earning a lot of money before I came here – and I had a company car, expense account and all the rest of it – but I think I'm far wealthier now than I was then. You see, on an island you think twice about buying unnecessary possessions, which then hang around in a cupboard and eventually go to the boot sales. When you buy something on Jura, you really ask what it's for. It's an older world, where possessions are to be treasured not piled up and never used.'

'What made you make the move to Jura in the first place?' I asked, gathering my coat-collar around me. I like to think of myself as a hardy individual, but it was bloody cold standing out there. Steve appeared not to notice.

'I am a trained accountant,' said Steve, 'and I was based in Yorkshire, specialising in helping small companies get their business in order. But I began to find the people I worked for were so amateurish it made me think I should be running a small business myself. The only thing my wife and I came up with was buying a shop in a nice part of the country which really needed one. We spent two years looking before we saw the advertisement for the Jura Stores. It was a bit remote, but we said we'd try it for a couple of years. We have been here for seventeen.'

'And you've never regretted it?' asked the Bart.

'Not now,' said Steve. 'But when my son was born, we thought we'd put the shop up for sale to get him a better education. Then we changed our minds – and it's the best decision we've ever made. When we see what's happening on the mainland! Our son would probably have been involved in gangs of yobs and have no respect for his parents or the community. My wife comes from Leeds, and at first she wasn't used to the friendliness here – you know, just walking down the road and being invited in for a cup of coffee. Now she loves it. You don't have to lock your door. You don't have to worry about someone stealing your property. It's a much better world, and I'd much rather be a big fish in a small pond.'

'What about your treatment as an incomer?' I asked. 'Was it hard to be really accepted?'

'Well,' said Steve, 'by making the stores a success, I'm helping the community, so I don't need to try and prove myself. I get really annoyed with some of the newer people who come here and don't visit the shop but go to the big supermarkets in Islay. They put nothing back into the place. I call it community rape. It's like a marriage where one party starts off by loving the other for their beauty, character and personality, and then spends their life trying to change them.'

I thought twice about asking the next question. Steve was a big man, and he obviously had a lot of friends – but I was curious. 'Do you think the islanders regard you as a local or an incomer?' I asked.

Steve thought for a long time. 'My son will be a local as he grows up,' he replied eventually. 'I know I never will be, but that doesn't bother me. I'm happy doing my bit for the island, and I know I'm respected for it. Anyway,' he finished with typical Yorkshire bluntness, 'if they don't like me – and some don't – they can bugger off.'

From Steve's shop we made our way to Ardlussa, the most northerly of the seven sporting estates on Jura, and the only one lived on all the year round. Life has not always been easy for its owners, the Fletcher family. Rose's adored husband Charles had recently died of MS. He was much loved on the island, and we were proudly told that as he was lifted into the helicopter for his last ride to the mainland, he was singing Scottish folk songs. His father too had died early, after suffering appallingly as a Japanese prisoner of war.

The journey north was through wild and beautiful countryside. The road climbed along the spur of a hill with a hundred-foot drop over the side. At one point the cliff had slipped away beneath and was in the process of being shored up, and I felt distinctly wobbly as the Bart drove gingerly over the dangerous bit. Then the single track ran along the seashore, upon which myriad birds were feeding. Knots and dunlin strutted with oystercatchers and herons. We could see deer in the distance, feeding on the seaweed.

I have never been good at map-reading and the Bart and I had our usual quarrel as, yet again, I got us lost. He seemed unaccountably unwilling to be distracted by my attempts to point out passing wildlife and kept muttering over and over again through clenched teeth, 'But where *are* we, Bounder? Never mind the bloody fauna!'

Eventually – and I doubt I could do it again if I tried – we arrived at Ardlussa. As we pulled up the drive we were greeted by a flock of curlews flying overhead. I watched them wheel into the distance against the beautiful backdrop of a mirror-patched grey sea and timeless islands. In front of us stood a large welcoming house of mellow red bricks covered in late-flowering clematis and wisteria, its peeling white-framed windows facing straight out across to the bay.

Inside, the house had all the cluttered comfort of an old family home. Rose Fletcher, a tall, elegant woman with a natural sense of humour, was presiding over the big kitchen. Here the dust of ages covered an ancient Aga and a central table was mounded with yesterday's mail and bills, and it was clearly here, as in all the best kitchens, that the family gathered for warmth. Today, however, the warmth was off and a small family crisis was on. The central heating oil had run out, and Rose's daughter had refused to get out of bed until the temperature rose a few degrees. Rose seemed to be taking these domestic upheavals in her stride and, settling herself comfortably with a large ginger cat as her personal central heating, she gave us her highly individual view of island matters.

'You've met Steve Martin at the shop,' she said. 'He'll get you anything and send it up on the bus service run by the McLean family. He's just as likely to ban you from the shop if he doesn't like you, but he's a real asset to the island.' She paused. 'Unlike the Scottish Executive, who are the bane of my life.'

'Aha!' said the Bart, who's had his own problems with such bodies. 'What do you mean?'

'Oh! They're so urban in their thinking,' said Rose, 'small-minded, jealous, even. We're not allowed to call ourselves "estate owners" any more – that's not "politically correct". We have to call ourselves "Land Managers", whether we own the place or not. We get endless surveys, endless questions and endless inter-ference – all of it completely pointless.'

By this stage I would have proposed marriage to Rose on the spot, and I could see that the Bart had a soppy look on his face, too. 'You don't look like a wealthy landowner, grinding the faces of the poor,' I said.

'We may own 30,000 acres,' Rose said, 'but almost all of it is bog or hill. Apparently, in the Exec's view owning this much makes us a class enemy – in your terms, an endangered species. It's hard to get grants, for example, unless the project is community-owned, even though the estate owners would like to help. The Exec has tried pouring money into the place, but some of their ideas are quite ludicrous. You see that little pier at the end of the garden? They wanted to put public toilets there – but who is going to maintain them, an hour's drive up a bumpy road?'

'But clearly, a lot of good has happened on the island the last few years,' ventured the Bart.

'It's a funny thing,' said Rose reflectively. 'The biggest change that I have seen is pride in houses and gardens. When we first came here, the little cottages were all run down and no one both-ered much about the gardens either. It was typical of Western

Scotland. Now there is huge pride in possession – and most people live a lot more comfortably than I do in this barn of a place.'

'And what about the young people?' I asked. 'Why are they coming back?' This was the key to Jura's whole future, and I wanted to ask the same question of everyone I encountered on the island.

Rose smiled. 'When my husband inherited the estate, most of the people on the island were old-age pensioners. The young ones had all left to look for employment. There was a lot less money about then and the estates, traditionally the biggest employers, had to reduce the numbers of their workers. In the past we would have employed four or five people: a gamekeeper, river keeper, stalker, gardener, and a youth as general dogsbody. Now there is only one person working here with us at Ardlussa, and he has to be a jack of all trades. The younger ones all try the outside world, but they find they really miss the island life. Young Ross, whom you met in the bar –' here Rose paused and looked meaningfully at both of us. Had news of our night-time exploits already reached this far north? But she continued with a twinkle in her eye – 'young Ross is typical of his generation. He's become a very good landscape gardener. When they come back they want to do something independent. They want the freedom that they missed in the outside world, not get stuck all day in community workshops. Maybe a new generation of islanders is being created with new skills. It's a good feeling.'

I asked the question that I had been puzzling over since I first saw a map of Jura. It has a huge, totally uninhabited West Coast, where there is not even the trace of a road. As Rose clearly knew all about our conversation the previous night in the pub, I felt I could ask her: 'With fewer people working on the estate, how can you stop poaching? There are supposed to be five thousand or so deer on the island and we saw some fantastic specimens all along the road on the way here. Surely a man with a good boat could make a killing.'

'It's not a huge problem at the moment, as the price of venison is so low,' Rose said. 'Mind you, we did have one man who came over from the mainland and made so much money at the game that he built a house called "Venison Villa". He poached the unin-habited side of the island but was never caught, despite the fact that some walkers took pictures of him hauling the deer down to the shore. They were handed over to the police who, strangely enough, lost them. One of the stalkers put a bullet through the bows of the poacher's boat – and was promptly sued for danger-ous behaviour! Luckily the case was thrown out of court.'

'What happened in the end?' I asked.

'Oh!' Rose smiled with satisfaction. 'Do you know? That poacher's boat mysteriously sank at anchor . . . I'd say it's the way things are done out here in the islands.'

Finally we asked about the English people who come to Jura. There had been a great deal of late-night muttering in the bar the previous evening about rising property prices and strangers.

'Some are fine,' said Rose, 'but others come here and then try and change the way of life they professed to love in the first place. They try to manage every committee they get onto and they make themselves really unpopular – although the islanders are usually too polite to tell them.'

It sounded to us like the classic 'incomer' behaviour we found all over the country in the course of researching this book. The difference in Jura is that the local community is still, for a while anyway, resistant to being ordered around.

Just then a tall figure rapped on the kitchen window and star-tled us. It was the oil man. Rose tipped the ginger cat off her lap and went to welcome him in with some relief. The still-slumbering daughter would be pleased.

Ardlussa is one of the most beautiful places we have ever seen anywhere. When Rose came back into the kitchen, I asked her about the future of the estate and whether she could ever bear to leave it. A look of sadness crossed her face.

'I'm going to hand it all over to the next generation,' she said. 'I might buy one of those warm little houses I talked about earlier. I suppose it should be on the mainland, but I'd really miss the independence of the islanders. Strangers might think we're all crazy, but I think there's more sanity in Jura than in the rest of the big world out there.'

As the Bart and I drove back to Craighouse, I thought about what Rose had said about Jura being saner than the modern world. Maybe she was right, and it really was Hinba, Columba's magical island of tranquillity. After all, George Orwell had spent two and a half years here writing *1984*. Had beautiful Jura given him the peace he needed to write such an apocalyptic vision of our world?

We headed back south down the island, passing the Paps, Jura's highest hills. They rose into the sky out of the stark landscape, and because it was a clear day we could see the peaks. There, wheeling high above on the thermals, was a pair of golden eagles. Cloud shadow passed over the brown and purple moorland. This, I thought, was indeed a land as God had made it.

I asked the Bart, who was driving, to stop at a bridge so I could look at a little river that flowed urgently with peat-stained water. Below us was a pool, only sixty yards from the sea, in which I could imagine sea trout stopping in season. As I looked into its depths, a sleek head showed above the surface, then a tail, and an otter climbed out onto a rock. I signalled frantically to the Bart to keep still, and we watched as the otter licked himself and then dived back into the pool to continue his hunting.

As a fellow fisherman, it is always a moment of wonder for me when I see an otter, but I was surprised to see the Bart so affected by this sighting. We watched in silence to see if our otter would surface again, but he had obviously gone on to other hunting grounds. As we clambered back into the car and set off again, the Bart told me a strange tale.

Fiction's most famous otter is, of course, the eponymous hero of Henry Williamson's book *Tarka the Otter*. Williamson re-wrote the book no fewer than 21 times before trying to get it published, only to meet with endless rejection slips. Eventually he managed to sell the worldwide rights for a paltry £500.

Williamson was one of the Bart's father's greatest friends, part of a rackety group of rebels that included T. E. Lawrence and Dylan Thomas. (He was also, incidentally and briefly, a lover of my mother's.) He was often a guest at Bellarena, the Bart's family estate in Northern Ireland, and the two old men would go on endless nature rambles to talk about their wicked past. Their favourite walk was beside an old millpond, long since silted up and overgrown, but the few remaining flashes of shallow water seemed to bring in every sort of water fowl and wild life.

Long after his father's and Henry Williamson's deaths, the Bart sold Bellarena. On his last day there, before he left the place forever, he decided to make a final pilgrimage to the 'writer's walk', as he called it, to say goodbye. The water as usual was still and placid, without a trace of movement. Suddenly, two streams of silver bubbles appeared, streaking across the dark surface in front of him. The Bart watched entranced as first one sleek brown head and then another appeared, and a pair of otters climbed up the bank. Here they licked each other clean and then stretched out under the trees. It was, he said to me as we drove across the deserted moorland of Jura in the twilight, one of those moments when he knew absolutely that there was an afterlife – even if it is just a couple of old Tarkas playing in the sun.

We had an appointment that evening with Scottie, the manager of the distillery, whose product had been our downfall the previous night. He turned out to be a hugely professional whisky man whose enthusiasm knew no bounds. He lived on Islay but commuted to Jura weekly.

'There has been whisky distilled here, both legally and illegally, for hundreds of years,' he said as we walked round the impressive plant. 'I love this building. It's still got some of the old copper vessels and not too much computerisation, so there is a sense of tradition about the place. The whisky is fantastic too. Even my wife prefers the Jura 21-year-old to anything else on the market – I reckon she'll get me to live here one day.'

Scottie had a wonderful and mischievous solution to the island's dislike for central government. 'The total tax on whisky produced in Islay and Jura', he said, 'comes to over £250 million a year. If they declared UDI they'd have a wonderful time!' Despite the historical precedent for a 'Kingdom of the Western Isles', we couldn't see the Scottish Executive agreeing to the scheme – but it was a lovely thought.

Much refreshed, in every sense of the word, by our visit to the distillery, we made our way back to the hotel. We were keen to spend some more time with Maggie Boyle, who had promised to talk to us about the new crofting initiative on Jura, which has really helped the island and encouraged the young to return. According to Maggie, it means that locals can get access to land very cheaply, then build a working shed and a house on it, all for less than a hundred thousand pounds. With Maggie on board we drove around the fresh communities, and were very impressed by the smart new houses and outbuildings rubbing shoulders with the old stone-built versions that had been around for two hundred years or more. Maggie knew every one of the young people and their history and, it turned out later, she knew the telephone number of everyone on the island as well. As she said, 'On an island this small, every family who leaves is a disaster, and every one that stays is a wonder. People are more important than anything, and that's what makes island life so special.'

As Maggie knew so much about the island, and as I sensed a kindred spirit, I plucked up the courage to ask her about the chances of achieving a long-held ambition of mine: to do a 'Macnab'. The original idea of a 'Macnab' appeared in John Buchan's novel *John Macnab*. It tells the story of three bored well-to-do Londoners who try to poach a salmon and a deer from various friends' estates, without being caught. This has subsequently metamorphosed into catching a salmon, shooting a brace of grouse and stalking a stag, all in twenty-four hours. To me, Jura seemed the ideal spot to recreate this – and I thought Maggie would be the ideal co-conspirator.

Maggie's eyes gleamed as we explored the idea in the bar that evening. Clearly she was the sort of woman who relished a challenge, and she thought that, as in the Buchan story, the island's landowners would treat it all as a bit of a lark. 'Well,' she said thoughtfully, 'the most difficult part will be catching the salmon. It really depends on the state of the water. The best river is next door to Donald Ewen's house – and if he's prepared to help you with the grouse and the stag, that could save a lot of time.

You'll need a spate, but rain is forecast for tonight so you could be in luck.'

'Bet you don't manage it,' said the Bart, ever the optimist, but a man who can sense a keen bet.

'How much?' I asked. I refused to be intimidated.

'Bottle of 21-year-old Jura malt.'

'Done,' said I didn't fancy my chances.

As Maggie had predicted, the rain duly came, and poured down for most of the night. The next morning I woke at 4 a.m. and drove through the darkness to the south of the island. It was a two-mile drive up a really rough track to the river, and I arrived just as dawn was breaking. I decided to walk upstream and fish the river down to the Sea Pool at the bottom.

I have always loved the freshness of a new day: it is like getting to it before anyone else has used it. The rainbow sun glinted on the wet bracken and heather as I tramped up the hill beside the river. The country smelt of new rain and the water was running high but reasonably clear – perfect for a fish. After I had walked for about a mile, I reached a really promising pool. Here, I thought, this is where I'll catch my salmon. And then, just as I was setting up the rod, there was a whirring of wings and cries of 'go back, go back' as a covey of grouse lifted from the heather on the opposite bank. You wait until later, I thought – if I can only find you again . . .

I began to fish the head of the pool and worked slowly down towards the end, letting my fly fish slow and deep. Just as I reached the tail, the line went tight and I knew I was into a salmon. But it was a mad fish, and immediately tore away downstream and out of the pool. I ran as fast as my poor old abused body would carry me, fell into a peat hole, and jammed the reel handle into the ground. There was a horrible jerk and the line went slack, broken at the fly. Bugger, I thought, there's my chance gone. And indeed, it seemed I was right. I fished on down the river with never another touch on the line.

As I came towards the Sea Pool, I saw a figure in the distance. Somewhat bleary-eyed after my early start and thinking it was Donald Ewen come to see how I had fared, I hailed him.

'Morning!' I shouted.

'So, have you had anything?' It was a woman's voice. I peered hard. Maggie Boyle was standing beside the pool.

'Just lost one,' I said ruefully. 'And what the hell are you doing out here at this time of day?'

'Thought you might need a bit of help,' she replied, and bending down, she picked up a beautiful fresh salmon. 'I needed a fish anyway,' she said, 'for a friend's birthday, and I thought I might as well take two while I was at it in case you'd had no luck.'

'How did you do it?' I asked, although I was not about to look a gift fish in the mouth. I'd keep the Bart in the dark, I decided, until the last possible moment.

'Never you mind,' said Maggie, with a wink, but I could see the net marks on the salmon's flank. 'Just don't tell Donald Ewen.' And she made her way, carrying the other salmon, to the boat which I had failed to notice moored on the sea shore nearby. It was a much easier route than by car, particularly if you were poaching.

I walked on to Donald Ewen's house, carrying my fish.

'Well done!' he said. 'You got one!'

I couldn't lie to him after all his kindness and, without mentioning any names, I told him the truth.

'Maggie Boyle,' he said with certainty and no hesitation. 'She always takes one at this time for her friend's birthday. Come in and have some breakfast.'

Over warming eggs, bacon and coffee laced with whisky I told him about the grouse that I had seen.

'Aye,' he said, 'we'll take those next as I think I know where they'll be.'

By four o'clock that afternoon Donald Ewen's prediction as to where the grouse would be was proving faulty, and my early rise was taking its toll. We seemed to have walked miles and I was pouring with sweat and utterly exhausted. I thought of the simple shot offered beside the river in the morning and cursed the Gods. We had not seen even a feather. It seemed my chances of shooting one grouse, let alone two, were hopeless. Donald Ewen's dog had been on a lead all day because, as he explained, he was only any good at retrieving. If he was let off to put the birds up, he was apparently likely to disappear for miles.

'Can't we let him have a run?' I asked at last. 'It can't do any harm. I don't think there are any grouse in this area anyway.'

The dog duly disappeared and we trudged on across the interminable high heather. The day had, of course, turned into a scorcher after the rain and at the next burn I laid my gun down and knelt, preparing to drink the wonderful clean, clear water. Suddenly, in the distance, I heard excited barking and then Donald Ewen shouting: 'Here they are!' I looked up just as the covey appeared two hundred yards away, coming with the light breeze downwind at fifty miles an hour. There was no time to stand up. I grabbed the gun and took the first bird sixty yards out, the second immediately afterwards. Both, to my amazement, fell. The dog hurtled up and retrieved them and suddenly I wasn't tired and exhausted any more – I was cheering and shouting, and Donald Ewen and I were dancing about and hugging each other.

After we had finished slapping one another on the back and taken a suitable pause to catch our breath, Donald Ewen said, 'Now for the stag. The one I've marked for you is a twelve-pointer, a Royal, but he's old and past his prime. We'll tie the dog up here at the burn so that he has water and collect him later.'

We walked on for another mile, although now I had a spring in my step and two birds over my shoulder. We had been steadily climbing and now, near the peak, Donald Ewen signalled for us to crawl. 'I think he'll be just over the top,' he said.

We wriggled forward and peered from the summit. Donald Ewen raised his binoculars.

'There he is!' he said triumphantly. 'Just where I thought he'd be.'

I took the binoculars from him and through the lens I saw a fine stag with several hinds about four hundred yards away. We came down from the summit and wriggled sideways until we were hidden in a burn which ran across the hillside to within a hundred yards of where the stag was feeding. After a slow stalk we peered over the top of the burn bank and there he was again, an easy shot of about a hundred and twenty yards. As Donald Ewen handed me the rifle I noticed that the breeze was perfect, downwind from the stag to us. I made myself comfortable in the classic spread-eagled sniper's position and looked through the 'scope. Magnified against the backdrop of the hillside, our stag stood with his head up, sideways to me, proud and majestic in all his glory with his antlers stark against an azure sky. And I suddenly knew that I couldn't do it. He was too beautiful.

I laid the rifle down and turned to Donald Ewen. 'I'm so sorry,' I said.

'You're not the first,' he replied, 'and ye'll no be the last.'

Back at Donald Ewen's house the Bart was waiting as arranged, comfortably ensconced in the kitchen. I entered in triumph, brandishing the salmon and the brace of grouse.

'Well, I'm buggered!' was his generous reaction. 'Well done!'

It took a lot to persuade him that I had had the stag in my sights and hadn't shot it, but on the whole he seemed suitably impressed with my day's efforts. 'I owe you a bottle of 21-year-old,' he said magnanimously.

I told him the truth. I've always been a shocking liar. 'But let's give Maggie the bottle,' I said. 'She's the one who really deserves it. And –' I knew this would be the clincher – 'she's a generous woman who'll be happy to drink with new friends.'

Postscript

Sadly, that great Jura character Donald Buie died shortly after this chapter was written. He is much missed by the whole island.

10

October

GYPSIES

We aren't all bad people
We want a chance to prove
That we have much to offer
The same as each of you.
So help us please achieve our goal
There's many a one amongst us
Who needs a settled site
Young or sick or weary
If only for a night

JULIA GENTLE

The Bounder and I spent last Remembrance Day with friends of ours in the Midlands. Peter's Guardsman son was serving in Iraq and this made the two minutes' silence even more poignant than usual. Underlying Peter's pride in his son, whose photo in full dress uniform hung on the wall, was his understandable concern about a war that grew more pointless and dangerous by the day. As we sat there remembering all those we had lost and those whose lives were currently in danger, a huge crash at the window suddenly shattered the silence. Shocked, I looked over to see a thick smear of egg yolk running down the pane.

Peter got to his feet and went over to look out. 'It's those yobs again,' he said heavily. John, his friend, shrugged.

From outside we could hear a volley of abusive language, which was followed by more eggs and then the sound of a racing car engine, which startled the rooks from the trees around the camp.

The Bounder and I looked at each other in amazement. 'What on earth ——?' I began.

'We're used to it,' John interrupted. 'Always happening.'

Louise, his wife, got to her feet and rummaged under the sink for a cloth. 'Outcasts,' she muttered as she rinsed it out, 'that's what we are. They're happy enough to let our son risk his life for his country, but we're still outcasts.'

Then we understood. Our friends were gypsies.

The gypsies comprise perhaps England's most discriminated-against minority group. It was hard at first to penetrate a community that has so little trust (with good reason) in outsiders, but we were determined to learn what we could about this most endangered of all country people. After all, the gypsies have been part of the English countryside for more than five hundred years and are as much guardians of its lore and skills as any.

Our quest began at the annual Horse Fair at Stow-on-the-Wold in Gloucestershire. We were introduced to it by Sir Mark Palmer, a cousin and godson of the Queen and the only man ever to phone Her Majesty from a public call box. Mark had floated out of London in the Swinging Sixties, dressed in Druid robes, and then bought a caravan from a gypsy when the weather turned cold. He lived this way for almost twenty years, perhaps the first of the 'New Age' travellers, before setting up as a horse dealer. He told us about fairs like Stow that the gypsies use for meeting and dealing, and about some of the families, both good and bad, who turned up each year.

On the morning we arrived, the pretty little Cotswold town of Stow-on-the-Wold seemed primed for imminent nuclear catastrophe. Most of the shops were shut and every pub closed and boarded. The few locals on the streets scurried past, heads muffled in their Barbours, or peered anxiously from behind net curtains. Police were everywhere.

The Bounder and I were loitering in Vera's curio shop, one of the few left open, gossiping with Vera Norwood, a still-sprightly 76-year-old and former Tiller Girl, independent local councillor and ex-Mayor. As we were chatting, the doorbell suddenly jangled. The Bounder and I peeped round a display of knick-knacks to see three adorable little girls smiling at Vera. 'Please, Missus Norwood,' said the eldest of them politely, 'do you have any colouring books with animals on them?'

Vera gave them what they wanted for free and then watched as the trio left the shop, shutting the door quietly behind them, before they went skipping down the street. She turned to us: 'Well,' she said, looking at us sternly. 'That's gypsies for you. I expect you're a bit surprised by those girls, aren't you?'

The Bounder and I both shifted about a bit awkwardly. The truth was, we *were* surprised – and felt thoroughly ashamed of ourselves for assuming that gypsy children were, as popular prejudice would have it, all dirty, snotty-nosed urchins. We were also surprised that a respectable shop-owner would be on the side of the gypsies, but Vera, it turned out, had always been a bit of a rebel. She told us how she came from a respectable professional background, but with a mother who had always harboured a secret longing for the stage, despite her family's disapproval. All her mother's thwarted ambition was focused on Vera. When war broke out and the family went to live in Stow, she would practise ballet in the churchyard, using the gravestones as an impromptu *barre*, as a result of which the vicar became her first fan and personally contributed towards proper lessons.

Vera told us her first stage role was in 'Eugene's Flying Ballet'. Life was tough for a young actress in post-war Britain. Digs were usually advertised as 'NBOLGL' – 'No Bath, Outside Lavatory, Gas Lights'. Proper stockings were available only for the lead players, and Vera and the rest of the troupe had to be content with 'Wet White', a mucky substance bought from Boots, mixed up in a bucket with red and yellow ochre powder to make a tan colour, and glycerine added to make it tacky, then painted on with a sponge.

After an audition in a bombed-out church in Soho, Vera became a Tiller Girl. The Bounder was typically eager to get to the meat of the matter. 'What about all those men hanging round the stage doors?'

'I had very good legs' – here Vera got up for a demonstration dance – 'and I was often used for publicity shots. Of course one or two famous names wanted to take me out, but I always preferred handsome and impoverished artists – they were the loves of my life.' Vera stopped, and smiled a secret smile.

'I suppose you could call *me* an impoverished artist . . .' the Bounder said hopefully. 'Would you like to come to lunch?'

We carried Vera off to The Lords of the Manor for lunch. 'What a treat!' she said as we settled down. The Bounder launched us straight off into the whole gypsy saga.

'It seems to me', he said, 'that the gypsies have held their horse fair every year in Stow for centuries, and all the locals loved it. Then along come a whole bunch of incomers, who think that horse shit all over the place will affect their rapidly rising property prices, and they're doing their best to bugger it up.'

'You're quite right!' said Vera. She seemed to be warming to him. 'The original fair was assigned by right of Royal Charter, but that hasn't stopped the new people trying to close it down. Things got even worse when the Smiths – who are a well-known family of gypsies we see every year – bought their own field. You should have heard the cries of outrage. How dare *gypsies* buy land in our wonderful little country paradise!'

'And you, darling Vera, being a natural rebel,' continued the Bounder, 'were determined to fight for the ancient rights. I'm the same . . .' He was obviously keen to establish a connection.

'Yes,' said Vera, 'but it wasn't just the new people who behaved badly, it was also some of the original Stow citizens who had vested interests – especially the estate agents and those who were making a killing on property they had bought cheaply. You see, I knew everyone in the town in those days. I settled in Stow thirty years ago with my lover . . .' (I could see from the twitch in the Bounder's prawn-like eyebrows that Vera's stock had just risen by a point or two) 'We were going to get married, but somehow never got round to it. I even bought the wedding dress, which we kept under the bed. I might even be buried in it,' Vera added wistfully. 'He was a real Stow boy,' she continued. 'I used to tease him that he thought Stow Square was Piccadilly Circus! But he knew every pub and everybody, and that was how I got accepted here – and I was eventually elected an independent councillor.'

The late-autumn afternoon light was fading outside and a wisp of mist was hugging the well-mown lawns of the hotel. We hunched closer to the burning logs in the bar's open fire. 'Last drink, Sir,' said the Polish barman, who had looked after us very well. We ordered three large whiskies and encouraged Vera to carry on with her story.

'You know, it was the attitude of the new people who made me stand for election in the first place,' went on Vera. 'It started with all the posh new antique dealers who tried to have the square closed off to coaches full of trippers, and then it was the gypsies. At first, everything continued as it had always done on Fair day. The gypsies camped along the roads; the independent traders and stall-holders made a fortune in their site on the cricket field; the established horse dealers used the opportunity to sell their wares to the country gentry and refreshed their stock from the gypsies. Everyone got on well together. The event was well publicised in the radio and papers and everyone enjoyed it enormously.

'The Royal Charter that protected the Fair was originally granted to the monks of Evesham Abbey, but by now had become vested in the rights of a Lord of the Manor. When he started charging higher prices, everyone got in a huff. The established horse traders set up their own fair on another day, and the council refused to loan their cricket pitch. This left the gypsies on their own with nowhere to park their caravans, and a whole parcel of wealthy locals trying to kill the fair with endless complaints.

'Well, the next thing that happened was the "new age travellers".' It didn't sound as if Vera had much time for the New Age. 'The following year every bloody hippy in England descended on Stow, believing there was a great human rights cause they could support. The trouble was that, unlike the gypsies, who just come for the Fair, these hippies came for the whole year. Oh, they were a terrible nuisance! They were dirty and unwashed, they stank to high heaven and had the morality of alley cats – do you know, I even found a couple making love on the top of a car in the Square in broad daylight! The gypsies couldn't stand it – they themselves are always very clean and many of them are born-again Christians. In a strange twist of fate, the police asked the gypsies for help, and the "new age travellers" were made to feel unwelcome and left.'

'And didn't that make the gypsies more popular?' I asked.

'Unfortunately not.' Vera shrugged. 'The additional rumpus was just one more excuse for the enemies of the Fair to make complaints – and they did. By this time I was a councillor and I was fed up with all these attempts to kill the Fair. I made quite a fuss, and drew quite a bit of attention in the media – and as a result of all that I was invited onto the Gypsy Council. Well, that was all very well, but on Stow Council itself, the situation had got even more ludicrous. The gypsies had now bought their own field, but were refused permission to build a road on it to provide access to the traders' stands – despite the fact that one was already there!

The reason given was that this was an area of outstanding natural beauty. I pointed out that a new Tesco had just been given permission in the same area, and this covered more space than a bit of asphalt, but it was no good. I've been fighting ever since against even more ludicrous legislation – do you know, the latest makes it illegal for gypsies to sleep in their own caravans on their own field, during Fair days? – but it's been a losing battle.'

The Bounder and I looked at each other and I could see the same feeling being born in both of us. Vera was biased in favour of her friends, of course, but we were both outraged by her story and by the way in which petty bureaucracy was being used to undermine a centuries-old tradition. We clinked glasses. 'It's our mission, should we choose to accept it,' I said to him. 'It's time we found out for ourselves.' We rose to our feet.

'It's been lovely being taken out by a couple of naughty boys – thank you both for the lunch and for listening,' Vera said. 'I share your enthusiasm and passion for life – it's what makes me feel still young at seventy-six. Mind you' – with a last long look at the Polish barman – 'I'm not finished yet!'

Our quest started that very afternoon. 'No time like the present,' said Vera, marching us firmly back to the car and hopping into the front seat. 'You have to see the Fair for yourselves.' It was complete chaos, as we drove through Stow. A mass of cars and caravans were crammed into a small road, made even narrower by a set of 'tank traps' that the local council had built to stop the traders pitching their stands along the way. Vera was greeted enthusiastically and waved through into the field, which was even more crowded, and swimming in deep mud. Somehow we found a space to park and looked around for someone who would talk to us. In front of us an immaculate 'Vardo', the traditional horse-drawn caravan, was parked. Against it was propped a hand-lettered sign: 'Christ Jesus Came into the World to Save Sinners'.

'Come on, Bounder, let's start here,' I said. 'You look in need of a little redemption.'

A compact, nut-brown man smiled down at us from the open door. 'Welcome to the Lord's House,' he said. And so we came to meet Sid 'The Deacon', our first real gypsy.

Sid's caravan was warm as toast. Most of the space was taken up by a massive and very comfortable-looking double bed – 'A real down mattress,' said Sid proudly. 'Our people have always lain on feather beds, even if they have no proper shelter. A good feather bed is a prized family possession.' Next to the bed, a small solid-fuel range blazed; and nearby stood a chest of drawers which had many uses for the travelling people. 'From table to cradle,' said Sid. We were to meet many older gypsies whose first bed had been the pulled-out bottom drawer.

The Bounder asked Sid politely what he preferred to be called, as the word 'gypsy' carried all sorts of bad associations.

'I don't really mind,' said Sid. 'Romany, Roma, Travelling People – these are the names we prefer. "Gypsy" is rather like calling a Pakistani a Paki – more often than not it's a term of abuse – and it's all based on an early mistake when people thought we were Egyptians. Yet,' Sid said, changing tack with alarming speed, 'at the end of the day a leopard cannot change its spots. God put us here for a purpose and we are all his disciples.' The Bounder coughed nervously.

Sid, it turned out, had joined the Born Again movement ten or so years back, and still shone with all the fervour of a recent convert. Throughout the hour that followed, I kept on glancing at the Bounder to see if Sid's hard sell on the advantages of a personal acquaintance with Jesus was irritating him. (I remembered only too well a boot in a persistent Mormon's backside a while back, when he caught the Bounder with a particular nasty Sunday hangover.) The Deacon, however, was so friendly and sincere, and his knowledge of gypsy history so fascinating, that the conversation flowed like the very water he would have baptised us with if he'd got the chance.

'Don't worry about the mud outside,' said Sid as the three of us somehow crammed into his caravan. 'We're used to the soil from the days when our life was spent travelling from one sort of picking to the next, hops, plums, apples. Now they are mostly picked by machinery, more's the pity. It was a great life.'

With a sideways glance at the Bounder, I plucked up the courage to ask Sid about his strong Christianity, and how common it was amongst gypsies nowadays.

'We're rebels and we're proud,' said Sid. 'That's our history. The man is the head of the family and his word is the law. We'll still abide by civil law, but we'll always bend it to our ways if we can, although now we live a more settled life we've got to learn to fit in with others. But God's law covers everyone, even the Queen of England.' He smiled beatifically at us both. The Bounder looked a little uncomfortable.

'But how did the gypsies become Christian?' I persisted.

'I've read that it all began in Paris,' said Sid, 'in a little back-street church with only one or two people in it. One day the priest noticed a gypsy standing at the back. When the service was over, he came forward and said that his mother was sick at home and would the priest come and pray over her. The priest followed him back to his caravan, laid his hands on the sick woman and found some fresh fruit to bring her – and she recovered. Six weeks later another six or so gypsies joined the congregation, and so it began. The new church brings us all a sense of rightness we've never had before. We can even get married properly – something that was impossible when you are moved on every couple of days.'

The Bounder pitched in on what he saw as safer ground. 'Why', he asked, 'have the gypsies been treated so much worse than any other minority for generations? And why does it still go on when the world is bursting with laws against racial intolerance?'

'I suppose it's a failure by everyday folk to understand how things have changed for us,' Sid said. 'Forty years ago, we were all travellers; then they started building the sites and making new laws against roadside camping. Being more settled allowed our children to go to school: before that, most of us couldn't read or write. It's been a big problem for us, learning to adapt, but at the same time keeping our traditional values and our language. If we stop travelling, we'll lose our language and culture and that'll be the end of us.

'The sites are all right as long as you have a good community of families, but one bad apple can give everyone a bad reputation. This is our world, but the *gaje*, the outsiders, just don't understand what the changes mean for us. The country folk understood us, the traditional travellers, but the law now pushes us together with the rest, and they have only their prejudices to guide them. I wish I could see more understanding and openness in all men's hearts,' he finished, 'but it's getting worse rather than better – and it's our children who bear the brunt of it.'

'And why is ownership of land such a big problem?' I asked. 'Vera has been saying that when Isaac Smith bought the field here, it started all sorts of ructions with the locals.'

'When you try to buy your own land,' said Sid, 'everyone is up in arms against you. It's four times as hard for a gypsy to get permission to use it as a *gaje*. I had a piece of my own land, just used it for myself. Went into work in the morning and came back at night. Never a word from anyone. The council man gave me seven years' stay, and when it was up I had to move, but it gave me the chance to get my kids to school, and that was a blessing. Then it was back on the road.'

'But why did you go back to a traditional gypsy caravan?' the Bounder asked.

'It's like this,' Sid went on. 'I said to my wife that our children will never know what it is to travel with horses. With a horse, you can see nature, not just fields rushing past the window. You can see the wild life, the plants, the trees, the animals. Travelling this way takes the stress out of life. You stop worrying about time for this and time for that. You don't need much money, just enough to live on, and that's another worry gone. I can honestly say that I don't owe anyone anything, and yet I read that over two million young people in this country are in hopeless debt. It doesn't make sense. People should stop and think what are they doing it all for.'

'When I was a kid,' the Bounder mused, 'we never used to look down on gypsies. In fact we used to envy the travelling life – I'd far rather have been doing that than be cooped up in school. Probably have learned more, too,' he added ruefully. 'What about the landowners, whose land you used to stay on? How did they see you?'

'I'll tell you a story,' said Sid. He reached forward to stir the coals in the old range – although it was at hothouse heat already – then began again. 'My Mum and Dad used to work fruit-picking on Her Majesty's estate at Sandringham. In fact, the old Queen Mum used to come round the caravans and give sweets to the children. We have a story of the old Queen, too, Queen Victoria. There was a gypsy couple, very poor with only a small cart and a tent. They were round by Windsor Park and it was snowing and very cold. The wife had young twin children and was expecting again, so could do little to help. The children did their best pitching the tent, and making a fire with damp wood.

'As they were at last getting a little warmth, up came the

gamekeeper from the Queen's palace. "Whatever are you doing here, you gypsy man?" he said. "Don't you know you can't put your tent up in the Queen's private park?" The husband lifted the tent flap and showed him the little family shivering in the cold. The gamekeeper took in the situation at a glance. "Oh!" he said, "she's got twins and all. I'll have to see what we can do." And he went off back to the palace to report to the Queen. A short while later, along comes a pony and trap full of warm clothes, food, wine, and even a pair of socks, knit by the Queen's hand. Now there's Christian charity for you,' finished Sid, 'and from the highest in the land, too.'

The vision of the little family in their tent and the Queen's generosity stayed with us as we said goodbye to Sid. 'God bless you,' he said. 'And mind you come back soon, and here' – he seemed to have the Bounder fixed in his beady gaze as he passed us each a brightly-coloured leaflet – 'is something to read when the spirit takes you.'

We set off again for the Fair. Behind the caravans and the traders stood a number of big horse-boxes, attended by solid-looking countrymen with outdoor faces. We picked one at random. As it turned out, we had got ourselves a *gaje*, not a gypsy. I asked him where we'd buy a horse. In reply, I got that long, slow stare that countrymen reserve for the big city idiot who is about to waste his time with dumbfool questions. However, George, a local farmer as it turned out, warmed up as we got around to his favourite subject.

'It's not too difficult,' he said. 'Just walk around, see a horse you like, pays yer money and you'll get it.'

I could see this was going to take time. George's daughter was leading round a beautifully groomed pony. 'That's a lovely animal,' I said in what I hoped was an engaging manner. '*Palomino,*' hissed the Bounder in my ear. 'Would she be worth a lot of money?' I asked. '*He,*' hissed the Bounder. We were in danger of becoming a pantomime act.

'I've already turned down an offer of seven grand,' said George, ignoring our cross-talk. 'But he'll be back later. The record is forty-two.'

'Why do you come to the Fair?' I asked. 'Are you a gypsy?'

'No!' said George, stepping back a pace to give me one of his long looks. 'I'm a farmer. I buy these horses in as yearlings from a gypsy who lives near me, I grow 'em on for a couple of years and then sell 'em.'

'Is it profitable?' I asked. Once started on the dumbfool questions, I thought I might as well continue.

'Not 'arf,' said George, giving me an old-fashioned look. 'They only cost me about a grand each, and as long as I stick to the right bloodline – the gypsies will sniff this out quick as a flash – I can make a tidy profit on each.'

I summoned up my courage to ask the killer question. 'And how do you find dealing with the gypsies?'

'I don't have any trouble with them,' said George quickly, with a nervous look over my shoulder at the swirling crowds. 'I won't say it's by choice, but the money is always straight as a die. You can't fault them on that. They'll even ask me if I'm short of cash "You're sure that's enough, mate? You can have some more if you want it." Very useful bank. Open all hours and friendly with it. Better than my bank manager.'

I told George, who seemed to be warming to me slightly, about the book, and asked for his view on the more contentious issue of 'bad' gypsy families.

'There's good and bad, like anything else,' he said. 'In fact, I've got some of the most "notorious" living near me. But if you play straight with them, they make sure that there'll be no trouble from the others.'

We said goodbye to George without making a serious bid for the Palomino and continued on our quest. A small tent with flapping canvas and a sign saying 'Gypsy Council' caught our eye. Vera had told us about the Council, so we thought we'd find out just how good they were at political action – from the size of the tent, it didn't look as if there was much serious money behind them!

As it turned out, Vera had warned the Council people to expect us, and we were introduced immediately to Peggy Smith. She is the closest thing you can get to gypsy 'royalty', and as a baby had slept in the bottom drawer of a chest in an old Vardo like Sid's. 'Can't you just imagine her having tea with the Queen?' whispered the Bounder, awed, in my ear. Peggy's son Charles had gone further than any others in climbing up the ranks of the Establishment, becoming in turn the first gypsy mayor, then first gypsy Commissioner for Racial Equality, before dying tragically of cancer the year before.

Peggy quickly got us up to speed on the creeping legislation that had changed the gypsies' way of life. 'In 1960,' she told us, 'the Caravan Act produced the first legislation affecting where we could stop. Then, in 1968, another Act required councils to build special sites for travellers, although this was left to local discretion. In 1994 a new Act abolished stopping on the road totally, and, much worse, abolished the 1968 Act providing sites. This threw about five thousand families back on the road with nowhere to stop and no education for the children. Various directives now "recommend" that councils build us more sites, but they always come up against the Planning Act. And in any case, when any plans get advertised, people's negative views of us usually result in complaint, and mostly the council backs down.'

'So for you it's a vicious circle,' I said to Peggy. 'Poor-looking sites will only reinforce people's perceptions that gypsies are a bunch of no-goods, which will stop them approving plans for better sites, and so on and so on.'

'You've got the right of it, Richard,' Peggy said, with a heavy sigh. 'We are in a trap, and there's no way to break out without the government forcing councils to give us good sites, and this they will not do. And even if we do get a good site, it can be shut down with almost no discussion. The plans for the Olympics involve closing a site in Docklands that has housed the same families for over fifty years. The council has offered them space in a children's school play area, but the residents are up in arms, so once again we'll be back on the road.'

'Where the hell do they build sites, then?' demanded the Bounder. 'On rubbish tips?'

Peggy and her fellow council members looked at each other. 'I think you'd better go and see,' she said.

'But what about the gypsies who still want to go travelling?' I asked.

'Well,' said Peggy, 'the only answer is to gather together into bigger groups that are harder to move on, but it's no real solution. The media and politicians will use any ammunition they can – getting us compared with the "New Age" travellers, who are nothing like us, or, more recently, the Irish travellers, who do not have our culture and take a much more aggressive attitude to the law and anyone else who gets in their way. My boy Charles would have told you,' said Peggy. 'He'd talk to anyone, he would, and believed passionately in making the outside world understand us. Mind you, despite everything he achieved, which no gypsy had done before, he was always saying that in terms of what needed to be done, he was still a failure. He wasn't, you know, but it's no use just talking. You'll have to see for yourself.'

Peggy was silent for a long moment, and we could see she still missed her boy terribly. As we made our goodbyes, she pointed at a bunch of pretty gypsy girls, swaying through the crowd on their high heels, sweaters cut short to show the jewels sparking in each navel, eyes swivelling like searchlights to see who might notice.

'Maybe they're our best hope,' finished Peggy. 'We always used to say Stow Fair is for trading daughters as well as horses. Makes me wish I was young again!'

The Bounder and I trudged back to our car (parked in a 'convenient' field at least a mile away from the Fair). My friend's mind was clearly more on the pretty gypsy girls than anything else, but his approval wasn't shared by everyone. A massive woman swathed in tweeds, with a voice like a ship's foghorn, was not amused. 'Look at those awful tarts in white boots! Time we got out of here, Penelope,' she boomed, as she herded her reluctant daughter back to the family Range Rover. I thought it looked as if Penelope would have preferred to stay for a chat with the girls instead. Maybe Peggy was right after all.

After we got back from the Fair, we decided to take Peggy Smith's advice and find out for ourselves. Our friend Jake Bowers, whose radio programme for gypsies, Rokker Radio, was now being broadcast by BBC Three Counties Radio every Sunday night and proving very popular, offered to help.

'It won't be easy to get you in with a gypsy family,' said Jake. 'It's not as if I could just give you a phone number and an introduction. Our people are very nervous of strangers and need time to get to know you, before they'll let you into their lives. I'll tell you what,' he went on, 'we're doing our first outside broadcast at a site in the Midlands next week. Why don't you come along and see how you get on?'

'What about a little Romany to show we mean business?' I asked.

Jake borrowed my notebook and wrote down two short

sentences. 'The first means "Look at the gorgeous girl (*Dik at the rinkeni rakli*)", and the second, "Watch out, there are police outside (*Kakk! the gavvers are jelling akai*)",' said Jake.

The Bounder and I agreed this covered most situations, so we memorised the words. In fact, when we tried them out later we had mixed results. Jake had actually given us the Romany for 'wrinkled old crone', not 'gorgeous girl', which got me into some trouble with a young gypsy actress we met, but that's another story. At least I discovered the gypsy sense of humour.

The day of our site visit was cursed with foul weather. We surfed our way up the A1, then struggled with satellite navigation to follow Jake's instructions. There was no street number and I had almost given up when, hidden between a supermarket car park and an industrial estate, I spotted a caravan. 'Here we are,' I said to the Bounder. 'Nervous?' We both admitted to a twinge of apprehension, and despite the friendly reception we had had from Sid and Peggy in Stow, I was not sure what we were letting ourselves in for.

The road into the site was pot-holed and the street lighting almost non-existent. A pack of unseen dogs warned off outsiders. At least we knew what we were looking for. 'You'll see a van with a bleeding great aerial,' Jake had said, and there it was, right in front of us. We parked and got out to face the music.

Jake was up to his ears. 'It's all going on here,' he shouted over to us. 'We've got an Eastern European Romany band made up from a bunch of guys who've got a pub down the road, but I'm having some real problems with the studio. Make yourself comfortable and we'll talk later.' We sauntered over as casually as we could towards a crowd of people clustering around the crew. A strongly-built bullet-headed man with a thick Eastern European accent was standing holding a selection of DVDs.

'Are the DVDs for sale? What's on them?' I asked. It sounded like a good enough pick-up line to me.

'Is like weddings, christening, travel, and like that,' said the man, who introduced himself as Roman Bartos. The friend standing next to him expanded on this description, but as he spoke only Czechoslovakian, the Bounder and I were none the wiser. None the less, I shelled out a tenner for the DVD and got a cup of sweet, milky tea as a bonus from a tall friendly man with a nice smile who was manning the till.

'I'm Richard and this is my cousin Mike,' I said. 'I'm a friend of Jake Bowers.' My 'Open Sesame' to the community worked like a dream.

'Jake's my friend as well,' said John. 'Welcome to my home.' Big sigh of relief – we were in!

John took us back to what he called 'the shed', a small prefabricated structure containing a kitchen and bathroom where we met his best friend Pete. We sat down on the comfortable sofa and John's wife Louise busied herself with preparing refills of nourishing tea which kept us going for the next couple of hours. I asked Louise about the living arrangements.

'Well,' she said, 'we do most of our daytime living in the shed, but we use the caravan next door for sleeping – and entertaining people we want to impress, rather than people we feel comfortable with.' She showed us over it later. It was absolutely immaculate inside and out, but I felt pleased that she had placed us in the 'comfortable' category.

The Bounder asked John about the site itself.

'It was built by the Local Authority under the 1968 Caravan Act,' said John. 'Before we came, it was a peat bog – and it still floods every year. The first families here spent so much money infilling the bog that at first there were only funds over for a tiny day-room, then these were upgraded ten years ago. We have twenty-four pitches here, spread across eight to ten families. We have all known each other a long time, and we work well together to keep things under control.'

'And do you still travel much?' I asked.

'No,' said John. 'I stopped my caravan here twenty-six years ago and haven't moved since. At the time my two kids were nearing school age and I felt they needed a proper education. One or two still travel every summer, but it's getting less frequent.'

The Bounder was staring fixedly at a picture of a young soldier in full dress uniform on the wall. 'Who's that?' he asked Louise.

'That's Pete's son,' she said. 'He's in the Grenadier Guards, serving in Iraq.' We were both very surprised. I had always assumed that gypsies would avoid military service, but it turned out that many had served in both wars, and that they even numbered a VC among their ranks. Pete himself had also been in the regular army, serving in Cyprus at the height of the conflict there.

John was involved in the Civil Rights movement, so I asked him why gypsies had made so little fuss in the past about obvious discrimination of the kind we had heard about from Peggy and Vera. 'It's our history,' he said. 'When we had trouble before, our first thought would have been to move away. Now there's nowhere to go, so we have to find a way of making ourselves heard.'

Jake and I talked about this later. He was not hopeful that the gypsy community would find a voice. 'Most of them are just banging their heads against a brick wall,' he said. 'Even Charles Smith was little known to outsiders. This is why I started Rokker Radio with the BBC. I'd've liked to have our very own radio station, but the economics were against us.'

Outside, Roman and his band had now launched into the

Romany national anthem 'I walk, I walk'. We listened to the wild, plaintive music until it was finished, then decided to seek out the younger generation. Pete's fifteen-year-old-son Nathan gave us a surprisingly lucid insight into what it is like growing up as a gypsy kid and attending the toughest school in town.

'Do the other kids give you aggro for being a gypsy?' I asked him.

'It was bad at the start,' said Nathan. 'Then I realised that unless I slapped a couple of the guys giving me trouble, it would get worse. So I did, and things have been better since. Mind you, every new kid who comes into the school finds out about you and wants to have a go. Last week, I got attacked by some new Polish kids, who wanted to prove how tough they were. I'm lucky – I've got a Russian friend, Dimitri, who is a real solid guy. When he hits someone, they stay down. No one touches the pair of us now – but the trouble is that any fighting is always seen as our fault. For example, if I see a boy hitting a girl, I'll tell him to stop or fight me for it. But then, I'm seen as the trouble-maker, because I am a gypsy, and get taken off school for a week and miss lessons. If more people knew and understood what it's like to be a gypsy, things would be better.'

'And what's going to happen when you leave school?'

'You can't really get a decent job round here,' went on Nathan. 'William' – he beckoned a friend over to us – 'applied to the local supermarket, but as soon as they saw the address "Travellers' Site", I reckon they just tore up the papers. I'm going to find a self-employed job, then join the army,' said Nathan, as if it was obvious.

'Hasn't any of this put you off risking your life for this country?' asked the Bounder.

'Nah!' said Nathan. 'Why should I worry about a bunch of ignorant people? My brother loves the army, and my dad and granddad did too. It's a family thing.'

'What about girls?' the Bounder asked (he would). 'Do you go out with gypsy girls or *gaje*?'

Nathan looked a bit embarrassed, but William jumped in. 'The problem is,' he said, 'if you go out with a gypsy girl, they expect you to marry them right away, then have kids. And before you can even go out with her, you have to ask her parents' permission first. Gypsy girls have higher aspirations in life than just having a bit of fun.'

'And what would you like to do?' I asked William.

William thought for a minute. 'I'd really like to do an apprenticeship in construction, but getting an application accepted is a big problem, like with the supermarket. I'll probably end up doing something on my own like Nathan. It would be good to earn some decent money. My dad's generation still want to go back to the old ways, earning very little and living on hedgehogs and stuff, but it doesn't appeal to me.'

'But don't you like the country? Do you keep dogs or birds?' the Bounder persisted.

'Oh, we all keep dogs,' said Nathan. 'Mine's a Yorkshire terrier. William and I are always out hunting.'

'What do you think of the site?' I asked.

Nathan looked at me with a certain contempt. 'We live between a great big transmission mast, which is going to fry our brains, and a council refuse tip, which will poison us sooner or later. So what do you think?' I guess this was the answer to the question we had asked Peggy Smith. The parents might put up with the limitations of the sites, but the younger ones, like Nathan, saw them with different eyes.

Both boys had a good deal of pride in their parents. 'They may not be able to read or write,' said Nathan, 'but they are wise and clever. And the women are brilliant at selling – you'd be amazed at some of the things they have done when money was short.'

Nathan had stood up for his family with more than words. 'Fighting is a tradition with us,' he told me. 'It's OK to fight and lose. There's nothing to be ashamed of as long as you fought the fight, but you can never refuse a challenge. My dad used to be a champion fighter, and although he's getting on now, young men will still challenge him so that they can claim they've beaten someone famous. If that happens, I'll stand in front of Dad and take the challenge. It means I get beaten sometimes by bigger blokes, but I'm not having them take it out of Dad.' Nathan's description of fighting for his father still stays with me today. I'd be proud of a son who did that for me!

Before we finally left the site, on the wall of the shed I noticed some pictures of Vardos on the road, and I asked Louise if she missed the old days.

'Yes,' she said. 'I bought the pictures because I remember so well that way of life. If I had a chance to go back, in five minutes I'd be on the road. It was a cleaner, better way to live. I feel that people respected each other and the country itself more in those days. We used to call it "living lightly on the land" – just take what you need and leave each place as you wish to find it. The cycle of picking was our life then. We'd start with the fruit: strawberries, then currants and apples, then work right through to the potatoes and winter vegetables. We'd always work for the same farmers, who got to depend on us. I remember one driving right across two counties to find us, when he had an extra crop to get in quickly. When the picking was over, we'd pack up the caravan and go hawking around the villages. The older women were best at it, and the younger ones would stay in the camp and clean up. Then on Saturday night we'd all go out together.' She sighed.

'It sounds a good life,' I said.

'It was a hard life,' said Louise, 'but a good one, because everyone worked together. Even the kids from four upwards would be found work in the fields, and it was healthy too, being in the open air all day. If they got sick, we had the old-fashioned remedies to cure them. Of course there was little or no schooling in those days, but our kids found out things about the country that few modern children would ever learn today.'

'Do you ever want to go back?' I asked her.

'I still go visiting the old places when I get the chance,' she said. 'I've been back several times to the farms where we used to do all the fruit-picking. And when we travel to Stow and the other fairs, we often take weeks to do it, taking all the small roads, stopping here and there as we used to.

'I've got a cousin in Hampshire with a nice three-room bungalow, but I could never be closed in by four walls. Sometimes, even when I am sitting here watching the television, I have to get up and go for a walk. I can only sleep in the caravan. Lying in the feather bed and listening to the rain on the roof – there's nothing to beat it! Do you know – if someone gave me a mansion, I reckon I'd end up parking the caravan in the grounds and living in that!'

Louise showed us all the traditional tools for a travelling life, which she still has stored above the roof in the shed: the painted water containers, the cooking pans and kettles, and the great curved kettle-holder for holding the pots over an open fire, which had been given to her mother as a wedding present. 'I never want to forget these things,' she said. 'That's why I keep them with me. They're like living people to me. Once a traveller, always a traveller. It's in the blood.'

Her husband John showed the Bounder and me the intricately carved and painted model Vardos he made in his tool shed, and sold for what seemed to us ludicrously small amounts of money.

'Will you ever build a real one?' we asked him, as we pored over the beautiful details.

'Of course,' he said. 'Before I get too old, I have to travel one last time, just me and the missus.'

I looked at the Bounder. 'Sounds like we know what to do next,' I said.

He snorted. 'You're not sharing my feather-bed, old cock,' he said emphatically.

John and Louise bid us goodbye and told us to come again whenever we liked. 'You are known now,' they said. 'The door is always open and the kettle is always on.' It was a good feeling.

It was not until the weather brightened the next spring that we were actually able to go travelling. Jake had introduced us to Jack Richardson, an influential gypsy at the site and he had agreed to help us realise our dream of sampling life on the road. Jack was a quietly spoken and sincere man with a warm smile who, although illiterate, clearly ran a successful business – admittedly, we never found out exactly what it was. He also exercised strong control over not just his children and grandchildren, but the site itself. He had two traditional Vardos, several fields full of horses, and the most splendid 1930s Bedford van, all freshly painted in gleaming new colours. 'Cost me more than building them in the first place,' he said. 'I've started a few families travelling the traditional way again,' he told us. 'It's amazing, the change in people's perceptions. Roll up in a Vardo and you are everyone's friend; park a trailer and you are a thieving gypsy!'

Jack, like many gypsies, was an enthusiastic bird-keeper, and he had suggested bringing along a real expert, 'Birdie' Smith, on the trip. In fact, strangely enough, we had met Birdie already.

The previous year, the Bounder and I had been making one of our regular visits to Brian Oliver and Pete Beech, stalwarts of the Royal Albert Ratters. Pete had taken us to see his extraordinary collection of birds, bred using the traditional methods his father and grandfather had taught him. It had proved another 'Endangered Species' story. The old craft of trapping birds has been made illegal, and new regulations for inspection and registration are emerging by the minute. Brian told us how, because it was near-impossible to say for sure whether a caged bird had been bred or caught, a new generation of 'snitches' had appeared. One of these had reported him to the RSPCA for keeping hawks' eggs, and got him arrested. A year on, he had just got his eggs back, after the 'experts' ('Everything they know about birds could be written on my right bollock,' said Pete) had admitted that his painted Tesco chicken's eggs were not illegal.

That Sunday we had gone with the two Yorkshiremen to a caged birds show in the local school. Pete had taken his prize 'Goldfinch Mules', a cross-breed of canary and goldfinch with extraordinary markings of red, cream and deep tannin that are especially prized in both the gypsy and *gaje* worlds. It had been a successful show, Pete had won a couple of the coveted 'Best in Class' awards, and we were heading across the car park to leave the birds in the car before celebrating in the local pub when we were stopped by a thin swarthy man with a beak-nosed face, two sharp black eyes and a mop of tousled, greying hair.

His eyes flickered quickly over the cages, taking everything in. His decision was immediate: 'Sell me that one, mister,' he said. 'I'll give you £400 for it.'

A short period of bargaining followed, then £500 in old notes changed hands and the deal was done. I asked him if he'd join us for a drink, and told him briefly about the book, the gypsies that we had met, and our plans to go travelling in the spring. 'Birdie', with whom Pete had done business before, sized us up, clearly reserving his judgement, but was agreeable to a pint or two. In an attempt to warm him up I asked him if his name was really Smith, as I had been told that a number of gypsies used it as a convenient alias.

Birdie's sharp eyes rested on me for a minute, and I was sure that one of them winked, but it was so quick that one could have been forgiven for missing it. He ignored the question anyway. 'What do you know about birds, then?' he asked.

We had got to know Birdie well since then, and recognised that the lightning wink was a closer indication of what he really meant than anything he said out loud; but there was nothing he didn't know about birds. We were delighted to see him again as the Bounder and I were bringing our children – my two teenagers and his younger ones – on the journey, and with Birdie on board we thought we'd see if they might acquire an interest in bird breeding.

The night before we set off we were invited over to the pub run by Roman Bartos and his Czechoslovakian gypsy community, whom we had met during Jake's outside broadcast. How he and fifteen hundred of his fellow gypsies had come to England and set up life over here was a story too good to miss.

Roman was pleased to see us. 'Eat, drink, later we have music, dance,' he said. A snap of his fingers brought a friendly girl fighting her way through the jumble of tough, swarthy-looking men who filled the bar. 'So, what you want to know?'

'What made you all decide to come to England?' I asked.

'Slovakia still very bad place for Roma peoples, even though no Communists now,' Roman said. 'They took away our caravans and made us live in villages, but separate.'

'What do you mean, separate?' asked the Bounder.

'Most village have river,' went on Roman. 'Roma live one side, *gaje* live other. But our houses very poor, no sanitation, no electricity. Like, what you say, shanty town. You know, after Communists, big prejudice started. In short time pub, restaurant, hotel, shop, all had signs say: "No Gypsy". Also, new kids with money give us bad time. They are like, what you had here once, Teddy boys. Dress funny, ride big bikes and carry knives. They kill you if you not polite. Police not help. Kids' dads all wealthy businessmen, politicians. Put us in prison, steal our land for development, if want.'

'So how did you make up your mind to leave?' I asked.

'We are not stupid people,' said Roman. 'We now have television, read free papers. We learn about democracy, what Communists would not tell us. So, one day, the elders say, "Why we not go and live in a democracy? Must be better life than here."'

'Why England?' asked the Bounder.

'Simple!' said Roman, with a flourish of his arms. 'World have only two good democracies: England and United States. US too far, so we come here, where we hear good things, especially monarchy. We read about Princess Diana, Prince's Trust. Sound good. Roma peoples like monarchy. Don't trust state.'

'But how on earth did you manage to move fifteen hundred people to a strange country where you did not speak the language?' I asked. It seemed an almost impossible task.

'We sent one hundred men who speak some English to start with,' explained Roman. 'I found charity to help, called Comic Relief. Very good people. First we rent houses and work in London. Then when no more Comic Relief money, I start charity myself with help from Pakistani peoples to help teach older people English, which they cannot learn in schools. Then we can bring in more people and whole families. Now we decide to move to Midlands where is more work. Then we know we need community centre, where we all discuss problems, help people, settle quarrels, like in old country. Heart of community in England is pub. So we buy pub. People meet and talk downstairs. Upstairs is, how you call it, "Command Control", with papers, computers, telephone.' I was astonished at what Roman had accomplished. I looked around the room, and saw he had what any true leader has among his people: real respect. He deserved it.

By this time the wild swirling music we had first heard in the gypsy site was spilling out of the next room. 'And now we dance and sing!' insisted Roman, and with a slap on the back he escorted the Bounder and me onto the dance floor. Well – what else could we do?

The rest of the evening passed in a whirl of music and laughter. The extraordinarily evocative, swirling singing stayed with me for days. The Bounder scored the most points for Roma/*Gaje* relations by picking one of the largest ladies and whirling her around the floor. Who was leading and who following it was hard to say. 'Your friend, he dance like dog on ice,' whispered Roman in my ear. I took it as a Czechoslovakian compliment.

The next morning it needed several mugs of thick, sweet tea to clear the cobwebs. The stuff Roman had given us when we were proposing the toasts must have been rocket fuel. The Bounder's children danced round him in delight: 'Daddy's got a hangover! Daddy's got a hangover!' It was obviously a regular event.

All four children had been up early and, along with some of Jack Richardson's own grandchildren who were joining us for the journey, had been making friends with the big cob horses which would be pulling the Vardos: big black or brown and white beasts, with great hairy fetlocks. 'Look directly in their eyes, then breathe slowly into their nostrils,' Jack told the children, who got the hang of it much quicker than I did. On reflection, my horse may have had an objection to a mouth-to-mouth infusion of Roman's rocket fuel.

When it was time to go Jack led the way, the Bounder and I followed behind in the two middle Vardos, and Birdie brought up the rear, his bird cages already alive with the sweet songs of spring. Jack's son John would follow us later in the Bedford truck, with the big water churns and other necessities.

I was surprised at how fast we were going – 'Fifteen mile an hour, they'll do, steady all day,' Jack had told me – and I felt a bit nervous with my one horse power, but he was no trouble at all. He just picked up the pace and kept at it: stopping and starting when the other Vardos did, almost as if he had had automatic transmission.

By lunch time we had pulled clear of the city, and Jack was leading the way down a winding country road. Soon a small village hove into view and we stopped on a village green, next to a traditional-looking pub. First contact with the *gaje*, I thought, feeling like ET. But it was just as Jack had told us. The gaily painted Vardos soon drew a friendly crowd of adults and children alike, and in no time at all we were all chatting away, the Bounder and I making out as if this was something we did everyday.

As we were preparing to leave, a tall, grey haired man asked us if we had anywhere to stop for the night. I noticed Jack and Birdie's exchanged glances, and then they shook their heads. 'I've got an empty field a couple of miles up the road,' said our new friend. 'Look, I'll draw you a map.'

Neither Jack nor Birdie could read a word, but they nodded sagely over the map, and we set off again. As promised, a gate next to a beautiful red-brick Georgian house was open, and a good-sized field beckoned. John and the Bedford were already there. For a moment I thought that John must be an adept at 'dukkering' – gypsy crystal-ball reading – to have figured out where we were, until I noticed Jack tucking his mobile phone into his top pocket.

Soon a blazing fire was lit, and the kettles had been set on the big curved stands. A simple lunch, and it was time for business – finding our dinner. We split up. The Bounder went with Jack after some game. He had already shown us his special catapult, which was one of the most extraordinary things I had ever seen, specially crafted from gold and ivory and studded with diamonds. The heel was weighted as a 'priest' to give the victims last rites. It was astonishingly accurate, firing large lead balls. I was later to see Jack kill a rabbit at a good hundred foot, from a moving Vardo. He also had a big, friendly lurcher, called Speedy, and a cage of ferrets. Together his animal armoury found us everything we needed, boosted by a pen of chickens to provide us with break-fast.

Birdie offered to take the children netting for pigeons. To my surprise this was still legal, using decoys and sometimes strange foods, like alder cobs, to entice the birds down, and a 'clap net' to trap them. Birdie is an astonishing mimic. He can 'call down' virtually any bird, using its mating call. Once he had a whole squadron of redpoles circling him, swooping and chirping, convinced that he was their spring date. Later he taught some of the calls to the children. A great favourite was the 'danger warning' that birds use among themselves. With it, Birdie could silence a whole hedgerow in a flash. It was uncanny. My sons are both actors and soon picked up the trick, even changing their mobile answering messages to bird calls.

I was consigned to the lowly task of vegetable collecting, and immediately got the wobbles. What if I was caught? I could just see the headlines: 'Baronet goes Pikey'. I hunted around for something in which to hide my spoils, and decided on my smart leather computer bag. Surely no one would 'stop and search' that? In fact, my task proved the easiest: there were fields full of late winter vegetables, and even new potatoes. After a time the guilt receded and I stopped looking over my shoulder. Live lightly off the land, I reminded myself. No one will miss a few cabbages.

The accumulated spoils were amazing, and set the pattern for the days to come. Rabbits, hares, pheasants, pigeons – even once a small muntjac deer, snared from a low-hanging tree – provided a series of wonderful meals, cooked slowly in the great metal pot over the fire, or baked in tinfoil, stuffed with apples and wine, in the ashes. I don't think I have ever eaten so well. Jack was not only a dab hand at cooking, but an expert fisherman. As we moved down through middle England into chalk-stream country he would set night lines, with as many as twenty separate hooks, by morning all usually taken by trout and grayling. Sometimes, when the conditions were right, he would stuff an old hessian sack with straw, cut holes in the outside and weight it with stones before sinking it in a dark river pool. The result – a sack full of eels, some up to five pounds, ready to be sprinkled with coarse salt (which cleans off the slime and kills the fish), cut into portions, then fried in batter.

In the evenings we would all climb into the Bedford and roar down to the local pub for a pint or three, then drive back, singing, for a last tune round the campfire accompanied by John's

squeeze-box. My new extended family made me feel like Pop
Larkin in *The Darling Buds of May*, and I wondered how he would
have got on with the gypsies at the fruit- and hop-picking which
they all shared. Later I would lie awake in the Vardo, listening to the
sound of the rain on the roof and my children's quiet breathing,
and remember what Sid the Deacon had said about slowing down
the pace of life.

All too soon our travelling week was over. For our last dinner
Jack promised us something special. When we got back to camp I
saw, to my alarm, a large lump of clay blackening slowly over the
fire. Oh, no! I thought, feeling like Lawrence of Arabia faced with
the sheep's eyeballs. I sat with the others round the fire, determined
to be brave. Jack peeled back the clay as if he was opening a big
chestnut, and forked me out some of the white meat. He was quite
right. If you close your eyes, hedgehog does taste like chicken.

The next morning Birdie had a present for us: two beautiful
wooden birdcages, each inhabited by one of the goldfinches he
prized so much. I didn't bother to ask where the birds had come
from – I'd only have got the lightning wink treatment. The children knew, but they weren't saying either. Halfway to gypsies
already, I thought.

My wife came to pick us up from Stow, and professed surprise
at how clean we all were. 'How did you get on with the gypsies?
You didn't get into any trouble, did you?' she asked the children.

'No!' they said indignantly, with a quick look at each other.
'They were great, Mum!' I could see Susie giving them both a
narrow look, but she left it there.

On the way back home to London, I reflected on just how
much I had learned. Above all, I felt an extraordinary sense of
comfort and familiarity with the countryside, unlike any I have
had before. I'd like to spend more time with these people, I
thought, who have so much to teach me about our land.

And the gypsies? What next for these most endangered of species? After our Vardo trip we went to talk with Charlie, a friendly ex-copper who has run gypsy sites for several years and takes a deep and encouragingly human interest in the situation. We agreed about the almost insuperable problems that the English Romany gypsies face: the lack of sites; the critical issue of how councils can face up to a set of electors, biased beyond belief against the travellers; the abdication of real responsibility by central government; the real anger genuine, English gypsies feel about being 'judged by association' with Irish and New Age travellers who do not have the same sense of responsibility towards the countryside. Charlie's last comments were the most interesting: 'I admit that when I was in the police, we were very biased against gypsies. Now I have to admit that we were wrong. This is a real problem we have to solve, not sweep under the carpet.'

Our final thought was that England will get the English gypsies that we deserve, and the decision is an important one for us all. One last little story from John Searl, our illustrator friend, gets to the heart of the matter.

'I was fishing on one of the most exclusive beats on the Avon,' said John, 'and there was a gypsy caravan parked right next to my pitch. Everyone in the party was moaning and complaining about these gypsies and how they stole everything. I didn't complain myself, but saw a couple of their kids on the bridge later, obviously up for a bit of poaching. They asked me if there were any salmon in the river, and I told them that there were plenty of trout instead and showed them where to fish. They were small kids and the river was over-stocked anyway.

'I never thought anything about it, but a few days later on the same beat I got locked out of my car late in the evening when the door jammed. I couldn't get anyone to come out to me, and was walking back past the caravan when one of the gypsies asked me if I needed help. When I'd told him what had happened he said, "Jump in the car. We'll run you home." It was a thirty-mile round trip, and they wouldn't take anything for the petrol. Just shows what a little politeness will do.'

Make your own mind up! As for the Bounder and me – we can't wait to go travelling again.

11

November

MAGIC CORNWALL

If you wake at midnight, and hear a horse's feet
Don't go drawing back the blind, or looking in the street,
Them that asks no questions isn't told a lie.
Watch the wall, my darling, while the gentlemen go by!
Five and twenty ponies
Trotting through the dark –
Brandy for the parson,
  'Baccy for the clerk:
Laces for a lady, letters for a spy,
And watch the wall, my darling, while the gentlemen go by!

RUDYARD KIPLING, 'Smuggler's Song'

I was bored. It was a familiar, yawning feeling of ennui that went deep into my soul. I was staying with my parents-in-law in Cornwall. They brought out the very worst in me – as they were the first to point out – and I knew my only chance of surviving the weekend was to make myself as scarce as possible. I'd smuggled my rods into the back of the car at the last minute under the disapproving gaze of the then Mrs Bounder. There was a small chance that I would be able to find one of the fabulous 'greybacks' – huge mythical salmon of more than forty pounds which supposedly ran the River Fowey in November. This was fifteen years ago, and in those days Cornwall was foreign territory to me. I had a strong sense that my father-in-law, who does not fish, would not be any help in locating a decent stretch of river. All was gloom until I remembered someone mentioning a man who lived in nearby St Neot who knew the rivers of Cornwall better than anyone. He had an uncanny gift for finding fish, they said. I wanted to meet him. He was disreputable, drank too much and was a womaniser, they told me. I wanted to meet him even more.

It was suggested, acidly, that I should try the local pub. I needed little persuading, and made my way there as fast as the tiny, winding lanes of Cornwall would allow. I enquired at the bar. The landlord pointed to a small man sitting alone on a bar stool

259

with a half-empty pint of Guinness in front of him. He was dressed in an ancient greasy Barbour and had the permanently tanned face of the perennial countryman. On his head he wore a battered old leather cowboy hat, beneath which dangled long unkempt locks of hair. A hand-rolled cigarette hung from the corner of his mouth. He was considerably the worse for wear.

'Are you Charlie Bettinson?' I asked politely.

He looked up at me from under his hat and stared for several seconds. Then, without removing his cigarette, 'What the bloody hell do you want?' he said.

From that lowly beginning developed a friendship which I value more than most and which has, so far, lasted for fifteen years – longer than any of my marriages. Charlie is a true country-man, at one with nature, and with a sixth sense about his beloved rivers. To walk along an overgrown bank in Charlie's company beside softly sparkling water while many of the trees are still in the glory of their autumn colours is always a wonderful experience.

'There's a big one there,' he says suddenly, pointing towards the opposite side. 'It's a salmon, about fifteen pounds.'

I stare myopically at where he is indicating, and can see nothing except an overhanging bank and the ebony water racing past.

'For God's sake, Mike!' says Charlie, exasperated. 'You're supposed to be a professional salmon fisherman and you tell me that you can't see that fish?'

'Oh, yes, of course. There it is,' I say, looking hard and seeing nothing.

We first went fishing together the day after we met. It was an entirely different type of angling to any other that I had ever done in my life. When I first looked at the River Fowey I could not believe that any piece of water so small and insignificant could possibly hold a good head of salmon and sea trout, until Charlie started to point out the lies.

'They're under the banks and in the white water beneath the falls,' he said. 'You rarely see them during the day, but they're there all the same. The sea trout particularly come out at night and, to a certain extent, so do the salmon. It's too late for the sea trout now. They start to arrive in April and May; big ones up to twenty pounds. Then the main run comes in 'round June and July time – small fish about a pound to three pounds.'

'What about these greybacks?' I enquired.

'They'll just be coming in now,' said Charlie, 'but they're only a few. We'll catch them on a worm. Just watch me and I'll show you.'

At the next waterfall we came to Charlie dropped the well-weighted worm into the rushing white water. 'It'll be taken into the back of the fall,' he said. 'It's where the fish hide. If he takes, you'll feel a small plucking on the line. Do nothin'. If he starts to run, wait until he stops and then strike.'

At the third pool we came to, Charlie suddenly stopped. 'There's a fish at the worm now,' he said. 'Here, take the rod and feel it.' I took it and felt the heavy line. At first there seemed to be nothing there, and then I felt a tiny pluck, and then another.

'Is it a greyback?' I was trembling with excitement.

'Well, it ain't a roach,' he replied sardonically. 'But it could be anything – small trout, eel – you name it. Now, you concentrate, and wait until he runs.'

Just then the line started to slip slowly through my fingers.

'Don't do anything,' said Charlie. 'Just wait.' The line stopped, and the air around me seemed to tingle. 'Right, give her a pull now,' he said.

I struck, and immediately knew that this was no monster. Eventually we beached a small, very black, male salmon.

'Little black cock!' Charlie laughed. 'Sounds just like you, Mike.'

We had no more luck that day, but in the pub that night, over several pints of Guinness, I realised that I was in the presence of a kindred spirit. Like me, Charlie loved the countryside and fishing, drinking and laughter, women and wickedness. So it was very late that night before I drove back drunkenly and dangerously to my parents-in-law's house and crept into bed.

'You were very late last night and you missed dinner,' my mother-in-law said accusingly. 'I suppose you were drinking with that Charlie Bettinson.'

I nodded cheerfully, mouth full of toast, but thought it wiser not to comment.

Cornwall is totally different from the classic English shires. It is not soft and gentle. It is wild and untamed, and its people are the same. They are of Celtic stock, with all the talents of that great race, and the uneasy peace between them and the incomers is the same now as it has been for centuries. In times past it was the Saxons or the Romans; now it is the tourists and the retired couples. The Celts have always been bards and poets, artists and artisans, with a natural love of drinking and laughter.

Charlie is a true Celtic countryman, the very rarest of an endangered species, and when I told the Bart about him he could not wait to meet him. Like me, the Bart has always been fascinated by the Celts: good-looking, quarrelsome, and passionate about songs, jewellery and bright clothes, they have a huge love of life and excitement. In ancient times theirs was a tribal society, loosely held together by their Gaelic language but also by the Druids, who administered healing, teaching and law-giving as well as exercising their mystical powers, of which even Julius Caesar was nervous.

In the five hundred years before Christ the Celts over-ran most of Europe and even extended as far East as Turkey and Armenia. In 390 BC the Celtic king Brennos even conquered Rome itself, and was only persuaded to leave after payment of a huge ransom – most of which, knowing the Celts' love of drink, he and his followers probably spent in celebrating on the way home. Everywhere the Celtic people left evidence of their passage in stone circles, graves, caches of gold and silver, and marvellously crafted weapons and chariots, which they would throw into sacred pools as offerings for the gods. Local Cornish myth still has it that the mystical lake into which King Arthur flung Excalibur was Dozmary Pool on Bodmin Moor.

Caesar came, saw and conquered England twice, but it was not until the Claudian invasion that the Romans settled. Those Celts who would not become citizens were pushed back into the wilder reaches of Brittany, Cornwall, Wales, Scotland and Ireland itself. They had a brief renaissance after the Romans left before succumbing once again to waves of Saxons, Danes and Normans. Yet among the poorer country people and even in the church itself, their presence is still obvious today.

In the Dark Ages that followed the collapse of the Roman Empire the candle-flame of Christianity nearly flickered out completely under a wave of bloodthirsty pagan gods. Only in Celtic Ireland was it kept fully alive, and the Celtic influence on modern Christianity is still extensive, with festivals (even the dating of Christmas itself), ritual and locations being copied freely. Celtic stories, once passed from bard to bard around the fireside, are deeply engrained in popular culture, especially among the young. Modern heroes like Obi wan Kenobi, Luke Skywalker and Gandalf clearly have their origins and forebears among the Celts.

Trick-or-treating at Hallowe'en, now so popular with our children, is an exact imitation of many of the customs practised at *Samhuinn*, the Celtic Festival of the Dead, held on the same calendar day.

In medicine, too, the Celts have played their part in our island heritage. Quite apart from its enshrinement in stories, music and strange country games, Celtic knowledge lies at the heart of much of the country medicine widely employed before the advent of the National Health Service, usually peddled by local 'cunning folk'. Warts and other disfigurements could be cured; cattle were freed from ringworm and other infections. Charms were concocted to stimulate a hesitant lover or discourage an unwanted one. On the darker side, curse magic or 'blasting' could be used against an enemy. The practitioners of these arts, the so-called 'white witches', reacted to the blessings of twentieth-century science in many different ways.

Charlie tells a magnificent story of a turn-of-the-century Cornish 'cunning woman', Granny Boswell, and her first encounter with a car. Granny, who was drunk at the time, was at first entranced by the strange monster. Swaying in front of it, she was heartily blasted with the horn by an angry driver. Shrieking with fury, she rained curses on the unfortunate vehicle and predicted it would never get further than the end of the street. Halfway there it broke down with a loud bang, and had to be towed away by a man with a horse.

I finally introduced Charlie to the Bart when I arranged for the three of us to go sea trout fishing at night on the Fowey. We met in The London Inn in St Neot at about ten on a warm July evening. I felt that if we had met earlier, too much Guinness would have been consumed for us to have any real chance of sensible fishing.

Midnight found us sitting on the banks of the weir pool. The moon had not yet risen, and the night was solidly dark. Under Charlie's expert tuition I had by now become reasonably proficient at fishing the worm. The Bart had never done it, and was being tutored by Charlie in this arcane skill.

'If you feel anything you must let it have line,' Charlie told him. 'Then, when you think it's had the worm for long enough, you give it a good pull.'

With Charlie's murmurings in the background, I sat fishing in peaceful contentment listening to the soft night sounds. In the distance a fox barked, and leaves rustled as a zephyr of night wind touched them. Further up the pool a fish jumped, and the ripples lapped against the bank. I pulled in the line and re-baited with another worm. Suddenly I felt something rub against my back. The hairs on the nape of my neck begin to rise as all my superstitions came to the fore: I was back in the caves with my primordial ancestors. I sat quite still and then I felt it again, only this time it was a push against my shoulder blades. Overcome with panic, I leapt to my feet and kicked out blindly.

'What the bloody hell do you think you're doing?' demanded Charlie. 'Why are you kicking my dog?'

I sat down sheepishly and tried to explain, while the lurcher cowered at Charlie's feet. The Bart was rolling on the ground laughing.

'Why do you think I have him here?' asked Charlie. He lowered his voice to a whisper. 'He keeps away the big bad wolf.'

The Bart sat up. 'The Beast of Bodmin,' he said under his breath. 'Have you ever seen him?'

'Yes, I have.' Charlie looked away and started fiddling with the fishing bag. A tawny owl hooted in the darkness, and somewhere in the distance there was the squeal of a rabbit as a fox attacked. He paused, and then went on. 'It was about ten years ago. I was out on my own fishing in the twilight for salmon at Golitha Falls, just on the edge of the moor. Suddenly the dog started barking. Wouldn't shut up. I looked up and there, just across the river, was this bloody great cat sitting on a rock. It was a huge black panther and it just sat there, staring across at me. Would have only taken one leap, I reckon, and it would have got me.'

The Bart shifted uncomfortably. I looked around nervously. Was that really a log, or . . .

'What did you do?' I asked in a low voice.

'Well, we both sat still and stared at each other for about thirty seconds,' Charlie continued slowly, 'and all the time that dog was barking its head off. Then The Beast stood up and slowly slunk off into the bushes. I sat there shaking like a leaf – I don't mind telling you, I've never been so scared in all my life, and I don't scare easy. Then I ran to my car and drove as fast as possible to the nearest pub for comfort.' He shivered, remembering. 'Got a fair few drinks for that story, though, I can tell you!' he added more cheerfully.

Just then the Bart stood up. 'I've got a bite!' he whispered excitedly. 'I can feel the line running through my fingers.'

'Let it run until I tell you,' said Charlie. 'Here, let me feel it.' He put his hand across and gently held the line. 'I don't think it's a sea trout,' he said. 'It's not a strong enough bite – but give it a pull, and we'll see.'

The Bart struck hard, and a very small eel flew over his head. He retrieved it from the brambles, cut the hook out of it, tied on another, re-baited, cursed thoroughly, and wiped the slime off his hands. Anxious to change the subject and give himself a chance to recover his dignity, he asked Charlie what else he knew about The Beast.

'Well, the government and officials, they all deny it exists,' he said. 'But I tell you, there are definitely several of them. There have been too many sightings by too many honest people, too many unexplained footprints found in mud and snow, too many lambs and sheep killed and their remains found half-eaten. Us locals, we know that The Beast exists all right. My dog, the one you tried to kick just now, will suddenly start barking when I'm out nights like this one. Now, he doesn't do that unless there's a really good reason. It might just be a fox or a badger that's got him going, but I know their smell. The Beast, he smells different. Sort of rank and bitter . . .' He stopped and cocked his head, listening to something only he could hear. Suddenly the old lurcher growled softly. Charlie put his hand on his dog's head and the serene summer night seemed a little less welcoming. As the moon rose, the shadows of the trees took on strange shapes, and all at once I no longer wanted to catch a sea trout.

'Come on, Charlie,' I said. 'Let's go home.'

Over the years Charlie and I have become very close. Under the rough country exterior is a highly intelligent and sensitive man. In his tiny cottage, which always looks as if a bomb has hit it, is a very good, impressionistic oil painting of his favourite fishing spot, Golitha Falls, on the River Fowey in south-east Cornwall. The first time I saw it I was drawn to it immediately. 'Who did that?' I asked.

Charlie shrugged. 'I did,' he replied, 'but I don't like it. I wasn't in the right mood to do it properly. Come with me and I'll show you some more.' He took me through to a back room where, higgledy-piggledy on the floor, leaning against furniture and hung haphazardly on the walls, were about fifty oil paintings. All of them were scenes of local Cornish rivers, lakes and hills. And all of them were very good.

I looked round, astonished. 'Where did you train?' I asked.

Charlie just laughed. 'Train?' he said. 'I wouldn't know what to do with training!'

The interior of Charlie's eighteenth-century cottage is messy but homely. A stone wood-burner that he built keeps the place very warm; there are stone flags on the floor, fishing rods hanging from racks in the ceiling, and a table stained with mug rings by the cracked window. It's comfortable, but it lacks, to put it mildly, the feminine touch. There have been many women in Charlie's life, but he has never married and has no children to which he will admit. No woman can hold him for long, as he is fiercely independent and either they tire of his lack of commitment or he tires of them. None the less, it is easy to understand why women find him so attractive. To see photographs of Charlie as a young man is to see an Adonis with a dark, moody face and the high cheekbones of the true Celt.

Because he is one of that rare breed of men who truly love women, Charlie has the great gift of managing to remain friends with all his ex-lovers. Over the years the Bart and I have met a number of his former partners and have marvelled at – and envied, in my case! – the fondness they plainly have for him. It's a fondness that is mingled with respect and a certain wariness, as the Bart and I found out when we met one of his former girl-friends, Lillian Oaktree, in a local pub.

Lil, now in her early fifties and beautiful, with long auburn hair, high cheekbones and translucent skin, is Dutch by origin but has lived in Britain since she was twenty-nine. 'From an early age', she told us, 'I knew that I wanted to live here. As a child my dreams were always of standing on a high cliff and looking out over the ocean. When I came to Cornwall,' she went on dreamily, 'I felt I had come home. It felt right. When I first walked on Bodmin Moor my feet sang.'

From dreams we went on to 'spirit guides', and by now the

Bart and I were feeling rather out of our depth. Eventually Charlie got up. 'Feet singing? Spirit guide?' He snorted. 'I'd rather have a drink than listen to all that crap.' He made for the bar, fast followed by an apologetic-looking Bart. Lil seemed a bit put out.

I liked Lil enormously, but I was surprised that she and the down-to-earth Charlie should have stuck together for six years.

'Didn't Charlie find all your strange beliefs and psychic powers difficult to cope with?' I asked. 'It's not his thing at all, surely? Is that why you split up?'

Lil looked at me as if I were completely mad. 'Don't you know?' she said. 'I thought you said you knew Charlie well?'

'Well, I do –' I began hotly, but she interrupted me.

'Charlie is the most psychic person I have ever met!' Lil said, staring at me pityingly. 'He has incredible powers – like all Celts – they come from his mother's bloodline.' She lowered her voice. 'Charlie's Mum is famous locally. They call her "The White Witch of Cornwall" – but Charlie's gifts are far greater than hers. He can pick up your hand, and without even reading the palm describe four or five generations of your ancestors, detailed physical descriptions and everything. He also has an uncanny ability to forecast the future, and doesn't need the tea leaves his mother uses, just to be near someone – and the reading comes through clear as a bell. Just don't you tell her I said that,' she added hastily. 'She's very jealous of Charlie.'

'Go on,' I said, leaning forward. I was desperate to hear more – but Lil had already clammed up.

'If you want to know about it, you must ask Charlie himself,' she said. 'If you don't know already, he may not want you to know, and it wouldn't be fair on him for me to tell you.'

Eventually Charlie and the Bart rejoined us with another round of drinks and we went on to talk about other things. But I couldn't get what Lil had told me out of my mind. On the way out, I took Charlie aside.

'I didn't know about your psychic gifts,' I said to him quietly. 'What's that all about?'

Charlie started. 'Lil been talking? I'm not saying anything in here. It's too public. Come round tomorrow morning if you really want to know about it.'

The Bart and I arrived at the cottage after breakfast and were greeted by the usual myriad dogs.

'You feeling a bit trouty, Mike?' Charlie asked with a broad grin on his face. He was obviously in a mischievous mood. 'I thought you might have been skanking off skibbing.'

I looked askance at him. 'What?'

'With your passion for English, I reckoned you'd be interested in a bit of pure Cornish,' he said with a wicked grin. ' "Trouty" means sexy,' he explained, 'and "skanking off skibbing" translates as disappearing for a bonk on the quiet. The way you and Lil were looking at each other last night, I wouldn't have been a bit surprised.'

I denied it vehemently. Determined not to let Charlie go off on a tangent, I pulled up two stools to the kitchen table, and the Bart and I sat down. 'Now look here, Charlie,' I said, 'I want to know all about these psychic powers.'

It was the first time during all the years that we had known each other that I ever saw Charlie embarrassed. 'I hate talking about it,' he said, reddening slightly. 'It's something I wish to hell I didn't have.'

'How long have you had it?' I asked.

Charlie was silent for a moment, and pensively rolled a cigarette. 'I was three when it first happened,' he said. 'My granny was going to baby-sit while my parents went out to the pub. I can remember screaming and crying and begging them not to go, because granny would be ill. They thought, quite rightly, that it was just a tantrum, and took no notice. They had only been gone an hour when my gran had a stroke. When they got home, they found me clinging to her, and trying to revive her with glasses of water.' Charlie paused and stared at the fireplace, and I felt a superstitious tingle run down my spine.

'When did it happen again?' the Bart prompted him. I wondered how he was so certain that it *had* happened again. Charlie appreciated that too.

'I can see you understand these things better than Mike,' he said. 'The next time, I was five years old. My dad and granddad always went to the pub on my granddad's motorbike of a Sunday evening to play darts. In those days, especially on a Sunday, everyone got dressed up. My granddad used to put on a highly polished pair of black shoes. Suddenly, about an hour before they were due to leave, I had one of my "feelings". I was certain that something awful was going to happen. I rushed upstairs and hid my granddad's shoes because I knew that he wouldn't go to the pub without them. But he guessed that I'd taken them, and forced me to tell him where they were. Even then, I was howling and bawling. I remember clinging round his legs, and my mother pulling me away. I told them that I'd had the same feelings as when my granny died. Now, my mother had "the gift" as well, and she was shocked and begged them not to go to the pub, too. But they took no notice – a child and a silly woman, they thought – and off they went on the bike with granddad driving and my father riding pillion. It was a bitterly cold winter's evening and there was ice on the road. They'd only gone a mile when the bike skidded out of control and hit a tree. My father was badly hurt but granddad was killed.' Silence fell. The Bart and I looked at each other. Charlie got up and went over to the sink. 'Coffee?' he asked us.

'And it has happened again?' I asked, taking the cup Charlie passed me.

'Yes,' said Charlie, 'it has. I was stupid enough, when I was pissed, to tell the boys in the pub about it. Of course, they didn't really understand, and one of them asked me to read his palm. Well, I can't do that, and I don't want to do it anyway, but just to stop them pulling my leg and talking about it I took his hand and turned it over. I didn't look at his palm, but I immediately had a "feeling". "You be careful come October," I told him, and then I went home. The next morning I regretted it as soon as I woke up, but eventually I shrugged it off and thought no more about it.' There was a long pause.

'You can't leave us there,' I said. 'What happened?'

'In October he died of cancer – although there had been no sign of that when we was in the pub.'

'So, what do you feel about this gift?' asked the Bart, gently.

'I fucking hate it,' replied Charlie. 'Wouldn't you?'

We both thought about it for a while and then: 'Let's go to the pub,' said Charlie. 'Cheer ourselves up.'

Once in the pub and with a few rounds tucked behind us, I felt bold enough to ask Charlie more about his life. I'd begun to realise that despite the time we had shared fishing side by side on river banks, I didn't know anywhere near as much about my friend as I thought I did.

'Well, of course I was hardly ever at school,' Charlie began. 'I was always playing truant so that I could go fishing. The local poacher was my best friend. He always carried a fishing rod, but he never used it. His speciality was gaffing the big salmon that lay under the bank, then selling them in the local market. We got good money in those days, mind you. His favourite were the huge greybacks that only run in November and December. I've seen them up to forty pounds in weight, and the river is pretty empty of fishermen at that time of year, so it's ripe for a little naughtiness.'

'Can you still catch the greybacks?' asked the Bart. 'I'd love to have a go if you'd take us.'

'I'll take you tomorrow,' said Charlie. 'November or December, that's the best time, but no gaffing, mind you – I'm a reformed character now.' He paused to take a drink and then went on: 'When I officially left school I went to work for a local farmer who owned a thousand acres of Bodmin Moor. He employed me to look after his cattle and horses, both of which were virtually wild animals. My main job was to round them up for the sales, and to stop people from rustling them. I did this all on a horse, so you could easily describe me as a cowboy in those days. Now, of course, it would all be done with a quad bike and be much easier; but I loved the riding.'

'Was there a lot of rustling in those days?' I asked, intrigued by the thought of Charlie as a cowboy.

'Oh yes.' said Charlie. 'If you could manage to get them cows into a lorry they were worth a lot of money – probably six or seven hundred pounds each. You only had to steal ten animals and it was a good night's work.' He paused. 'I remember one night when I hadn't been at the job long. It were the lorry I saw first, miles in the middle of the moor it were, with the tailboard down and a barbed wire fence leading out in a huge "V" shape away from it to guide the cattle in. Well, I knew that trouble was afoot, and I hid beside the truck. Then I heard the cattle coming and I counted six go in. I waited 'til they was all done, and then I confronted the two men who was driving them. I only had a cudgel, but I waved it at them fiercely. They stood like statues, they was so surprised.

Then one of them says: "That you Charlie?" And I recognised my friend the salmon poacher.'

'What on earth did you do?' asked the Bart, horrified. 'I couldn't run in a mate. It would be like me handing in the Bounder, and he's deserved it enough times.'

'No more'n could I,' replied Charlie. 'But what was I to do? Eventually we agreed that he would let the cattle go and we'd say no more about it. He went into the truck and drove them out. But I tell you what – I only counted five go out, so he made a bit of cash for his night's work. And I felt that I'd paid him back a bit for all the money he'd split with me at the salmon. And nobody would miss one beast.'

The Bart and I laughed, and I went to buy another round.

'One day,' Charlie went on when we were settled again, 'I saw an advertisement in the local paper from the Forestry Commission for someone to take over the felling of the trees in a section of their land, and then to clear the wood. It was good money, and I told them that I had been doing it for ages, though I had never seen a chainsaw in me life up 'til then. They hired me, and I learnt the trade. Then I decided to do it on my own, as I hate being told what to do by anyone. I approached a local landowner and asked if I could buy the timber rights on some of his land. He was knocking off my auntie at the time, so was only too happy to oblige. Think he felt he owed it as they'd been together at least ten years. Every Sunday they met up and he used to tell his wife he was going to church. Only hymn they sang were "Abide with me".' He stopped and took a long appreciative draught of his Guinness. 'Anyway,' he continued, 'I've been in timber ever since and that's where I make my real money. Of course I take people out fishing and some of the townies buy two days of my life, but that doesn't make me a living – it's just great fun.'

The Bart lent forward over the table. 'Now, Charlie,' he said, 'what about all the mystery of Cornwall, the witches and the Celtic legends, that I've been reading about?'

Charlie was not to be drawn so easily. 'Only Celts I know are like the two fish I caught last week,' he replied. 'They were marked nicely red, just like that bugger over there by the bar.' He pointed at a heavy-set man laying down the law to a group of locals. ('Kelts', by the way, are salmon which have spawned and return to the sea.)

Charlie was taking the piss. 'Come on,' I said. 'I know you're proud of your Cornish Celtic blood – and you're as Pagan as all hell!'

Charlie gave one of those impish smiles he uses to avoid difficult questions. 'All right, I'll admit it,' he said. 'I'm Pagan and proud of it.'

'Ah,' said the Bart, rubbing his hands together. 'Your Mum – is she really a White Witch?'

'Yes, she is – and she just revels in it,' said Charlie. 'She loves the publicity, and she's very good at curing ringworm in cattle and warts on people. If you like, I'll arrange for you to go and see her tomorrow.'

'Can she cure warts without seeing the person?' I asked nervously. I was harbouring a few beauties, but was suddenly shy of meeting the White Witch face to face.

'Over the phone,' said Charlie. That wicked grin of his spread over his face. 'Especially if you've got a credit card handy.'

The next day the three of us set out for Common Moor. I had made more than the usual effort with my *toilette* and the Bart was, of course, as suave as usual – but I was most surprised of all to see Charlie wearing a clean shirt. When we arrived at the tiny bungalow, I was glad I was wearing my second-best neckerchief. To say the White Witch had a beady eye was an understatement.

Charlie's mum was a sprightly 89-year-old. Disappointingly, she didn't look anything like my idea of a witch at all – in fact, she appeared very ordinary – except for her eyes, which were alert and piercing. She shook our hands, invited us in and, after she had poured us a disappointingly ordinary cup of tea, I plucked up the courage to ask her how she had discovered that she had psychic powers.

'I was a postwoman for many years,' she said, 'and of course that involved visiting a great many farms. I've always loved cattle, and one day I stroked one of the farmer's beasts. The next day when I went to the same farm, the farmer asked me to stroke some more of his cattle, ones that he picked out. Well, I thought this a bit odd, ringworm was very common in those days, and later he told me he had noticed that all the cows I had touched had been cured of the ringworm. Word spread, and soon all the farmers wanted me to cure their animals. They thought I was wonderful, and used to give me a small tip as I left. The same', she said, and gave me a penetrating look, 'went for warts on humans.'

'But do you have to see the person and touch the wart in order to cure it?' I asked. I was very ready to make a run for it.

'No,' she replied. 'I can do it just as easily over the phone. I just have to concentrate on the *particular part* of the body where the wart is.' She looked at me again. A huge smile spread over her wrinkled face, and she leant forward. 'The other day,' she said, fixing me with those strange eyes, 'a woman called. She said that her husband had grown a huge wart on his penis. It was "*most uncomfortable*" she said, if you know what I mean . . . Although' – Charlie's Mum cackled like one of the witches in Macbeth – 'I thought as it might have been quite an asset! Anyway, this woman asked if I could cure it. "Send me a photograph of your husband," I said, "and I'll do it straight away." Well, she sent me a photo of him, and he was this ugly little man and I had to imagine his penis with a wart on it!' She cackled again. 'I couldn't decide whether to think of it up or down.' She collapsed into peals of laughter.

In the car on the way back to the pub I couldn't contain my curiosity. 'Have either of you ever had a wart on your cock?' I asked the other two.

'No,' said the Bart firmly.

'I did,' said Charlie.

'And did your Mum cure it?' I asked.

'I wouldn't bloody well let her near it.'

Later on in the pub Charlie said, 'You know, all that second sight stuff, that isn't me. I hate it. I'd much rather be in the woods or beside a river. When I take people fishing they buy a day of my life, but they don't really understand the river, the fish or me. I try to explain it, but it's quite beyond them and they can't wait to get their mobile phones out of their pockets and return to the world that they know.' He was silent for a moment and then perked up. 'Tell you what,' he said, 'why don't we have a look for a greyback tomorrow?'

When I awoke it was a beautiful mid November day with a weak sun glinting on the last of the autumn leaves and a soft zephyr of a westerly wind. When Charlie collected us after breakfast, he seemed to know exactly where to go. The woods were thick and the footing slippery and treacherous after recent rain, but Charlie said that the water was just right for the greybacks. As we passed the falls, there was a long stretch of bank with a tree at one end. Charlie stopped for a second his face alert and intent.

He was all but pointing like a dog. I could swear his ears twitched.

'If there's one here,' he said, 'it'll be just this side of the tree, right up against the bank.'

We kept well back, and both of us stared hopefully into the fast-flowing river. At first it seemed that the lie was empty, and then the Bart gasped. It was the sheer size of the fish that had confused us. It could have been a big black rock or a sunken log – but then I noticed a massive tail moving leisurely in the current. Charlie, who handles his tiny fibreglass rod (£5 at any sporting tackle shop) with the delicacy of a calligrapher's quill, tossed the worm upstream with hardly a splash. At first the giant salmon ignored the bait, then our hearts stopped as we saw the white of a mammoth mouth opening to suck in the morsel. Charlie let the fish hold the worm for a minute and then, when he was sure that it was well down, he struck. To my amazement, nothing happened. There were no mighty splashings, no heart-stopping runs. The rod bent, but the fish remained where it was.

'He's a big bugger,' said Charlie. 'Could be as much as thirty pounds.'

'What will you do?' I asked.

'Well,' said Charlie, 'I'm not waiting here all night. Why don't you kick him in the arse?'

At first I thought he was joking but then, realising that he was serious, I dangled a foot in the water and gently nudged the massive tail. All hell broke loose. With the surging strength of a Polaris submarine, the greyback turned and headed for the falls. The reel screamed and the salmon turned just as it reached the waterfall, went round a rock, and the line broke. We watched as the bow wave surged past us, and then there was a pregnant silence.

'Pity we didn't bring the gaff,' said Charlie.

12

December

CHRISTMAS

And is it true? And is it true?
The most tremendous tale of all,
Seen in a stained-glass window's hue,
A Baby in an ox's stall?
The Maker of the stars and sea
Become a Child on earth for me?

JOHN BETJEMAN, 'Christmas', 1954

I have never yet spent Christmas in a city. For me the festival demands the warmth, friendship and beauty of the country village I remember from my childhood. The excitement of going to bed on Christmas Eve; the hanging-up of the largest shooting stocking available ('Don't you dare lose that. I'll need it on Boxing Day!'); and the determination not go to sleep, so as to catch Father Christmas in the act. I never did stay awake. Every year I woke up to the thrill of the bulging stocking, never knowing what it contained. Then smoked salmon and scrambled eggs for breakfast ('I think that was a fifteen-pounder from the Dee') and being made to go to church, where the decrepit vicar once wished my family 'Happy Easter' on Christmas Day. In my memory those Christmas days were always cold. There was a heavy frost on the grass, which crunched underfoot, and cock pheasants strutting arrogantly on the lawn. Little did they know . . .

Lunch was always a huge turkey that had gone into the oven at 4 a.m. that morning. Once my uncle, who had had one too many glasses of sherry, tripped over the dog and rolled on the floor with the bird. Spike the Labrador pounced but my aunt, who had been the early-riser, was quicker, and grabbed both the turkey and my uncle before there was a disaster. There were stories and laughter among friends and relations, for there were always at least a dozen staying for the holiday. For me the best part of the day, even from a very early age, was the traditional reading at the cracker-festooned table of Oscar Wilde's *Selfish Giant*, arguably the greatest fairy tale that has ever been written. The wonderful ending to the story, when the Christ Child says to the dying giant: 'You let me play once in your garden. Today you shall come with me to my garden, which is Paradise', to me epitomises the whole spirit of Christmas.

I'm a sceptic about organised religion, but both the Bart and I have a soft spot for the Church of England. As he says: 'It is the bastard child of a king's lust and a pope's obstinacy and yet there is a gentleness, tolerance and essential Englishness about it that appeals to me. It doesn't rant or rave or preach hellfire. Anyone and everyone is welcome through its portals and I, who am essentially agnostic, am very fond of it.' I agree entirely – although I've known very few churchmen who genuinely had the true gift of virtue. Perhaps the one who had the most profound effect on me was the vicar of Pyrton in Oxfordshire, the village in which I grew up. Even then I recognised him as someone special. He had taken over from the old vicar (the one who thought Christmas was Easter), who had at last gently succumbed to Alzheimer's.

The Reverend Richard had the beautiful Anglo-Saxon surname of Mickaelroth. He was a man in his mid forties with a fine-featured face and dark hair. But it was his eyes that were different: they were piercingly blue and seemed to blaze with religious zeal, yet when he talked it was quietly and hesitatingly, and there was an aura about him which spoke of kindness, gentleness and love. He fulfilled few, however, of what would nowadays be considered the key functions of a vicar. He did not rush about the parish doing Good Works; there was no Mrs Mickaelroth to run the Women's Institute and comfort unhappy wives; and he quite often forgot some important duties.

We had been expecting old Mrs Taylor to die for several months. She was in her nineties and had been bedridden for a long time. Eventually, in the early hours of a bitterly cold November night, she succumbed. Her family had lived in the village for centuries, so that almost everyone was in the church for her funeral. All were in their best Sunday clothes, the coffin stood in the aisle, the choir and organist waited to sing the first hymn, and the usual baby was crying. But there was no vicar. The congregation began to grow restless. Eventually my uncle stood up rather sheepishly. 'I think I know where he'll be,' he told the gathered throng. He left the church and hurried off towards his lake, only two minutes' walk from the church.

The Reverend Mr Mickaelroth was a passionate fisherman: my uncle's guess proved correct. There, sitting on an old milking stool, in gum boots and a torn tweed jacket, was the vicar, contentedly watching a pike-float bobbing merrily near a reed bed. My Uncle Jack was an old-school colonel of the Edwardian era and would normally have given the vicar a strong piece of his mind but, as he said afterwards: 'For some reason I couldn't chastise him. It would have been like tearing a strip off St Peter.' Richard Mickaelroth wound in his tackle, leant his rod against the old cedar tree and walked back to the church. As he made his entrance everyone looked round. 'I'm so sorry,' he said, 'I completely forgot. I went fishing instead. It's a pastime on which some of Our Lord's friends were rather keen, and so am I.' He then conducted the service with such passion, feeling and sensitivity that everyone forgot that he was wearing his fishing clothes. The village not only forgave him, they adored him.

Mr Mickaelroth saved his best mistake for Christmas Eve. The capture of the enormous pike in my uncle's lake had become the focus of his life. After Sunday Matins he used to rush straight from the church to the lake, still in his cassock, and hurl out his live

bait, which he kept in the font for easy access. By this time the elo-
quence of his services had spread and their fame had reached the
ears of the Earl of Watlington, who on Richard Mickaelroth's first
Christmas Eve in the village had booked him to christen his son.
What the earl had not heard of, however, was the vicar's penchant
for fishing – or his forgetfulness. He was therefore somewhat surprised to have his heir, the infant Lord Chinnor, sprinkled with
minnows and baptised with roach. Known neither for his humour
nor his charity, after the service the earl nevertheless invited the
vicar to fish Watlington Castle moat whenever he wished.

That first Christmas of Richard Mickaelroth's at Pyrton the
church seemed, to my twelve-year-old eyes, to be at its most
lovely. Great bunches of holly decorated the pulpit and font, children's paper chains hung between the beams, and someone had
placed an optimistic cluster of mistletoe over the porch. And it
was packed. The whole village was there, as well as people who
had come from distant parishes. They were standing in the aisles
and doorways to hear the vicar conduct his service. They were
not disappointed for he excelled himself, explaining the beauty
and wonder of the Christmas story so simply and with such
power that children stopped crying and listened and grown-ups
listened and cried. Even the Bart, who had joined us for
Christmas and rather pretentiously claimed to be an atheist, was
seen to wipe his eyes, although he alleged it was a draught that
had made them water.

Then it was back to the manor for Christmas lunch. Richard
Mickaelroth had cast his allure over my uncle and aunt and had
been invited to join us. As we walked past the lake there was a scattering of small fry on the surface as a big pike struck, and I saw the
vicar looking with longing. 'No,' said Uncle Jack, not unkindly.
'You can bloody well wait until tomorrow.'

What I had not known until then was that Richard Mickaelroth had been padre to one of the fighter squadrons during the war, and so had known a great many of The Few. Over Christmas lunch I asked him where he had learnt to fish. He told me he had found out that some of his squadron were keen on the sport. 'To take their minds off the misery of the Battle of Britain', he told us, 'I found a lake near the station and got permission for them to fish it. I didn't fish myself but then one of the young pilots, who was mad about it, took me with him. He was very kind to me and taught me all about angling and I became, almost instantly, hooked. He was shot down in 1940 and spent the war in a prison camp. He managed to escape six months before the war in Europe ended. His name was Hugh Falkus.'

My young ears were suddenly alert. 'Hugh Falkus?' I asked. 'I'm sure he's a friend of my father's. I think they flew fighters together before the war.' And indeed that turned out to have been the case. But from that holy and charismatic priest came some significant details of the man who came to have more influence on my life than anyone else.

I had of course known of Hugh Falkus for most of my life, but it was not until I was in my early forties that we became firm friends. I had always hero-worshipped him from afar. I had seen the films *Salmo the Leaper* and *Self Portrait of a Happy Man*, I had read the books *Salmon Fishing*, *Sea Trout Fishing* and the little-known *The Stolen Years*, which I always thought was the best, but I had never spent any time with him.

For fifteen years I had run my fish and game company in London, supplying delicacies to directors' dining rooms in the City and the West End. This had grown from being just me and a van to a fleet of 22 vans and their drivers. Over the years I had found myself doing more and more that which I had sworn I would not do: sitting in an office and administering the company. I therefore sold it, and celebrated for a boozy fortnight after the contract was signed. The 'phone rang in the flat just as I was thinking of going out for yet another drunken lunch.

'The Chelsea Home for Destitute Prostitutes,' I announced foolishly.

'Is that Little Daunty?' asked a distinguished voice. 'I can't call you "Daunty". That's your father's name. It's Hugh Falkus here.' I mentally stood to attention. 'Now listen,' continued Hugh, 'you've done very well, but what are you going to do now?'

'Very little for a year,' I replied. 'I intend to go round the world, do a bit of fishing and enjoy myself.'

'Very bad idea,' said Hugh. 'You'll probably drink too much and almost certainly get the clap. Much better to come and work with me. We'll have a lot of fun together.'

I couldn't believe my luck. To be asked to work with my hero was beyond my wildest dreams. I accepted immediately, and from that strange beginning came a friendship that changed my life. I loved Hugh as a father. We shared a passion for many things: fishing, of course, but also shooting, the countryside, literature, poetry, and women. Hugh and I used to sit in his study after dinner until the early hours, with the inevitable glass of whisky, discussing every topic imaginable, but always coming back to our mutual passion for poetry. He loved Chesterton, whom he once met as a very small boy in a pub in Fleet Street with his father. The great man had apparently patted Hugh on the head and then moved as far away from him as possible in case he was sick on his shoes. He used to quote great chunks of his poem 'The Secret People':

We only know the last sad squires ride slowly towards the sea,
And a new people takes the land: and still it is not we.
. . . .
But we are the people of England; and we have not spoken yet.
Smile at us, pay us, pass us. But do not quite forget.

'Doesn't that epitomise England?' he used to say.

Hugh also enjoyed Dylan Thomas, whom he had met in London before the war. At that time Hugh used to work for the BBC, and at weekends he would travel by train to the river that was to become his home, the Cumbrian Esk. Here he relaxed and caught the fish that later made him famous, the sea trout. On a Sunday night he would travel back to London, taking his catch with him. At lunchtime the next day he displayed it proudly on the bar of the local pub near the BBC and encouraged anyone who wanted some to help themselves. One Monday the sea trout were spread out, and Hugh surrounded by an appreciative audience. A North Countryman, not knowing the tradition, looked at the show. 'Are those roach?' he asked. Before anyone could put him right, a male voice with a lilting Welsh accent split the horrified silence. 'No, they're sewin, the finest fish that swims,' said Dylan Thomas.

Hugh was never an easy man. His mind was too quick and demanding for the niceties of life and he did not suffer fools. Nor did he tolerate pretension. Once while fishing a river I met a very amusing middle-aged peer. As is often the case in fishing lodges, after dinner we had been discussing women in general and our wives in particular. The peer had been silent during this idiotic chatter until there was a small silence, when he interjected in a sad and doleful voice. 'Do you know,' he remarked wistfully, 'I have never seen my wife naked.' As they had four children, my imagination ran riot. He was, however, a very kind and funny man – a great fan of Hugh's, too – and extended an invitation to me to fish his piece of Tweed if I was ever in the area. Later that year Hugh and I were fishing on the Junction Pool of that same river, and I suggested that we should ask the 'Luckless Lord', as I had christened him, and his wife to dine with us at our hotel. Apart from anything else, I badly wanted to meet his modest wife.

I briefed Hugh. 'I'm going to seat you next to the Lady

Margaret at dinner,' I said. 'And for God's sake chat her up and be nice to her. She and her husband own one of the best beats on Tweed, and we'll be invited to fish if all goes well.'

'Don't you worry, Daunty,' replied Hugh. 'I'm very good at that sort of thing.'

We sat down to dinner, and it soon became apparent why the Lady Margaret had never displayed herself to her husband. She was an overweight and overbearing battle-axe, stupid and boring. She was also ridiculously pretentious.

'Do you know,' she said, turning to Hugh, 'I do a lot of Good Works. I visit all those poor gals who have gorn orf the rails and ended up in prison. Many of them are, of course' – and here she whispered the word as if it was very daring – '*prostitutes.*'

Because I knew him so well, I could see that Hugh was about to say something awful. I kicked him hard under the table.

'Why are you kicking me, Daunty?' he enquired loudly. Then he turned back to the Lady Margaret. 'Please tell me something, Lady Margaret,' he said. 'Didn't you ever have a fuck before you married?'

Not surprisingly, we never were invited to fish the Famous Beat.

To his close circle of great friends Hugh was enormously kind. 'In this life,' he used to say to me, 'kindness is all.' And he lived by his own maxim. On that same trip to the Junction Pool we had been fishing all day and had had some success, with eight fish between us including two twenty-pounders (we were sharing a rod), and had returned to the bar to celebrate. As we were drinking our first whisky the telephone behind the bar rang and the barman answered it. He turned to me. 'It's for you, Mr Daunt,' he said. 'Take it in the booth in Reception.' My mood plummeted. I had been dreading this 'phone call. I knew that it would be from my wife, and we were going through a very bad patch. I picked up the receiver. 'Hello,' I said. A stream of abuse hurtled down the wires. 'Darling,' I said, in my most conciliatory tones, 'if you tell me quietly what the matter is, I'll try and sort it out.' There was another series of screeches from the 'phone and then a click as the receiver was slammed down. I walked back miserably to the bar.

Hugh immediately saw by my face that something was very wrong.

'That was my wife,' I said. 'I don't know why these bloody women bother to ring up if all they are going to do is scream.'

'Oh, I understand it very well,' said Hugh. 'You see, every time you go fishing they always think that you've got another woman with you.' And the previous year, on one of the courses we ran together, he had indeed been seduced by an attractive forty-year-old. There was a long pause, and then a wicked smile spread over his face. 'And, of course, they're usually right!'

The most extraordinary Christmas of my life was spent with Hugh. I had arrived at 4.30 p.m. on Christmas Eve, 1993 to pass the holiday with him and his wife Kathy at Cragg Cottage, their home just outside Ravenglass in Cumbria. I had been asked specifically to arrive early. 'Any particular reason?' I enquired, because I had noted something in Hugh's voice that boded a plot. There was that huge enthusiasm with which he threw himself into everything, however mundane. 'Wait 'til you get here,' he replied. 'All I'm going to say is that I've got a tremendous plan, and you'll love it.'

I arrived promptly, and was ushered quickly into his study.

'Now listen, Daunty,' he said. 'I'm reviving an old tradition. You and I are going carol singing tonight. We'll go round the neighbours, sing for them, and collect our well-earned tributes.'

'Er, tributes?' I asked uncertainly.

'Well, whisky, of course. What do you expect? Strawberry jam? You'll sing and I'll play my banjo to accompany you. Thus we'll have a small snifter at every house we go to. Talking of which, let's have a quick one now while we rehearse.'

I didn't demur, as I always found that with Hugh there was little point, as his huge love of life carried everyone along with him.

'Right,' said Hugh, holding his very old banjo at the ready. 'Here we go.' And he broke into a considerably jazzed-up version of 'Good King Wenceslas'. I sang loudly, and we managed one verse before I forgot the words.

'Brilliant,' said Hugh. 'That'll do. It's quite good enough. I knew it would be. Let's have another snort.'

'Shouldn't we do something else as well?' I suggested.

'No, no, *no*, Daunty, that's quite enough! We don't want to spoil them. They're bloody lucky to have us at all. Now, we should be able to get round at least ten houses, so we'll have a good evening.'

At six o'clock sharp we left the house to do our rounds.

'Just before we leave,' said Hugh, 'we'll serenade Kathy. She's gone to bed with a headache, but this will wake her up and she'll love it.'

We started 'Good King Wenceslas' again and had hardly reached the Feast of Stephen when Kathy's bedroom window flew open, and with unerring accuracy she flung a china ashtray at us. It struck Hugh a glancing blow on the forehead before smashing on the ground. Kathy's window was firmly slammed shut.

'Oh, my God,' shrieked Hugh, clutching his head. 'She's killed me!'

I inspected the damage, of which there was little – although blood was pouring down his cheek and, as is the case with most head wounds, it wouldn't stop. After I had patched him up we set off into the night, looking a bit battered and already rather the worse for wear. I remember little more of that evening. I know that we reached Hugh's nearest neighbour and sang lustily outside his house before being rescued and given more nourishing whisky, and dinner, and that I am sure is as far as we got. But I do remember driving Hugh home to the tiny, windswept cottage on the bleak fell-side in the early hours of Christmas Day with the snow gently falling on the windscreen. He was singing softly to himself the bawdy version of the German national anthem.

THE BART . . .

If Hugh Falkus taught the Bounder all he knew about fly-fishing – not to mention carol-singing – my father had left me a rather more uncertain legacy. The family estate in Bellarena in Northern Ireland was where I spent my family Christmasses as a teenager, but we were poor as church mice and that made it all the more fun.

Father returned from the Second World War to claim his inheritance on the death of his uncle and aunt, who were wealthy. Great Aunt Flora was a Walter from the family who owned *The Times*, and an extraordinarily forceful character. She had kept the army from destroying the great house during the war by complaining at every conceivable opportunity whenever the war machine offended her sense of civilised behaviour. One day she rang up the Group Captain of the local aerodrome. 'There are annoying little aeroplanes circulating my house and making a terrible noise,' she boomed. 'But they are Spitfires, my lady,' replied the astonished airman, placatingly. 'And what exactly are Spitfires *for*?' demanded Great Aunt Flora. Fighting the Germans must have been an easier business.

My father returned from his last wartime job in the Allied Control Commission in absolute disgrace. This was the time when every German town had a mayor from the conquering Allies, and my father's fluent German, learnt when he was directing films in Berlin in the 1930s – that period Christopher Isherwood captures so well in *Cabaret* – should have made him a natural candidate. But he had got appallingly drunk from the moment he arrived and been sent home in handcuffs, guarded by two large military policemen. Characteristically, he had inveigled them into a bar *en route*, and all three went AWOL for several weeks.

He was still well under the influence by the time he turned up at Bellarena, where Great Aunt Flora was on her last legs. No doubt he hoped to smooth his inheritance, but one night after a particularly long evening at Brolly's pub he decided to show the locals his rusty army .303 rifle, and fired off a scattering of shots through her ladyship's bedroom window. She was not amused and cut him out of her will, so that when she died shortly afterwards he inherited just the house with hardly a stick of furniture, but a sizeable trust fund – worth about £500,000 in today's money. Letting the mansion to a local farmer, who ploughed up the lawn to grow potatoes, my father headed for the bright lights of London and checked in at the Ritz.

The money did not last long. Every day Father would unlock his old bicycle, which he kept chained to the pillars in front of the hotel's Piccadilly entrance, and leave to do a round of the picture galleries by day and serious damage to the clubs and bars by night, until he was broke again. A pompous uncle from my maternal side was sent to sort out the mess, and wrote to my grandmother: 'I have managed to save a little from John's disaster. The Mayer Gallery very kindly took back two dreadful pictures I found under his bed. I received £30 for one by someone called Paul Klee, and £40 for another by an unheard-of Spaniard called Picasso.'

Back home at Bellarena Father led a squalid existence in one of the old estate houses, until he had the bright idea of marrying a county lady who could look after him and get the big house back in order. Dora had been living in an even more impossible mansion on the wild north coast of Donegal and was trying to bring up five daughters on the pittance paid to her by an absconding husband. With relief she accepted Father's proposal and made plans to move her family to Bellarena.

There was only one small hiccup on the way. Father, sent to London to post the banns, got up to his old clubbing tricks. My stepmother-to-be first heard of it from the society column in the *Daily Express*. 'Baronet to marry night club hostess', the paper trumpeted. Somehow, the sultry eighteen-year-old Russian lady was paid off and the wedding, as originally planned, took place. What Natasha would have been like as a stepmother, I never got to find out.

Dora and the girls brought life and fun to Bellarena, and even kept Father partially off the bottle. He grew healthy again, mowing the five acres of lawn (now recovered from the farmer's potatoes) with his old Atco, while we, his willing slaves, humped the grass cuttings into the shrubberies. There was no money to spare for any modern luxuries – no car, no heating, no holidays; but Christmasses were wonderful. I best remember the one just before my sixteenth birthday.

The night before the girls, helped by a smattering of cousins, sat around the huge, scrubbed pine table in the kitchen, the only warm room in the house. The previous evenings had been spent tying up bunches of holly and mistletoe to sell in the local market for a little spending money, but tonight we were working on our own account. I can still see the row of blonde heads bent to their task. As dusk drew in the aged generator which lived in a corner of the stables would thump into life with an asthmatic cough, and a puff of black smoke drift across the cobbled courtyard. Automatically we would look up at the single bulb over the table, which would glow dimly yellow, flicker and then brighten. We all offered up a short prayer to the gods of ancient Lister diesel engines.

The talk around the table was usually of men and making 'good' marriages – Jane Austen would have been very welcome. Most of the girls did pretty well as it turned out, but there were one or two missed chances. My prettiest cousin was denied a proposal from a penniless army subaltern, and forced to marry a local landowner. After leaving the army, the penniless subaltern metamorphosed into a multi-millionaire chairman of a well-known chain of estate agents. I guess you can't win them all.

Christmas morning dawned bright and clear. I scraped away the ice which covered my bedroom windows on the inside: there was still no heating in the house. There was a thick carpet of frost on the lawn and a white cap to Binevenagh, the mountain that dominated the skyline behind the house. I dressed as quickly as I could and ran downstairs.

Morning church was obligatory. We cycled up the winding mountain road to Tamlaghtard, the tiny Protestant chapel that was still filled with family memorials and bore testament to the time when good King James had planted the fertile Magilligan peninsula where we lived, our land originally rented from the Bishop of Derry and Earl of Bristol. He had spent most of his life trundling around Europe in his coach collecting antiques, then having the local hotels named after him in thanks for the enormous tips he left. The name Bellarena – meaning 'beautiful strand' in Italian – had been his idea.

The Service over, there was a mad ride down the mountain and a dash for the kitchen, filled with steam and our occasional but willing helper, Kathleen (a Catholic, so she had gone to Mass early), who as Rex Harrison pointed out in *My Fair Lady* had a laugh that 'would shatter glass', but infectious with it. The girls shooed me out of their way, and I went for a Christmas walk with Father. He was in a good mood for once and full of stories about the 1930s, peopled with its legendary characters: Evelyn Waugh, whose wife he had stolen, the Mitford girls, Oswald Mosley and the British Fascists, my godfather, the writer Anthony Powell, with whom Father had toured Nazi Europe in an open-topped MG, and many more.

By the time we got back, everything was ready. The dining room was set with all that remained of the Heygate finery. An enormous fire roared in the yellow marble fireplace and lit up the purple and gold of our prized Crown Derby dinner service, cracked a little, but still bearing the family crest of a wolf's head. The Heygate pictures, recently cleaned as a favour by one of my father's chums in the Tate, smiled down on us, headed by the first Baronet, Sir William – a well-known Alderman and Lord Mayor of London, who had been personal banker to the Prince Regent and his family.

The meal was traditional, of course, a huge turkey crammed full of chestnuts, picked by Father and me, stuffing mixed with sausage meat and wild sage; countless roast potatoes and a massive bowl of Brussels sprouts. There were not quite enough of the Crown Derby serving dishes left, so we had to make do with an old pudding basin or two. The Christmas pudding was brought in as the light started to fade. Somehow the girls had managed to hide a small bottle of brandy from Father, and a whoosh of blue flame announced its arrival. I noticed my step-mother watching him anxiously in case the smell set him off. As it turned out, she knew her man only too well.

After lunch, it was dressing-up time. By dint of necessity, the girls were brilliant seamstresses. I can still hear the hum of the hand-driven Singer sewing machine, turning to the creak of our wind-up gramophone and its set of scratched records, which lived in the small book-lined nursery, the second warmest room in the house. Tonight the results justified the effort. Shrieks of self-congratulatory excitement rang through the house. They were even nice about my first proper suit, topped with Father's Etonian tie.

The local bus picked us up at the lodge gates – much appreciative chat from the driver – 'My, you're the spitting image of the old Lady Heygate' (they were, of course, no relation) – and we were away. On Christmas night, as always, we were going to our sister house, Drenagh, an even larger and more imposing mansion than Bellarena, owned by Marcus McCausland, my impossibly wild and eccentric cousin. (He was later shot as a spy by the IRA after he decided to celebrate a successful romantic evening with a 3 a.m. drink at an illegal bar in the intensely Republican Bogside of Derry.)

Marcus was in high good humour. Tall and good-looking with a devilishly naughty Irish smile, he had the ladies falling over him in every direction. The customary Drenagh entertainment was Irish reels, the music coming from a local 'squeeze-box' merchant who could be guaranteed to be drunk by midnight, so you had to get your reeling in early. Tonight there was a new addition – case after case of champagne. Where had Marcus found the money, we all wondered. The answer was not long in coming. A slash of white lightning and a booming clap of thunder shook the house, precursers to a downpour of torrential rain. But there was one small difference – it was just as wet inside as out. Water streamed down the walls and spouted in a gush from the ceiling roses. The truth soon emerged: Marcus had sold the lead off the roof to pay for the champagne.

No one minded. It was totally in character, and by now the drink had taken hold. The squeeze-box man played for all his worth until midnight, when as usual, his head bowed over his instrument, he slid to the floor, It was time to catch the last bus. The girls had been working the local 'eligibles' to good effect and there was plenty to talk about on the way home. Outside Brolly's pub we came across a tall figure swaying in the road – it was Father, very much the worse for wear after his own Christmas celebration. A helping hand from the driver got him into the front seat and we were away, the whole group of us stifling our giggles in the back of the bus in case he recognised his own family.

Home again, father was clearly in a cussed mood. The Bellarena drive winds this way and that, but he was determined to take the direct route. This involved wading through a number of deep ditches, overflowing with dark winter flood-water. We watched in amazement as Father's dimly seen figure splashed down one side of each ditch, disappearing completely before emerging dripping up the other. I have rarely seen anything so gloriously funny.

Back in the warm kitchen again, it was time for a long post mortem over mugs of cocoa. The girls were still full of who had said what to whom, but I felt the urge for bed. Lighting a candle – the generator had long since gone to sleep – I crept through the dark house and up the long stairs to my room. Father was still awake somewhere. The odd crash of furniture showed he was re-hanging the pictures, a regular late-night eccentricity of his. I reached my room in peace and closed the curtains on the thick layers of ice on the panes – inside again, as always. Quickly undressing in the freezing cold, I snuggled under the many layers of old army blankets which were Father's only concession to winter. A few deep exhales with my head totally covered built up a comfortable warmth, and sleep came easily. It had been a Christmas to remember.

I inherited Bellarena after father died, bored and lonely once cancer took Dora from him. At first I rather fancied the life of a country squire after ten years in the corporate world, but the excitement soon wore off. The estate had not been farmed for a hundred years and the land was all let. My fellow squires seemed sunk in perpetual whiskey-soaked gloom over the cost of repairing roofs and the price of home-grown strawberries, and the tough Ulster businessmen did not seem very interested in spending time with an amateur ex-management consultant.

I started my career as a salmon smoker out of boredom. The idea of doing something with the natural resources of the area appealed. The tidal waters of a good salmon river flowed past the house, and we had the netting rights.

The sea lough at the end of the estate was also crammed with old mussel beds, and entrepreneurial folk were talking about reviving the oyster industry. Thinking back on happy memories of picnicking by Irish loughs with the Bounder and smoking the delicious pink-fleshed trout in a little Abu smokebox, I had a blinding flash of inspiration – I would start a smokery. The Bounder thought I was mad. 'The whole countryside will steal you rotten and you'll go broke,' he said. As things turned out, he was not far wrong.

A chance meeting with a local entrepreneur, Saville Hicks, who was growing oysters in Strangford Lough, led me to talk to Richard Pinney in Suffolk, who like me had left the business world in London and moved to the country, to a small cottage near Orford. He had spent some time researching ways of reviving native industries. He had started with oysters but, discouraged by the problems of artificial cultivation, where a whole crop could be wiped out in a sudden frost, he had turned instead to smoking.

'Don't touch those modern electric kilns,' he told me. 'And don't go near those violently coloured smoke dyes the mass-market smokers use – who wants to eat bright yellow fish?' Richard discounted all the modern electric kilns and was determined to smoke the old way, with oak and natural slow draughts. An engineer by trade, he was unhappy with the inconsistent results of using banked sawdust to smother the flames and allow the natural smoking oils to condense and flavour the fish, so he designed a metal contraption that produced the same effect from small oak blocks, but was much more reliable. He set up a small shop in his local village that was immediately successful – and is still there today, run by his son.

Richard Pinney was all enthusiasm for my venture. He built me one of his special smoke-boxes and lent me plans for the smoke house that surrounded it. It was complicated, full of cunning air passages, dampers and racks. Luckily a solution was ready to hand. The Bellarena estate was dotted with outbuildings, some left over from the army's occupation and still marked with indecipherable army hieroglyphics and rusting pot-bellied stoves. An old coach house which my father had used for chickens proved the perfect size, and now all we needed was to rebuild Pinney's smokehouse in the space. But we needed someone who could cope with all the complicated carpentry . . .

Jim Wilkinson was an old Northumbrian carpenter. Jong-Ja, my second wife, and I had met him as an odd-job man in London. He had lost his old carpentering skills as well as almost all his confidence, and was in a bad way. The death of his beloved mother had combined with a heavy drinking habit to make him capable of only the simplest jobs, and he was unable to support himself properly. To make the situation even worse, some lunatic doctor had authorised a double pre-frontal lobotomy – an operation of almost medieval barbarity, involving two holes being driven straight into his skull – apparently to release the pressure on his brain which was causing so much distress.

Since no one else would look after him, we took him across to Ireland and settled him down in the old butler's sitting room next to the kitchen – another of the few warm spots in the big house. Giving Jim back the confidence to do proper carpentry was a problem. Then Jong-Ja came up with the idea of renewing the massive coach house doors that led onto the courtyard at the back of the house. These had been hand built of local timber over 150 years ago, but were now rotten and sagging on their hinges. No local carpenter would look at them.

At first Jim flatly refused to try his hand at the repair. But slowly, by dint of regular visits to wood yards and long measuring sessions, we felt we were bringing him round. Eventually we bought the timber, and had it delivered, in a great pile outside Jim's window.

We held our breath. Jim stalked around the pile, like an ancient explorer circling a lost city in the high Andes. We held our breath. He set to work. We left him to it.

Slowly the huge doors came together, until at last they were ready for the final hanging. Jim threw another wobbly and pleaded that they were still not 'right', but we went ahead anyway. The doors swung to with a satisfying clunk, like old Rolls-Royce coach-work, with barely a gap between them. Jim broke down and cried.

With the doors behind him, Jim made short work of the Pinney smoke house. As Richard said when I sent him some photos, the copy was even better than the original. What I did not expect was that Jim would come to be our new 'smoker'. The operation of the complicated dampers and vents fascinated him, and he would stand for hours just peering into the innards of the box, making sure the smoke density was right. He even acquired what I called 'the mark of the smoker', a dark yellow stain to the forelock which covered his two lobotomy dents.

The only time Jim went off duty was when he was allowed out on his weekly day at the pub. He was always met off the bus in the local town by a fine parcel of fellow drunks, who would help him drink his wages, then load him back for the home run. Jim was, in his old Northumberland way, proud of his prodigious appetite for drink. 'There's not many of us left,' he would always reply to any criticism of his habits.

Jim also adored animals. Our over-bred London cat had gone native and sired a huge mixed brood of feral kittens. He would only come to Jim's call. The dogs loved him, too. His other joy was growing tomatoes. He had repaired a corner of the rotting wooden greenhouses in the deserted walled garden that had needed six full-time gardeners in my grandfather's day, and here he grew prize specimens. He always swore by his special feed mixture, which he kept in an evil-smelling rainwater butt. Sheep shit and water were the major ingredients – God knows what else he used, but it worked wonders.

The final touch to Jim's new life came with the arrival of our daughter, Eun-Hee. Her Korean name means 'Silver Child', child of good fortune, in English. Jim adored her. 'I've got dogs and cats, and now a baby as well,' he told anyone who would listen – and she became the frequent toast of all the pubs in Limavady, the local market town.

Our smoking operation was fairly small-scale to start with. At first we smoked just our local salmon and a few farmed trout, together with mackerel in the summer months, but an inter-country friendship visit to a food fair at Hamburg organised by the Northern Ireland peace movement gave me a new idea. Just next to our stand there was a traditional eel smoker.

He was a large, jolly fellow with a red nose that had been in the bottom of a lot of Schnapps tumblers. His technique was simple. He would make a lot of noise to attract a crowd, then pick out the plainest and shyest lady. He would give her all his attention, involving some very obvious gestures with his largest eels, and some of the thinnest-disguised lewdities I have ever heard. His target would lap up the attention, grow pink in the face with embarrassment and pleasure, and buy the biggest eel, just to get away. With one sale made, all the other housewives would swiftly follow. He never failed.

I got talking to him and he told me a huge amount about eels: the way they run for the Sargasso Sea on cold windy nights in autumn, then drift back on the currents as tiny elvers, before struggling through streams and even wet grass to their lifetime home. Horst, my eel friend, took me one evening to a net shop in Hamburg, and when I loaded up the car I had a complete set of fyke nets with which to try my luck. The Bounder was staying that summer and we perfected our techniques, laying the nets along the edges of wild lakes in the nearby mountain. The most unpromising dark pools would yield up a treasure of struggling eels – sometimes as many as fifty in a single trap.

My smoked eels became so popular that I could hardly keep up with the demand, and soon had to look for additional sources of supply. I could never have imagined that the solution to my eel problem would lie with a man of the cloth.

Father Kennedy had taken over the Lough Neagh eel fisheries, once the most famous in Europe, from the Dutch company who had given up trying to control the poaching. The bottom end of the lough is in real deep Armagh bandit country, and the locals don't take too well to foreigners. The Father soon solved the poaching problem: as well as any threats of hell fire he might deal out, he roared around the lough day and night in a powerful speedboat, putting the fear of God into anyone who stepped out of line. Soon the fisheries were running smoothly again, and to see the 'silvers' running in September, the prized, succulent eels that have built up fat in readiness for migration, was an amazing sight. A wet, windy evening was best, although you could never be sure when the eels would react. Suddenly, lemming-like, they would respond to some powerful yet undetectable signal and cram the sluices and nets of the fishery. Father Kennedy's men would work like demons to pack the catch live into boxes and then ship them off to the markets in Amsterdam created by the original owners. It was fascinating to watch – a night of pure excitement.

After our first year of smoking, we settled down to celebrate at Christmas with some of our closest friends. Garech, my globe-trotting friend and member of the Guinness family, with whom I had shared many an adventure, had driven up from the South the night before. He looked a little shaken when I came out to welcome him, and I asked what was the matter.

'There's a body lying in front of the back door,' he said, rather nervously.

I went to have a look. It was Jim, home – more or less – from his own celebration. We lifted him up, log-like, and carried him to bed to sleep it off.

Garech had brought with him Paddy Maloney, leader of the traditional Irish music band The Chieftains. He had discovered them, and then set up his own record label to launch them. Paddy's tin whistle-playing was the most atmospheric I had ever heard. Once we'd dispensed with Jim we all went down to Rosie's, the tiny pub at the end of the drive, for a pre-Christmas glass of Bushmill's. I knew there was an old whistle there behind the counter, a discarded relic of some long-gone musician. Paddy nursed beauty from it that stopped even Rosie's customers in their tracks, glasses halfway to their mouths – no mean feat, I can tell you. My stock in the village shot up to its highest ever.

Our other guests were an assorted lot, but enough to make a decent showing in the big dining room. It had once seated seventy to breakfast, but now the ceiling was falling down and there was a damp patch the size of a small table in the far left-hand corner. When Jong-Ja and I moved to Bellarena our first guest had been Patrick Chabrier, an enormously sophisticated Frenchman. Patrick always had his doubts about my country ways. One morning, shortly after she and I met, Jong-Ja told me her latest dream. 'You were teaching Patrick how to fish – how out of character!' she said.

'And what was Patrick teaching me?' I foolishly asked.

'Why! How to make love, like any good Frenchman,' she said, smiling sweetly.

I really walked into that one.

That night we sat down to a lengthy Korean meal, which I had cooked – my new party trick. Suddenly Patrick looked up. 'Now I feel really at home,' he said. 'Your beautiful 'ouse so reminds me of my chateau in Burgundy.'

'You mean the gloriously high ceiling and the gold cornices?' I asked.

'No,' said Patrick. 'I mean the water that is pouring down the walls!'

Perhaps our most eccentric guest for Christmas was Mariga, the Princess of Urach, a European aristocrat, partly Scottish, partly Bavarian, partly Norwegian, with a claim to rule Lithuania and Monaco. Mariga had been educated by no fewer than seventeen governesses, and still retained a unique and regal way of

speaking which entranced everyone who met her. She sometimes introduced herself with the words 'I am related to the
Wittelsbachs and a little bit mad.' Mariga was the estranged wife
of Desmond Guinness, heir to the brewing fortune, but was now
living in a deserted court house on the Antrim coast without electricity or, often, heating. She had also lost her driving licence,
having been discovered well over the limit, entangled in a road
works in Ballymena.

'Have you been drinking, Mrs Guinness?' the local policeman
had asked unnecessarily.

'If I hadn't been feckin' drinking, I wouldn't have driven into
this feckin' road works!' the Princess replied robustly. After losing
her court case – which she vigorously defended using ancient
European royal precedence – she lent her battered Citroën Safari
to a local farmer to use as a chicken coop. When she recovered her
licence she reclaimed it, drove it down to Dublin and parked it,
still thickly covered with chicken poop, on the immaculate drive
of her ex-husband Desmond's castle. I heard it speeded the
divorce settlement considerably.

The Bounder was staying as usual, this time between wives.
He had become fascinated by my Korean mother-in-law, who
claimed to be a direct descendent of Ghengis Khan. Her family
was known, Jong-Ja informed me, as 'The Golden Family',
because when they are cross, their eyes go bright gold. If this
happens, your best option is to run for the hills. I became the
model husband while the mother-in-law was with us.

My mother-in-law spoke not a word of English, but was a
fervent Buddhist and would get up to chant at 5 a.m. every
morning.

'What on earth is she doing?' I asked my wife.

'She is appeasing the spirits of the house,' was her enigmatic
reply.

After a week, this stopped. Apparently the spirits, scores of red-coated horsemen who circled the lawn, were too miserable to be appeased, which was an interesting reflection on Irish history, which had seen my forebears hanged by the English as often as they had later been potted at by the Fenians.

The last member of the party was my best friend and solicitor, Bruno Brown. A tall, commanding figure with a booming voice, Bruno had taken a degree in advanced alcoholism at Trinity College, Dublin before settling down to being a surprisingly successful lawyer in his father's practice. He and I always knew when it was time to kick over the traces a little. One or the other would call with a lunch invitation to a favoured hotel, and we'd take it from there. Once I was away for 48 hours. To this day, I have no knowledge of where we went. I woke to the sun streaming in through my bedroom window, a sense of pure relaxation and a dent in the car. We all need friends like Bruno.

But the star of the evening would be Eun-Hee, now three and still the apple of Jim's eye. She spent most days either in 'Jim's Kitchen', the huge stone-flagged room kept at hot-house heat by an old range, or in the deserted walled garden, following Jim everywhere like a little shadow. She had also started to attend the local day school, and had picked up a Northern Irish accent as thick as Ian Paisley's. Jim now came out 'Dim', but he didn't seem to mind.

The dining room was elegantly set for dinner. Candles flickered on the last of the Heygate silver. Father had been arrested while dragging a trunk-full to Christie's in South Kensington. ' 'ello, 'ello! What 'ave we 'ere?' asked a passing copper. Father drew himself up to his full height. 'I am Sir John Heygate and this is my family silver,' he said. The obvious lack of a recent razor and the strong smell of drink did not impress the constable. 'And I am the fairy queen and this is my magic wand,' he replied. A wave of the truncheon and my father was nicked.

Still, what we had left made a jolly show. A great fire, Jim's creation, roared in the high marble fireplace and set the mood. Of course we started with smoked salmon and eel, the latter washed down with shot glasses of Danish Royal Schnapps, ice cold from the freezer. Then came turkey. My mother-in-law had insisted that we daub this with a thick coating of soy sauce, and it came out a curious dark brown colour, but no one noticed in the candle-light, and it tasted good, heaped around with fresh vegetables from the garden.

The grand finale followed. The dancing notes of Paddy's whistle came from the kitchen to announce a procession. Eun-Hee and her grandmother led the way, both wearing traditional Korean costumes in shimmering green and blue silk. Between them they carried a big plate of fried rice, a single candle and sprig of holly on the top as a concession to the day.

We all took a big spoonful. Jim got a mouthful of one of the hot red peppers I grew in the hall as Christmas decorations. 'Very tasty,' he said, choking (he described everything he ate as very tasty). Then he made a run to the kitchen to put the fires out.

Then it was time for the stories and the toasts. I liked Bruno's best. He stood with difficulty and raised his glass. 'Here's to . . .' he managed, before his six-and-a-half-foot length toppled, like a giant tree, onto my one remaining Sheraton chair, reducing it to matchwood.

Mariga left at 3 a.m., only to return half an hour later, smelling strongly of cow dung. 'My driver has driven into a pasture,' she declaimed with great dignity. Another guest for the night.

As I drifted off to sleep, my last waking memory was of Eun-Hee's warm brown eyes reflecting in the candle-light as she oh! so carefully carried in the rice to the sound of Paddy's magical music. Truly, Christmas is where the heart is, I thought.

The New Year took us back to England. Jim stayed on in the

big house, helping the manager of the growing smokery. His life ran on much the same for six months until he died from cancer of the colon, the curse of all beer drinkers. I came over for the funeral and afterwards carried his ashes down to the old walled garden to be scattered as he had asked. The garden was more overgrown than ever, but Jim's restored greenhouse was immaculate. It was filled with massive tomato plants, now pendulous with ripening fruit. I bit into one, and tasted that sharp sweetness, straight off the vine, that you can never buy in shops.

The barrel of Jim's magic tomato mix still stood nearby, filled to the brim. I packed Jim's ashes carefully around the plants and watered them well in with a healthy dose of his feed. He would, I know, have approved.

ACKNOWLEDGMENTS

To my wife and family who have had to put up with my frequent grumpiness and varying enthusiasms while researching the book. To our friend, editor and publisher, Kate Parkin, without whose constant diplomacy and endless patience the book would never have been started, let alone finished. Finally, to all the wonderful people we have met on our travels. May they thrive and flourish and, above all, continue to bring out all that is best in the English countryside we love.

R.H.

There is one person above all others without whom this book would have been only a pipe dream. After we had appeared in 'The Bart and the Bounder' on BBC2 we were telephoned by Kate Parkin of John Murray (Publishers). Over a very giggly lunch (which finished at 6 p.m.), she asked us to write this book. There was an instant clicking of minds and much laughter. As we swayed happily from the restaurant we all agreed that if nothing else we would have serious fun writing it. We have – and it is all due to the best editor that any writer could ask for. Thank you, darling Kate, from the bottom of our evil old hearts. Some of the material in these chapters has previously appeared in that marvellous champion of the British countryside, *The Field*. My thanks to its editor, Jonathan Young. I also want to thank Daniel Busk for all his help and innovative ideas. There is no one like him. He is kind, intelligent and gentle, the epitome of all that is best about an English country gentleman: a truly endangered species. I feel very privileged to be able to call him a close friend.

Another great countryman and close friend is Charlie Bettinson. We have drunk, laughed and fished together for many years. In his mastery and originality of the gentle art of angling he is in the same class as my dear friend, the late Hugh Falkus, and I can pay no one a higher compliment. Sir Edward Dashwood, who opened his door and his heart to me and showed me great kindness, is another person with a great passion for, and knowledge of, the countryside. His enthusiasm for all things rural shines through, which is why he is known affectionately to his friends as the 'Bouncing Baronet'. Thank you, Ed. Another Ed – or Eddie – is the Earl of Leicester who, despite being poached for forty years by my wildfowling mentor Kenny Cook, held him in high respect and helped us enormously in researching Kenny's mastery of the nefarious art. Thanks, Eddie. And lastly, to all the gamekeepers, tractor drivers, ghillies, poachers, river keepers, farmers and landowners with whom I have drunk in smoke-filled taverns and laughed with in wind and rain on swollen rivers and dripping woodlands, huge thanks for your quiet advice, soft wisdom and comforting companionship.

M.D.

The authors and publisher wish to thank the following for permission to reproduce copyright material: A. P. Watt on behalf of Gráinne Yeats for 'The Song of Wandering Aengus': David Higham Associates for 'Ballad of the Long-Legged Bait' from *Collected Poems* by Dylan Thomas: John Murray (Publishers) on behalf of the Estate of John Betjeman for 'Christmas'. The authors would also like to thank Julia Gentle, whose work has been quoted.